A WOMAN'S ISSUE

Recent Titles in
Contributions in Women's Studies

The Paradise of Women: Writings by Englishwomen of the Renaissance
Betty Travitsky, compiler and editor

The Origins of the Equal Rights Amendment: American Feminism Between the Wars
Susan D. Becker

European Women on the Left: Socialism, Feminism, and the Problems Faced by Political Women, 1880 to the Present
Jane Slaughter and Robert Kern, editors

Toward the Second Decade: The Impact of the Women's Movement on American Institutions
Betty Justice and Renate Pore, editors

A Conflict of Interest: Women in German Social Democracy, 1919-1933
Renate Pore

The Second Assault: Rape and Public Attitudes
Joyce E. Williams and Karen A. Holmes

Oppression and Resistance: The Struggle of Women in Southern Africa
Richard E. Lapchick and Stephanie Urdang

Against All Odds: The Feminist Movement in Mexico to 1940
Anna Macías

Pariahs Stand Up! The Founding of the Liberal Feminist Movement in France, 1858-1889
Patrick Kay Bidelman

Separated and Divorced Women
Lynne Carol Halem

Female Soldiers—Combatants or Noncombatants? Historical and Contemporary Perspectives
Nancy Loring Goldman, editor

A WOMAN'S ISSUE The Politics of Family Law Reform in England

Dorothy M. Stetson

CONTRIBUTIONS IN WOMEN'S STUDIES, NUMBER 34

GP

GREENWOOD PRESS
Westport, Connecticut • London, England

Library of Congress Cataloging in Publication Data

Stetson, Dorothy M.
A woman's issue.

(Contributions in women's studies, ISSN 0147-104X ; no. 34)
Bibliography: p.
Includes index.
1. Married women—Great Britain—History.
2. Divorce—Law and legislation—Great Britain—History. 3. Domestic relations—Great Britain—History. I. Title. II. Series.
KD758.S74 346.4201'5 81-13465
ISBN 0-313-23087-0 (lib. bdg.) 344.20615 AACR2

Library of Congress Catalog Card Number: 81-13465
ISBN: 0-313-23087-0
ISSN: 0147-104X

First published in 1982

Greenwood Press
A division of Congressional Information Service, Inc.
88 Post Road West
Westport, Connecticut 06881

Printed in the United States of America

10 9 8 7 6 5 4 3 2 1

To
Louise Lilly Albertson

Contents

Tables and Figures

TABLES

FIGURES

Preface

This book describes and analyzes the process of change in English public policy toward the status of women in the family. Through a series of reform statutes since the mid-nineteenth century, Parliament has greatly altered official values regarding the rights and responsibilities of women in marriage. Several generations of feminists have taken up the issue of family law reform. Despite legal and political handicaps, they have successfully pressured English lawmakers to abolish common law rules that gave married women the same status as children and idiots and to treat marriage as a partnership of equals.

These changes in public policy happened gradually and are still going on. This study focuses on the process of policy change through eight statutes reforming divorce and marital property rights. In examining the way conflicts were resolved among feminists, lawyers, and politicians, an explanation of the nature and direction of policy content emerges.

Statutory reform of married women's rights in English family law has been a long struggle to overcome the common law doctrine of coverture. *Coverture,* a concept placing married women in a special legal category, was the basis of family law throughout common law countries including the United States. Under this concept, married women could not own property, had no standing in court, were not liable for contracts and torts, and could not sue for divorce.

Common law has deep roots in English custom and tradition, and politicians are reluctant to make sweeping changes in the law. The legal status of married women had been so inferior for such a long time that the move toward a policy of equality has been halting and tedious. Demands for reform surfaced in the 1830s. By the 1930s, after the enactment of six reform statutes, married women finally achieved equal legal status with married men concerning divorce and personal property rights.

Family policy also assigns responsibilities to husband and wife in marriage and divorce. In this area, English law presently is in transition, combining traditional and contemporary values. The traditional approach maintains a division of labor between husband and wife: husband is responsible for economic support and wife is responsible for the home and children. Reforms in divorce and property laws in the 1960s and 1970s have introduced a new standard of marriage that requires spouses to share responsibilities for the marriage and permits them to share family assets upon divorce. If the contemporary trends in family law reform continue, English family policy will eventually accept the interchangeability and equality of the husband and wife in marriage and place family responsibilities on the spouses jointly.

The study of the events that have led to these major changes in English family law reveals stories of personal influence, petition drives, investigations, ponderous judicial opinions, and back-room political party deals. Over the years, political leaders and lawyers have not drafted massive and rational reforms of laws to bring them in line with social realities. Rather, they have reacted to conflicting demands for change and against change. The process of resolving these conflicts leads decision makers to adjust values and distribute benefits and disadvantages.

To compare the pattern of decision making and determine the influence of feminists on the outcome of each reform, the events in this book are presented according to a common conceptual framework. This approach focuses on the point in the process where conflicting demands are finally resolved. Parliamentary committees and Royal Commissions resolve some conflicts over what the law is to be. Administrative officials and the Cabinet monopolize other issues. Both the content of the law and the influence of feminists depend on the type of political structure, whether parliamentary or administrative, that dominates the crucial step of conflict resolution.

The most interesting result of this study of law reform is the extent to which feminists have, since the mid-nineteenth century, been successful in achieving equality for women in marriage and divorce. Their influence has been primarily felt through their personal and organizational contacts with the legislature. They have had less success in gaining a sympathetic ear among members of the executive or judiciary. This study shows that if feminists are interested in the outcome of a particular reform proposal, they are able to force Parliament to take their demands into account. Otherwise, conflicts are resolved by administrative and legal leaders in the government departments without feminist input. Most of the clauses that close the gap between the sexes have been included in the statutes as a result of the demands of feminists.

Research for this study was conducted in London. The British Library, University of London, London School of Economics, Public Record Office, Fawcett Library, the House of Lords Record Office, and the Labour party provided necessary primary and secondary materials. British library staff offered welcome assistance to me in tracing events leading to the enactment of the various statutes. Busy politicians, lawyers, activists, and officials took time to recount events surrounding reforms in the 1960s. Without the help of the twenty-five people listed in the bibliography, an accurate account of the Divorce and Matrimonial Proceedings and Property Acts would have been impossible. I am also indebted to the keen interest and dedication of British feminists in fostering women's studies, sharing ideas, and providing materials. I especially want to thank the founders, members, and staff of the Women's Resource and Research Centre for continuing to offer an intellectual and emotional home to women scholars.

Abbreviations

CMW	Council of Married Women
CPC	Conservative Political Centre
DLRU	Divorce Law Reform Union
EJ	*Englishwoman's Journal*
LAS	Law Amendment Society
LRC	Law Revision Committee
MP	Member of Parliament
MPPA	Matrimonial Proceedings and Property Act 1970
MWA	Married Women's Association
MWPA	Married Women's Property Act, 1882
MWPC	Married Women's Property Committee
NAPSS	National Association for the Promotion of Social Science
NCCL	National Council for Civil Liberties
NCEC	National Council for Equal Citizenship
NCW	National Council of Women
NUSEC	National Union of Societies for Equal Citizenship
NUWSS	National Union of Women's Suffrage Societies
PLP	Parliamentary Labour Party
RCMD	Royal Commission on Marriage and Divorce
RGSR	Registrar General, Statistical Report
ROW	Rights of Women
WFL	Women's Freedom League
WLM	Women's Liberation Movement
WNAC	Women's National Advisory Committee
WSPU	Women's Social and Political Union

A WOMAN'S ISSUE

Introduction 1

According to English custom, all women are wives, potential wives, or former wives. Therefore, laws defining the status of married women affect opportunity for all women. Under common law, married women had few independent rights: their husbands were responsible for their domiciles, property, torts, debts, and children. English family life has changed considerably since the feudal times that gave rise to the common law. Patriarchy has given way to companionship and sharing. Family law has changed as well, removing legal disabilities from married women in property; liability for debts, torts, and contracts; guardianship of children; and divorce. These changes represent a fundamental shift in English public policy toward women by recognizing that equality before the law does not disappear by virtue of marriage and that married women are not a separate and inferior category of citizens.

Few areas of law affect women more than family law. English feminists from the eighteenth century to the present have recognized the profound importance of this woman's issue. To them law is not a remote and technical subject but a matter of political, moral, and economic values that defines their place in society. Successive generations of activists have joined in the controversies over the proper place of women in marriage and divorce. Gradually, through a series of reform statutes, the law has evolved to guarantee greater legal equality and opportunity for women.

Do feminists deserve the credit for this change in policy? Or is it part of an overall trend in modernization? It is true that laws have changed in all Western countries to improve the status of women. In fact, social forces common to industrial societies have coincided with the overhaul of laws and entire legal systems to make them more equal, uniform, and specialized. These major changes in public policy appear to be the result of social and economic modernization, not country-bound politics. Yet although general trends are noticeable, laws in various countries have not followed identical paths in content or rate of change. Similar problems face all industrial societies, but solutions vary in style, timing, and content.[1] The specific policies governments enact are the result of the way decisions are made. In law reform, for example, groups compete for control over the policy process. The clauses in reform statutes reflect the outcome of this struggle. It is not futile, therefore, to wonder about the political influence of feminists over the changes in family law and to discover the connection between social change, feminist politics, and public policy. Family law is a woman's issue. In England, is family law also the issue of women?

FAMILY LAW: A WOMAN'S ISSUE

Family law is important to women in several ways. Law is the official judgment of a society about accepted values and standards of proper behavior. It can have both educative and regulative effects on private values and behavior.[2] If people view public authority with respect and consider government action the guide for social good, they are likely to learn some of the cues to proper behavior from public symbols. Administration of the law effectively regulates private behavior by rewarding those who conform to official standards and punishing the rest.

Through family law the government sets standards and regulates the responsibilities, rights, and status of husband and wife with respect to each other, their children, and their property. A particular law might be based on one of several views of the proper role of woman and men in family life. For example, separate and unequal legal responsibilities are consistent with the belief that women's duties as wives and mothers should be substantially different from men's duties as husbands and fathers. Such laws usually require women to be responsible for child care and men to provide economic support for women and children. On the other hand, family law need not differentiate between the responsibilities and status of spouses according to sex.

The rights of women and men in the family affect their status outside the family. For example, the legal requirement that a husband support his wife and family both during and after marriage has been used to justify paying men higher wages than women. Limitations placed on financial rights of married women has handicapped their using property to raise capital and enjoy the privilege of managing a successful business. Laws that regulate and reinforce dependent roles for women in the family lead to their inferior status in the labor market, business, and politics.

Of all policies affecting the family, matrimonial property and divorce laws have the most direct and widespread effect on women's rights. Rules about matrimonial property involve the financial status of women both during and after marriage. Divorce procedures are based on assumptions about responsibilities of husband and wife. Divorce and matrimonial property issues are usually interrelated. The law may set guidelines about ownership of property only when the marriage has ended. This is especially so in common law systems such as in England and the United States where rights and responsibilities during marriage are only partially provided for and rarely enforced by the courts. It is when the marriage breaks up that the state applies public values to settle conflicts in a private relationship.

FAMILY LAW AND WOMEN IN ENGLAND

Traditional family law in England and Wales has roots in judge-made common law modified by equity and ecclesiastical law. Parliament was not often involved in issues of family law until the nineteenth century. Then in response to demands for reform stemming from the effects of economic and social modernization, Parliament periodically enacted statutes amending and revising the official policies toward wives and husbands along with reforms in other areas of law. Official norms of proper and expected behavior in the family have changed substantially in the last 150 years.

Before 1857. Before the nineteenth century, English family law was based on the common law doctrine of coverture.[3] Taken as a whole, coverture provided that marriage encompassed separate and unequal roles for the sexes. Upon marriage a woman became *feme couverte:* she lost her separate legal status of *feme sole* and came under her husband's tutelage as though she were one of his children or part of his property. She had no legal rights, no right to own or use property, and no right to custody of her children; her husband was responsible for all of her acts, torts, and liabilities. Since he was legally responsible for her, he had the right to restrain her and mete out moderate correction. If she left his house, without due cause, she could be legally forced to return.

The husband's responsibility was to support his wife according to his taste and ability. In practice, this meant that he had to keep her off the streets and out of the county poor house if he had the means. She could act as his agent to pledge his credit for necessaries if he did not choose to provide them himself. He was not required to give her any money.

The wife's responsibility was to be chaste, and she could be punished for her adultery. In addition, the husband could sue his wife's lover for damages. This suit was called *criminal conversation* and was based on the principle that an adulterer damaged a husband's sexual property. The wife involved in a case of criminal conversation could not appear in court to defend herself. On the other hand, it was acceptable for husbands to have sexual relationships outside marriage if they continued to perform their marital duties.

Wealthy families appealed against the strict property requirements of common law coverture to the equity courts. They sought to prevent scoundrels from marrying heiresses and making off with the family fortune. A marriage settlement in equity court before marriage guaranteed that the wife's money would be held in trust for her. She could use the income and under certain conditions the property itself. However, if her family wanted to protect property further from both the son-in-law and the daughter (who might be easily swayed by her husband), restraint on anticipation was made part of the settlement. If so, the wife could not sell the property itself. Marriage settlements had the effect of raising the legal and economic status of wealthy women above that of their poorer sisters under coverture, but in all legal and most financial matters, women remained inferior to married men.

There was no civil divorce under common law. Both marriage and divorce were handled by the Church of England in ecclesiastical courts. These courts would grant divorce *a mensa et thoro,* from bed and board, to a wife whose life was in danger from her husband's cruelty or to a husband whose wife committed adultery. Such a divorce was really a separation since spouses were not permitted to remarry. It suspended marital obligations of the innocent spouse: a husband did not have to support an adulterous wife; a wife did not have to cohabit with a cruel husband.

Since the Reformation, however, there had been demands, especially from the wealthy, for divorce *a vinculo* that would allow spouses to remarry. During the reigns of Henry VIII and Edward

VI, a church group proposed changes in canon law. *Reformatorium Legum Ecclesiasticarum* recommended that the church grant divorce *a vinculo,* allowing remarriage on grounds of adultery, deadly hostility, absence without tidings, and incorrigible violence. These reforms were not adopted and from the seventeenth century on, nobles petitioned Parliament for relief. Divorce *a vinculo* was granted by private act of Parliament for each case. It was an expensive procedure that involved obtaining divorce *a mensa et thoro* in ecclesiastical court and a favorable judgment in a civil suit of criminal conversation. By the nineteenth century more than 200 such divorces had been granted. Only four were won on petitions of women, and the ground for the men was always the wife's adultery.

The divorce law in England before the nineteenth century, therefore, was a combination of canon law and acts of Parliament. It was based on the doctrine of matrimonial offense. Divorces *a vinculo* were granted for the most part to men on the basis of their wives' adultery. A wife's suit for divorce *a mensa et thoro* typically charged the husband with extreme physical cruelty. Husband and wife had different responsibilities in marriage. Couples might part if either spouse violated his or her respective duties. The only offense thought to be grave enough to warrant divorce *a vinculo* was the wife's adultery and then only for those who could afford the high costs of obtaining an act of Parliament.

Changes in English family law began in the early part of the nineteenth century. Through statutes, marriage became a civil matter (1837), and married women gained some rights to their children (1839). It was not until 1857 that a statute provided for civil divorce *a vinculo.* After 1857 there were other major reforms in divorce and matrimonial property law. The reform statutes can be classified in four major periods: *1850s:* Divorce Reform and Matrimonial Causes Act of 1857; *1857-1882:* Married Women's Property Act of 1882; *1920-1937:* Matrimonial Causes Acts of 1923, 1937, and Law Reform (Married Women and Tortfeasors) Act of 1935; *1960s and 1970s:* Divorce Reform Act of 1969 and Matrimonial Proceedings and Property Act of 1970. Statutes passed during these periods of reform have drastically altered the common law doctrines of coverture and the equity doctrine of marriage settlements that were both in effect at the beginning of the nineteenth century. As a result, official standards with respect to proper sex roles in the family have also changed.

First Reform: 1850s. The Divorce and Matrimonial Causes Act establishing civil divorce and remarriage in secular court was enacted in 1857. The act permitted divorce on the grounds of adultery by the wife and adultery plus incest, bestiality, sodomy, or cruelty by the husband, as long as there was no collusion, condonation, or guilt on the part of the petitioner. Women separated from their husbands had the right to keep their own earnings and property.

The first period of reform began to erode the rigid distinctions between the sexes upheld by English family law. Women were, for the first time, allowed to sue for divorce, and they obtained some control over their earnings and property. However, the laws maintained the traditional pattern of separate responsibilities and unequal legal and economic status between the sexes. Although divorce was available to both men and women, the grounds were unequal. The property and earnings of a wife living with her husband continued to belong to him.

Feminists protested about the unequal grounds and property rights of husband and wife. The prevailing view in Parliament, however, was that adultery was a much graver offense when committed by the wife, not only because it might result in "spurious offspring" but also for the moral effects of the act on wifely and motherly duties. Adultery by a male might be equally wrong from a religious standpoint, they argued, but its social and moral consequences were insignificant. Furthermore, the Cabinet refused to consider the separate issue of property rights during marriage in a bill for civil divorce.

Second Reform: 1857-1882. The feminist campaign to extend to married women the right to own and use property began soon after the passage of the Divorce Reform Act. The first reform that passed the House of Commons was drastically cut by the Lords. As a result, the Married Women's Property Act of 1870 allowed married women ownership of earnings, savings, and investments only. The campaign for equal rights continued another twelve years. The final Married Women's Property Act passed as a government measure in 1882.

Under this act, a married woman retained ownership and control of her earnings, property, inheritance, and gifts. A wife also became liable for contracts and torts, but only to the extent of her separate property. She was not personally liable for debts as were her husband and spinster sisters. Thus although married women finally gained the right to own property and earnings, they remained handicapped in their ability to operate independently in the economy.

By the close of the second reform period, therefore, married women's legal status had been improved considerably over the common law *feme couverte.* They could sue for divorce, retain earnings and property, and use such property without their husband's consent. However, their status remained separate and unequal. Grounds for divorce emphasized different moral responsibilities for men and women. Women were not personally liable for their own actions, and a husband could be sued for his wife's torts.

Third Reform: 1923-1937. Demands for reform in divorce and matrimonial property laws reappeared in the wake of the suffrage movement. After votes for women were obtained in 1918 and 1928, feminists demanded the removal of the more obvious inequalities in the law, such as in divorce grounds and married women's economic status. There were also demands for a liberalization of the divorce law to accommodate increasing demands for divorce. Three statutes were enacted in the interwar period. The Matrimonial Causes Act of 1923 allowed women, like men, to sue for divorce on the grounds of simple adultery. The Law Reform (Married Women and Tortfeasors) Act of 1935 made women personally liable for contracts and torts and placed them on the same legal/economic status as men and single women. A further reform of the divorce law in the Matrimonial Causes Act of 1937 expanded the grounds for divorce to include cruelty, desertion, and insanity.

This third reform period established equal legal status for men and women in marriage. The anomalies of the separate property doctrine that allowed married women to own property but limited their use of it were removed. Women were subject to bankruptcy and were personally liable just like everyone else. The property of a marriage was composed of the property owned separately by each of the spouses.

The norm of separate responsibilities for husband and wife in marriage remained in the law at the close of the third reform period. Obvious inequalities in divorce grounds had been removed in light of the argument that there should be moral equality between the spouses. However, legislators favoring the liberalization of divorce in 1937 expected the new grounds to be more important to women than to men. They thought husbands were more likely to be physically cruel and to desert their families. They assumed that married women in their roles as wives and mothers were more likely to depend on marriage for both social status and financial support.

The new law made it easier for a wife, if deserted or not cared for properly, to end an unsatisfactory marriage and find a new husband.

Fourth Reform: 1960s. The first three periods of family law reform achieved equal legal status for men and women, but a separation of roles in marriage left women at an economic disadvantage. Under these laws, property in marriage consisted of what was owned separately by each spouse. The extent to which wives were actually responsible for childrearing and homemaking limited their abilities to earn income and buy property. Husbands, earning income to support their families, placed most of the property in their own names. The effect was the de facto economic dependency of women in marriage unless they had family wealth or full-time careers.

The Divorce Reform Act of 1969 and the Matrimonial Proceedings and Property Act of 1970 (MPPA) represent the latest change in reform of divorce and matrimonial property law in England and in public policy toward the pattern of sex roles in marriage. The idea that the separate spheres of husband and wife lead to separate bases for divorce was inherent in the old divorce law. The new act recognizes the principle that marriage is a relationship of shared responsibilities rather than separate roles for males and females. No one is considered to be entirely responsible for the maintenance or breakdown of marriage. The fault principle has not been totally removed; fault as well as consent are proof of breakdown.

This reform coincides with a shift from strict separation of property to the idea of family property. The MPPA gives the courts, for the first time, the power to transfer property to an unemployed spouse upon divorce. It takes a step toward giving the unemployed spouse (or secondary earner) a stake in the assets of the marriage based on the work of childrearing and maintenance of the home. However, despite the trend toward shared responsibilities and the concepts of family property, husband and wife have unequal economic status with respect to the family assets. Separate property principles remain and work to the disadvantage of an unemployed spouse, usually the wife. The act does not contain guidelines regarding the division of property. Courts tend to award one-third of the property acquired during a marriage to the wife rather than one-half as proposed by community property schemes. The fourth reform period has introduced the values of shared responsibilities and family assets into the law. The status of the spouses vis-à-vis these assets remains unequal. Notions of separate but equal roles have not been removed and for the present coexist with the new norms.

FAMILY LAW AND SEX ROLES

The first judges and priests to set forth rules for the community to follow in the practice of mating and marriage believed that family life was fundamentally different for women and men. Contemporary judges and politicians act on the assumption that women and men have a wide variety of common experiences in marriage. Despite these differences in belief, both the ancient and modern lawgivers had to settle two policy problems: What should be the responsibilities of wives and husbands under the law? What is the proper status of wives and husbands under the law? The review of English family law reveals a complex and shifting pattern of solutions to these problems. It will help clarify trends in policymaking to compare opposing concepts of family roles: separate versus shared responsibilities in marriage and equal versus unequal status of the sexes.

There are two views of the responsibilities of husband and wife toward each other: separate and shared. If the norm is marriage with separate responsibilities, then, by virtue of sex, each spouse has different duties and activities. Successful marriage consists of a husband and wife performing their proper work. If the marriage fails, it is because one spouse failed to fulfill those duties. Norms of shared responsibilities mean that responsibilities of the spouses in marriage are not assigned according to sex but according to the individual circumstances of the spouses in the marriage.

There are two kinds of marital responsibilities: labor and moral. Labor in the family consists of providing child care and economic support. Moral responsibilities involve personal codes of sexual conduct of the spouses. Sex roles based on separate labor responsibilities assign child care duties to the wife and economic support to the husband. Separate moral responsibilities means that a wife and mother should restrict her sexual life, but her husband could be involved with others. Shared labor responsibilities allow the husband and wife to share the work, both contributing to child care and economic support. They would have similar moral responsibilities, and the stricter code of sexual conduct would not necessarily fall on the wife.

The second dimension of sex roles is status. Family law confers both legal and economic status on husband and wife. Such status could be equal or unequal. An example of unequal status was the common law that limited the rights of married women as a group to own property, to appear in court, or to sue for divorce. Equal status would be conferred by laws that do not differentiate between married men and married women with respect to rights to property and employment.

The evolution of public policy through divorce and matrimonial property law reform in England has gradually changed the responsibilities and status of women in marriage from separate and inferior toward a shared and equal partnership with men. It has not been an even progress, but each statute contributed some, however small, step toward the overall trend. The first laws improved the status of married women by giving them some right to divorce and to property. Gradually, the wife gained equal legal status with her husband. Recently, policy has begun to incorporate the idea of marriage as a shared rather than a separate relationship. Although distinctions between husband and wife remain in the law, they are giving way to the recognition that marriage is a common experience. In the 1970s work continues to remove vestiges of separation and inequality from family law.

FEMINISTS AND FAMILY LAW REFORM

The transformation of the legal status of the wife from chattel to equal partner coincides with the development of feminism as a political movement in England. The first women's rights organization formed over the issue of matrimonial property rights in 1856. Since then, the question of family law has never ceased to be a major goal of the feminist movement, although other issues, such as the vote and equal pay, have frequently received more publicity. Specific demands have changed over the years. In the 1850s and 1860s the issue was the rights of a poor woman to her own earnings. Before 1920 suffragists sought an equal moral standard for women and men in marriage and divorce. In the 1950s financial safeguards for dependent wives stirred women much as the idea of legal and financial independence affected their daughters in the 1970s.

Through the decades of agitation for reform, feminists have used a variety of tactics and resources to influence Parliament. Prominent women have worked through personal friendships and in some cases family relationships to persuade top government officials. Single-issue feminist interest groups have concentrated their efforts with petitions, deputations, and private member bills. Large women's rights organizations have campaigned to improve women's legal rights, status, and opportunities.

The central concern of this book is to determine the extent to which feminists, that is, groups and individuals who claim they want to improve women's legal rights and status, have influenced Parliament in enacting family law reform. There is no question that the eight statutes affecting divorce and matrimonial property have been important in improving the status and opportunity of women in English law along the lines feminists have demanded. It is more difficult in light of the large numbers of political, social, and economic changes during the various reform periods to determine the influence of one group of interests. The entire process leading to the enactment of reform statutes must be studied.

The following section describes the approach that will be used in this book to analyze policymaking processes during the several reform periods. The framework helps to organize the events leading to the adoption of reform statutes by Parliament and to compare trends in policymaking over time. Most importantly, it sets forth criteria for estimating the influence of feminists over the reform process.

FAMILY LAW: THE ISSUE OF WOMEN

All acts of Parliament must complete the familiar stages of the formal legislative process.[4] Knowing this formal process, however, does little to help us understand why a statute contains certain provisions and eliminates others or why it advances some values and denies the rest. The substantive content of policy is the result of the particular set of events leading to its enactment, that is, of the informal decision-making process.[5] At its heart, this process is the story of conflict, of what befalls competing demands as they weave in and out of formal parliamentary channels. First, demands for change come to public attention. Then, the nature of the policy conflict becomes clear as opposing issues are defined and redefined by competing groups. Finally, the conflict is resolved, setting the stage for the formal enactment of the statute. The study of a particular policy involves answering a series of questions about these stages.

First, what is the origin of demands for change in the law? The search for the source of demands must begin in the social and economic environment of politics. People often see a need for change in law when they consider it outmoded by the realities of people's lives. Demands for change in family law arise from changes in family life, especially in the activities of women. In a larger sense a connection also exists between specific issues of family law and the achievement of equality and rationality in law as a whole. Proposals for reform may come about as part of a review of the whole body of civil law.

Second, how do demands come to the attention of public authorities? No public official will spend time on even the most worthwhile subject unless the demands make their way to arenas of public discussion. Parliament has limited time, and only a few issues receive more than perfunctory treatment. Proposals about law have special difficulty, because they are frequently seen as technical, not political, issues. For Parliament to undertake to make a decision about law, some members must be convinced of the importance of the issue. At this stage, those making demands, such as feminists, begin to compete with other groups to get the attention of politicians.

Third, how are the issues defined? Gaining public attention for demands results in conflict. Proposals for change provoke counterproposals and direct opposition. At this stage of analysis, it is necessary to describe all sides of the conflict and the definition of the issues as confronted by lawmakers. The way the conflict proceeds will be affected by the political context. During the period of reform people will be accustomed to a particular pattern of group interaction. Since the 1850s organizational complexity has increased and technological advancement has altered the way groups seek to influence Parliament. The context of group politics is important in understanding the definition of issues and the elaboration of the conflict.

Fourth, who resolves the conflict? The central problem in making policy is to form acceptable policy alternatives out of the conflict among demands. In British politics several kinds of political structures can resolve conflicts: groups of legislators, parliamentary committees, Houses of Parliament, political parties, the Cabinet, groups of ministers, higher civil servants, administrative committees, and regulatory boards. Which of these structures is most likely to have the final word on an issue will be affected by the relationships among formal political institutions at the time the political reform is considered. Therefore, conflict resolution must be studied in the context of executive-legislative relationships, the size and strength of the bureaucracy, legal institutions, the powers of the House of Lords, and trends in the power and organization of political parties.

Fifth, how is the conflict resolved? The result of conflict resolution is contained in the substance of the statutes passed by Parliament. Each act is the tally of success and failure for the contending sides in the conflict. The outcome of divorce and matrimonial property reform records the extent to which feminist demands were incorporated in the law.

Sixth, were feminists influential? Potentially, feminists, or any other group, could have an impact on policy at any stage, by making demands, gaining public attention, and defining the issues. However, conflict resolution is the crucial step that determines the outcome of policy. Those groups and individuals present during conflict resolution have an opportunity to influence policy outcomes. Feminist influence is defined in this study according to the presence of feminist individuals, groups, or their representatives during crucial stages of conflict resolution leading to change in policies toward sex roles. The level of influence is assessed by comparing the demands of feminists for changes with the actual policies.

PLAN OF THE BOOK

The purpose of this study is to determine the political influence of feminists on the development of divorce and matrimonial property law in England. The exploration of feminist influence focuses on the presence or absence of such groups during crucial stages of conflict resolution.

Material on each of four reform periods constitutes a separate chapter. After a summary of the statutes, each chapter is divided into four sections: The first section locates the demands for change in the law in the context of the social and economic environment and describes the events that brought the issue to public attention. The second section analyzes the boundaries of the conflict over policy change, the opposing interests, and their political activities, with the goals and organizations of feminists and lawyers receiving special attention. The third section describes the events leading to the resolution of conflict and the enactment of the statute; this crucial decision-making stage is discussed in terms of the general pattern of institutional relations for that period such as the power of the executive and the role of the parties. The last section in each chapter contains an analysis of the lawmaking events using the decision-making framework and gauges the influence of feminists on the political outcomes.

The final chapter presents the results of the comparison of the four periods of family law reform, offering conclusions about trends in public policy toward sex roles, the process of decision making, and the influence of feminists in divorce and matrimonial property law.

NOTES

1. Recent discussions of theory and methods of comparative policy analysis include: Douglas Ashford, *Comparing Public Policies* (Beverly Hills, Calif.: Sage Publications, 1978); Charles W. Anderson, "System and Strategy in Comparative Policy Analysis," in *Perspectives on Public Policy Making,* (eds.) W. B. Gwyn and G. C. Edwards (New Orleans: Tulane University Studies in Political Science 5, 12, 1975), 219-41; Leon Dion, "The Politics of Consultation," *Government and Opposition* 8 (Summer 1973), 332-53; Elliott J. Feldman, "Comparative Public Policy: Field or Method?" *Comparative Politics* 10 (January 1978), 287-306; G. Gustafson and J. J. Richardson, "Concepts of Rationality and the Policy Process," *European Journal of Political Research* 7 (December 1979), 415-36; M. O. Heisler, *Politics in Europe* (New York: David McKay, 1974); Richard Rose, "Comparing Public Policy: An Overview," *European Journal of Political Research* 1 (1973), 67-93; F. Scharpf, "Comparative Policy Studies: Cases in Search of Systematic Theory," *European Journal of Political Research* 6 (March 1978), 117-25; Philippe Schmitter, "Modes of Interest Mediation and Models of Societal Change in Western Europe," *Comparative Political Studies* 10 (April 1977), 7-38; T. A. Smith, *The Comparative Policy Process* (Santa Barbara, Calif.: ABC-Clio, 1975).

2. A wide range of literature deals with the relationship of law to society: Henry Ehrmann, *Comparative Study of Legal Culture* (Englewood Cliffs, N.J.: Prentice-Hall, 1976); Wolfgang Friedmann, *Legal Theory* (New York: Columbia University Press, 1967); Morris Ginsberg, *Law and Opinion in England in the 20th Century* (Berkeley: University of California Press, 1959); Stuart Nagel, ed., *Law and Social Change* (Beverly Hills, Calif.: Sage Publications, 1970); Lawrence Friedman, *The Legal System* (New York: Russell Sage, 1975); Michael Barkun, ed., *Law and the Social System* (New York: Aldine-Atherton, 1971).

3. Sir William Blackstone, *Commentaries on the Laws of England* (1764-1770; reprint ed., Philadelphia: Geo. T. Bisel Co., 1922).

4. All statutes pass both houses of Parliament and receive the Royal Assent. In each house a proposed bill must complete four stages:

1. *First Reading.* A member announces the intention to introduce a bill, and the bill is printed and circulated.

2. *Second Reading.* Formal debate is followed by a vote on the principle of the bill, which may require either a formal division or an informal voice vote.

3. *Committee and Report.* The committee may be a special committee, a standing committee, or a committee of the whole (as is usually the case in the House of Lords). Each clause of the bill is debated in committee and again during the Report stage. The entire house reviews amendments offered by the committee and additional amendments from the floor.

4. *Third Reading.* Debate is followed by a final vote on the bill, which may require a formal division. The bill is sent to the other house for action. Any changes made by the other house must be reviewed and accepted. The Royal Assent is the symbolic acceptance in the name of the sovereign and signals the completion of formal legislative stages.

A law reform bill may be introduced by the government or a private member. Government bills proposing legal changes usually originate in the House of Lords with the Lord Chancellor. They enjoy the resources of the government majority in the Commons—time for completing all parliamentary stages and the Whip. Private member bills are usually introduced by a backbencher in the Commons and sent to the Lords. Such bills have limited time, and the sponsors are responsible for delivering necessary votes at several crucial stages of the consideration of the bill in both houses.

5. This framework draws on the work of several analysts of the policy process: Samuel Beer, *Patterns of Government* (New York: Random House, 1973); Roger Cobb, Jennie Keith-Ross, and Marc Howard Ross, "Agenda Building as a Comparative Political Process," *American Political Science Review* 70 (March 1976), 126-38; Patrick Dunleavy, "An Issue-Centered Approach to the Study of Power," *Political Studies* 24 (December 1976), 423-34; Peter Eisinger, "Understanding Urban Politics; A Comparative Perspective on Urban Political Conflict," *Polity* 10 (Winter 1977), 218-40; Michael Hayes, "The Semi-Sovereign Pressure Groups: A Critique of Current Theory and an Alternate Typology," *Journal of Politics* 40 (February 1978), 134-61; J. J. Richardson and A. G. Jordan, *Governing Under Pressure: The Policy Process in a Post-Parliamentary Democracy* (Oxford: Martin Robertson, 1979); E. E. Schattschneider, *The Semi-Sovereign People* (Hinsdale, Ill.: The Dryden Press, 1960; reissued, 1975); Joan Stringer and J. J. Richardson, "Managing the Public Agenda: Problem Definition and Policy Making in Britain," *Parliamentary Affairs* 33 (Winter 1980), 23-39.

Divorce Reform in the 1850s | 2

THE ACT

The Divorce and Matrimonial Causes Act, which received Royal Assent on 28 August 1857, established new public policies in both divorce and matrimonial property law.[1] The act provided for the first time rules for civil divorce and judicial separation, as well as nullity and restitution of conjugal rights. It set guidelines in financial settlements in divorce and separation cases. Courts and judicial procedures were established to handle the new public responsibilities in the matrimonial area. The Divorce Act was widely hailed as a major law reform; in fact, there were only two basic changes in the practice of law brought about by the act. First, it removed the divorce issue from the control of ecclesiastical courts and Parliament and placed it in a regular civil court, thus increasing the uniformity and secularization of the legal system. Second, it provided the first property rights for married women, a crack in the common law doctrine of coverture.

All matrimonial matters were to be decided in The Court for Divorce and Matrimonial Causes. The new court was small but staffed with top-level judges, including the Lord Chancellor and the Chief Justices. Three judges were required to rule on divorce cases. The Divorce Act offered two alternatives for ending marriage legally: judicial separation and divorce *a vinculo* allowing remarriage. Judicial separation could be awarded on the application of either spouse proving adultery, cruelty, or desertion by the other spouse. The grounds for divorce were different for husband and wife. The husband could sue on the basis of a single act of adultery by the wife. The wife had to prove that the husband had committed intolerable adultery, that is, adultery accompanied by incest, bigamy, sodomy, desertion, rape, or "Adultery coupled with such cruelty as without Adultery would have entitled her to Divorce *a mensa et thoro*" (Clause 27). These grounds were based on the principle that marriage could be legally ended only when an innocent spouse had proved the guilt of the other spouse. If it were found that the petitioner was not innocent of adultery or had condoned or connived in the offense, the court could dismiss the petition.

The court was empowered to require a husband to pay alimony and child support. The act instructed the court to take into account the wife's wealth, the husband's ability to pay, and the conduct of the parties in making a financial settlement. The wife had no legal right to maintenance, and whether any award was made depended on the discretion of the court. The husband could sue the alleged adulterer of his wife for the damages and use such a settlement for benefit of his children or maintenance of the wife if so ordered by the court. The wife was not allowed to sue for damages against the husband's lover.

Although the act did little to change the financial status of most married women, it did guarantee property rights while a wife was living apart from her husband. If the wife were deserted, for example, she could apply to the local magistrate for the right to own and control her own earnings and property. Upon the judgment of legal separation, the married woman immediately assumed the property rights and status of a single woman or *feme sole,* equal with men, as long as she remained apart from her husband. The husband kept the property of the marriage.

Clauses 25 and 26 provided rights for the separated wife:

a. *feme sole* with respect to property of every description which she may acquire or which may devolve upon her;
b. *feme sole* for the purposes of contract, wrongs, and injuries (torts);
c. *feme sole* in suing and being sued in every civil proceeding;
d. husband not liable for any Engagement or contract she may have entered into; or for any wrongful Act or omission by her.

In other words, the disabilities that a woman assumed at the time of her marriage under common law doctrines of coverture were lifted for the first time in English statute law. Although it applied only to a small number of married women, this reform constituted the beginning of changes in legal and economic status of women in matrimonial matters that have continued to the present.

The 1857 Divorce Act retained the official standard that marriage requires separate responsibilities according to sex. The unequal grounds for divorce reflected different moral standards for men and women. Since the wife was expected to be morally pure and sexually innocent, a single act of extramarital sex constituted a violation of marriage duties so severe that the marriage could be dissolved. However, a husband's adultery was considered less serious due to his lesser moral responsibilities. His extramarital sex had to be aggravated by other offenses before it was serious enough to justify divorce. The divorce policy further maintained that marriage involved separate spheres of activity for men and women. The act allowed only the husband to be liable for alimony and child support, since the husband was the breadwinner and had the wife's property. Similarly, only the husband was permitted to sue his spouse's lover for damages. Women were not considered responsible for the financial effects of adultery and divorce.

A small but significant reform in the legal and economic status of women took place with the restoration of *feme sole* property rights to separated or deserted wives. These rights included ownership of earnings and property. Perhaps more important, they meant that these married women had legal standing in court to sue and be sued for contract and tort on an equal basis with their husbands. The policy of the government toward family sex roles thus changed slightly with the passage of the Divorce Act of 1857 in the direction of an improved legal and economic status for women.

THE DEMANDS

Major changes in family life throughout England during the period 1815-1851 encouraged Parliament to consider a major overhaul of the divorce law. A small but steady increase in parliamentary divorce had been evident since Elizabethan times. In the 1700s bishops and nobles had tried to save upper-class marriages and discourage disgruntled husbands from petitioning for the special act. After 1800, petitions for parliamentary divorces multiplied.[2] The divorce business among the nobility alone threatened to overwhelm Parliament and required some streamlining of the state's role in matrimonial causes.[3]

The growing and wealthy middle class, meanwhile, was busy elaborating a code of "respectability" that linked lifetime monogamy with economic prosperity.[4] To have the proper kind of family life—a docile, well-dressed wife, obedient children, and an imposing household—a man had to work hard and accumulate capital. Setting forth the ideal family as a goal implied that a man had the right to end marriage to a wife who violated her marriage vows and the ideals of respectability. He had the right to share his wealth with a proper, well-behaved wife. However, the poor had little cause to complain about their own unhappy marriages. Some reformers responded to the plight of the workers by telling them to fight their way to middle-class wealth and respectability.

In fact, it was the social upheaval attendant to industrialization of the English economy that both produced middle-class wealth and placed great strains on the family life of the workers.[5] The stability of the preindustrial land-based economy depended on lifetime monogamy. The family home was the center of production in farms and villages, and all of its members contributed to economic output. The factory system gradually replaced home industry and changed the living and working patterns of husbands, wives, and children. In various ways their interdependence was lessened. Wages were such that for a family to maintain a minimal living standard, most members, including the children, had to work. At first, with the adoption of factory labor, a father would transfer his entire family from the home to the factory. But various reform acts limiting hours of work for women and children and specialization in jobs separated the family members, the women and children working different hours and often in different places from the father. Factories employed workers, not families. Industrial production, unlike agricultural production, was not based on indissoluble marriage. Wives and husbands were more dependent on the factory owner for survival than on each other. Factory growth also coincided with population growth and urbanization. More and more young people were forming new families in the perilous atmosphere of smoky factory towns.

In the midst of these changes, the Church of England provided little support to troubled families. During the early nineteenth century, the church was at the center of a controversy over its power and role as well as its doctrine and teachings. It was considered part of the old aristocratic order, a stagnant impediment to development of the modern society. Attacks on the church exposed its corruptness, the nonreligious nature of its clergy, and its irrelevance to modern problems. A large number of dissenting faiths—Methodists, Congregationalists, Baptists, Quakers, and Presbyterians—mounted campaigns against the Church of England and sought support among the workers. None of them had the strict proscriptions against divorce that were found in the Anglican Church. By 1851 the census showed that 38 percent of the population attended no church and one-half of the rest, 31 percent of the total, were dissenters.[6] That left the Church of England speaking for less than one-third of the population, mostly the upper and upper-middle classes.

While the wealthy continued to seek relief from unhappy marriages through Parliament, the workers had no choice but to live together under impossible conditions, to separate and live alone, or to form new illegal families despite the unavailability of legal divorce. Through the plight of Stephen Blackpool, the "poor but honest" weaver of Coketown in *Hard Times,* Charles Dickens made an eloquent case for civil divorce. Blackpool asked his employer Mr. Bounderby if there was a law to help him end his miserable marriage to an alcoholic and marry his true love. Bounderby said, "There is such a law," but it was not for Blackpool:

> "Why you'd have to go to Doctors' commons with a suit and you'd have to go to a court of Common Law with a suit, and you'd have to go to the House of Lords with a suit, and you'd have to get an Act of Parliament to enable you to marry again, and it would cost you (if it was a case of very plain sailing), I suppose from a thousand to fifteen hundred pound," said Mr. Bounderby. . . .
>
> "Why then, sir," said Stephen, turning white, and motioning with that right hand of his as if he gave everything to the four winds, "*tis* a muddle. Tis just a muddle a'toogether, an the sooner I'm dead, the better."[7]

Although the Bounderbys told their workers to suffer silently at their looms, others of the middle class sought to reform society to ease the burdens industrialization had placed on the workers' lives. The decades before the 1850s were rich in reform movements that subjected all institutions to review and revision. Of special concern to the issue of family law reform were the ideas of Robert Owen, the Chartists, and the utilitarians.

Robert Owen and the Owenites criticized middle-class control of the factory and argued that the labor of the workers belonged to the workers themselves. They proposed a full-scale overhaul of the social system to improve the conditions of the workers.[8] Such a change included improved education, housing, and social relations, especially in and between families, through community reform. The nuclear family hindered the development of a cooperative community, and the Owenites offered evidence that enforced monogamy led to injustice and cruelty, especially for the children. They advocated a sharing of family roles and responsibilities. Although the communitarian movement was short-lived and became a utopic dream, the ideal of the separate and equal worth of the workers to the society and the dignity of every man and woman challenged the assumption of middle- and upper-class dominance through family respectability and profits.

As Owenite communities were disappearing, Chartism exploded in the 1840s with an intense but brief attack on privilege. The Chartists' list of political reforms reflected their optimism that social justice could be achieved by gaining political equality.[9] They challenged the dominent view that the wealthy classes could take care of and provide for the "lower orders." They proposed that the workers take responsibility for themselves. The misery of workers was not, as the middle-class "do gooders" believed, due to their moral depravity, but to exploitation by those in power. The only way to improve the condition of the workers was for them to get control of the legislative process so that proper social legislation could be passed. Then Parliament would direct its attention to the real problems of the workers and their families.

The utilitarians, following the philosophy of Jeremy Bentham, advocated law reform; it was a means by which Owenite goals of cooperative family life and Chartist demands for worker equality could be achieved. The state was caught in a snare of ambiguous, inconsistent, and unjust laws that prevented it from reaching out and solving great social ills of industrialization. Utilitarians wanted the law to be clear and rational and to further goals of equality, individual achievement, and happiness.[10] The divorce law, for example, not only was inadequate to social need, it favored the rich at the expense of the poor. Those who wanted to end marriages and remarry but could not afford the procedure formed consensual unions. Among the more uneducated and economically deprived classes, a husband leaving his first wife and family and marrying another woman opened himself to a charge of bigamy in common law courts. Utilitarians argued that Parliament should take the divorce question out of the eccleiastical courts entirely and establish separate civil courts and procedures.

The demand for civil divorce arose from both practical and intellectual needs. The practical need was for some means to accommodate the increase in broken marriages resulting from social and economic strains on families. The ecclesiastical courts could separate husband and wife but prevented couples from remarrying. Parliamentary divorces were too slow and too expensive. Ideas of equality, of cooperative families and communities, and of law reform offered ways in which practical needs could be met. They pointed to a uniform new law for civil divorce, available to all, and a special court to administer the law. But issues affecting marriage inevitably produce questions about the relationship of husband and wife. Therefore, the special practical and intellectual needs of women in the early 1800s produced additional demands about divorce reform.

Industrialization brought about fundamental changes in the economic status of all women, both decreasing and increasing their dependency. Factory, mill, and mine labor, for all the exploitation, risk to health, and grossly unequal pay it entailed, gave poor women for the first time the economic independence of paid employment.[11] Middle-class reformers were greatly alarmed at the threat to the moral health of families and therefore all society of the presence of mothers and young girls working alongside men. This "poison," as Lord Shaftesbury put it, in "the waters of life at its very fountain" caused more official concern than the ghastly working conditions and mind-numbing hours women endured for inferior pay.[12] Laws were passed that restricted the use of women's labor in the mines and mills, but failed to recognize their need and desire for paid employment. Working-class women, both married and single, earned money in a wide variety of ways. By 1851, 30 percent of the married women in the cotton districts were employed.[13] Women also pursued needlework, dressmaking, costermongering, hatting, bookbinding, and domestic work. Despite all efforts to reclaim working wives and mothers, their number continued to increase during the century. The law that denied a married woman the right to keep her own earnings seemed increasingly unjust, especially when that same law bound her for life to a layabout, drunkard, or worse.

The women who lived comfortably in middle-class families became increasingly dependent. The cult of family respectability centered around the presence of an emotional, warm, loving, pure, ignorant, and dependent wife and mother under the control and protection of a male.[14] Men monopolized the work that women had once done. Teaching, medicine, nursing, and business became professions, and women were denied formal education necessary to enter these fields. Marriage was viewed as the only acceptable career for women in the middle and upper classes. As their families got more property and wealth, women became poorer and more dependent on marriage for their food and shelter.[15] The economic plight of all middle-class women was poignantly demonstrated by the 1851 census, which reported a dramatic increase in the number of "redundant," that is, socially useless, women. These middle-class women were in poverty; they had to work, but there were no jobs. The great protective common law of coverture did nothing but add further burdens. Unlike their working-class sisters, however, some middle-class women had resources to fight against the law.

Words were the principle resource for educated women: through writing and through persuasion. Between 1820 and 1850 they joined with men in a spirited discussion of "The Woman Question."[16] They mixed in circles of dissenters, liberals, and utilitarians who discussed equality, freedom, and the individual pursuit of happiness, and they applied these notions to women as well as men. This discussion produced the first feminist literature and articulated the demand of middle-class women for an equal share of the benefits of the new society. In accordance with the liberal thought of their time, they expected to obtain social gain through law reform.

A disagreement among utilitarians over the status and rights of women produced some of the best feminist literature of the period. James Mill's famous "Article on Government" in the *Encyclopedia Brittannica* of 1823 argued that there was no need for women to vote since their husbands and fathers could adequately represent them and protect their interests. This view prompted William Thompson to write *An Appeal of One-Half of the Human Race, Women* . . . in 1825. He characterized marriage as legal slavery of women to men and argued for equality for women. He attributed many of his ideas to Anna Wheeler, who was also an influence on Owen and Bentham.[17]

John Stuart Mill was the most famous utilitarian to support the cause of women. He was a feminist who considered the status of a woman in the family basic to her social and political opportunities. He too attributed much of his thinking to a woman, Harriet Taylor. His early interest in the subject of women's status is revealed in letters to Taylor in the 1830s and 1840s. In an essay written in 1831, Mill demonstrated how marriage indissolubility related to women's general condition. He was critical that women's entire status depended on her marrying and on the indissolubility of marriage. This was so because women were brought up unable to subsist for themselves. Marriage was the only status for women. "A married woman is *presumed* to be a useful member of society unless there is evidence to the contrary; a single woman must establish what very few either men or women ever do establish, an individual claim."[18]

For a woman to seek a life not limited to marriage, she must be educated to be independent. This education must accompany a change in the law of marriage. "The indissolubility of marriage is the keystone of woman's present lot, and the whole comes down and must be reconstructed if that is removed."[19] Equality of woman depended on her education and her ability, although not always used, to support herself. When women are thus equal with men, marriage can be based on love, he argued, and when love no longer exists, divorce would be best to achieve the happiness of both.

> The arguments, therefore, in favor of the indissolubility of marriage, are as nothing in comparison with the far more potent arguments for leaving this like the other relations voluntarily contracted by human beings, to depend for its continuance upon the wishes of the contracting parties. The strongest of all these arguments is that by not other means can the condition and character of women become what it ought to be.[20]

This review of changes in social and intellectual aspects of marriage and women's rights provides the context for enactment of the divorce law. Such changes alone do not cause policy; deliberate government action is required to make new laws. Demands are always found in society, but only when government agrees to consider demands can policy be made. Demands for divorce and women's rights are, in some form, as old as marriage itself. English public officials have been making speeches about them since before Henry VIII sent his first wife away. Mill, Thompson, Owen, and

Bentham, like others before and after them, made proposals in response to the economic and social conditions of their time. But it wasn't until 1850 that the government of England agreed to consider the issue of divorce and make a definite policy. Various threads from social needs and ideas about law came together in the mid-nineteenth century to attach the issue of civil divorce and women's rights to a place on the public agenda.

The first attempt to gain serious consideration for divorce in the House of Commons failed. In 1830 Dr. Phillimore introduced a motion to ask the government for a Royal Commission on Ecclesiastical Courts for England and Wales to consider the law of divorce and "the expediency of enabling persons to obtain Divorce from the bonds of matrimony in cases of adultery, by legal processes in courts of competent jurisdiction."[21] He argued that Parliament was not the proper body to grant divorce *a vinculo*. The government and conservative MPs opposed the proposal and after a brief debate defeated the motion 45-102.

Fifteen years later, a sensational bigamy case finally aroused public attention to the injustice of the divorce law that the government could not ignore. In *Regina v. Thomas Hall,* 1845, Mr. Justice Maule asked the defendant, who was convicted of bigamy, why he should not be sentenced. The prisoner is alleged to have replied: "My wife was unfaithful; she robbed me and ran away with another man and I thought I might take another wife." Maule's tongue-in-cheek response was widely publicized:

> You are quite wrong in supposing that. You ought to have brought an action for criminal conversation; that action would have been tried by one of her Majesty's judges at the Assizes; you would probably have recovered damages; and then you should have instituted a suit in the ecclesiastical court for a divorce *a mensa et thoro.* Having got that divorce, you should have petitioned the House of Lords for a divorce *a vinculo,* and should have appeared by counsel at the bar of their Lordships' House. Then, if the Bill passed, it would have gone down to the House of Commons; the same evidence would possibly be repeated there; and if the Royal Assent had been given after that, you might have married again. The whole proceeding would not have cost you more than £1000.
>
> The prisoner: "Ah my Lord, I never was worth a thousand pence in all my life."
>
> J. "That is the law and you must submit to it."[22]

Prime Minister Lord Russell appointed the Royal Commission on the Law of Divorce in 1850 to review the policy on divorce and recommend changes in the law. John Lord Campbell, Chief Justice, chaired the group of lawyers and judges. They turned their attention to resolving three issues concerning the substance of reform: whether to allow divorce *a vinculo* or only legal separation; which court—civil, ecclesiastical, or parliamentary—should be responsible for matrimonial matters; and what grounds should justify divorce or separation. Once divorce received official attention, the government found it also had to deal with feminist issues before reaching a final decision.

THE CONFLICT

The Royal Commission, with one dissentng vote, decided that there should be civil procedures for separation and divorce. However, the grounds were to remain the same as those used by ecclesiastical courts. The issue, as the commission saw it, was to discourage divorce, not make it easier. As Lord Stowall had stated in *Evans v. Evans,* people must learn to take their responsibilities seriously:

> When people understand they must live together, except for a very few reasons known to the law, they learn to soften by mutual accommodation that yoke which they know they cannot shake off, and they become good husbands and good wives from the necessity of remaining husbands and wives—for necessity is a powerful master in teaching the duties of life.[23]

The report of the commission, published in 1853, proposed legislation to transfer the jurisdiction on separation and divorce cases from ecclesiastical courts and Parliament to a special civil divorce court, but to leave the grounds unchanged: adultery for divorce and adultery, cruelty, and desertion for separation. Adultery was the only grounds for divorce justifiable in the Bible and acceptable to the church. The commission concluded that there is always the possibility of reconciliation in a marriage except when the wife commits adultery.

The commission also considered the question of the wife's right to divorce, but saw little justification for it. A wife could easily condone adultery in her husband—in fact, it was in her interest to do so—but it was impossible for the husband to forgive his wife for such a violation:

> Two propositions may therefore be affirmed: First, that the wife has no title to ask for divorce *a vinculo,* when she is aggrieved only by adultery; and secondly, that the husband aggrieved only by adultery can demand, as it were, a divorce *a vinculo,* unless his own conduct has been censurable.[24]

However, the commission wanted to follow precedent. Since four parliamentary divorces had been granted on the petitions of women and since three of them involved incestuous adultery, it recommended one tiny ground by which a wife could sue for divorce: adultery by the husband plus incest.

The Royal Commssion's report was greatly influenced by the legal community, especially Lord Brougham, whom it quoted, and the Law Amendment Society, whose recommendations it copied. Lord Brougham, himself influenced by Bentham, had led the parliamentary battle for a complete overhaul of English law, achieving reforms in business and employment laws; the poor law; criminal law; marriage law; and contract law in the 1820s and 1830s.[25] In 1844 he organized the Law Amendment Society (LAS), composed of lawyers and judges who shared his utilitarian views of law reform. The LAS was one of the growing number of pressure groups in English politics.[26] As social, legal, and political issues became more complex, reformers increased their influence by studying issues and organizing opinion outside Parliament and then presenting specific proposals. Pressure groups enjoyed a special burst of power during the 1840s and 1850s when the fledgling political party system was temporarily weak.

The goal of the LAS was to maintain interest in the continuing need for law reform: "We must have in this country a simple and intelligible body of law, administered for the benefit of all classes by a simple and intelligible procedure."[27] The society drafted bills for Parliament and, through its many connections with prominent individuals in the Commons, the Lords, and especially the Royal Commissions, gained a hearing for its proposals.

In 1848 the LAS formally resolved to pressure the government for a new civil court: "the absolute necessity of a surrender by parliament of its existing jurisdiction."[28] It pointed out that most church officials agreed that the church should turn its control of divorce completely over to lawyers and judges. It refused, however, to depart from the views of its founder that it would be dangerous to make divorce too easy for women. The courts should continue parliamentary practice of granting divorces to husbands for simple adultery by their wives. Brougham feared that if both spouses had the same remedy, a husband could force his wife into a divorce merely by keeping a mistress. Besides, as Dr. Samuel Johnson had said, "The difference is boundless. The man imposes no bastards on his wife."

One distinction must always be kept in view—the distinction between cases of accidental and cases of systematic infidelity—the one admitting the other excluding all reasonable hope of permanent reformation; for so long as a husband is merely chargeable with occasional delinquencies, we agree with Dr. Johnson that a wife should endeavor rather to reclaim her erring spouse than try to get rid of him.[29]

In June 1854, when Lord Chancellor Cranworth introduced his divorce bill based on the Royal Commission's report, he probably felt fairly confident of quick success. After all, the commission enjoyed the support of the legal community and the church. As the commission had recommended, the bill provided for a civil court and divorce *a vinculo* on the grounds of adultery by the wife or adultery and incest by the husband. The Lord Chancellor tried to anticipate the possible opposition.[30] To the opponents of divorce *a vinculo,* he pointed out that the church itself had proposed divorce in the *Reformatorio Legum* in 1549. To those who wanted to expand the grounds for divorce, he argued that adultery was the only grounds justified by the Holy Bible and, also, the only offense that would truly destroy a marriage and prevent all hope of reconciliation. On the subject of equal grounds for men and women, he noted that although provisions of the bill might seem unjust, they were in fact to protect women. If there were equal grounds, he said, a simple act of adultery by a husband, at no loss to his status or reputation, would force his wife into a divorce. Unequal grounds protected the rights of married women to stay married as long as they were chaste. As Lord Campbell, chairman of the Royal Commission, had said (as had Brougham, Bentham, and Johnson), adultery by a husband, although reprehensible, did not make marriage intolerable.

The opponents of the bill made few arguments in this initial debate. Lord Redesdale and the Bishop of Oxford opposed divorce and suggested that adulterers at least should be prohibited from marrying to protect the sanctity of marriage. No one brought up the issue of equal rights for women. As the Second Reading debate droned on, a visitor in the gallery raged at the peers' total neglect of the plight of married women under common law. This spectator, Caroline Norton, prepared to fight the government on the divorce question. As a result of her efforts, the arena of conflict over divorce broadened from a simple debate over legal procedure to a major contest over women's rights.

Caroline S. Norton was the granddaughter of writer Richard Sheridan.[31] Her family were Whigs, and she was in a circle of influential politicians and writers; she herself was a successful writer of plays, poetry, and songs. However, in the 1820s she was a poor marriage prospect. Although she was beautiful and intelligent, she had no money and was too quick-witted to be a docile wife. She became a *mal mariée,* a woman who married the wrong man, and who perhaps shouldn't have married at all. (But in the 1820s to die was better than not to marry!) She separated from her husband, George Norton, shortly after their third son was born.

Mrs. Norton suffered all of the worst fates of a *feme couverte* as a result of her separation. Her husband exercised his legal right to deny her visits to her children, kept the money from her writings, and even sued Prime Minister Lord Melbourne for criminal conversation in 1836. Melbourne was acquitted of the charge, but the well-publicized case damaged Mrs. Norton's reputation, and, as in all such suits, in her case she was unable to defend herself against the charge of adultery. Melbourne even berated her for not being able to handle her brutish husband.

The suit against Melbourne by George Norton "may have done a good deal towards drawing attention to the injustice of the divorce laws of the time."[32] Mrs. Norton had no right to sue for divorce, and her husband had no grounds. He was able to keep her money and pay her only meager amounts for support. At one point, when he reneged on an agreement with her to pay her some maintenance, she found she had no redress; the court did not recognize such an agreement between husband and wife, and she couldn't sue anyone anyway since, as a married woman, she had no standing in court. But she did have her pen and her political connections.

Her first effort was a pamphlet on the guardianship laws: *A Plain Letter to the Lord Chancellor on the Law and Custody of Infants,* written under the name of Pearse Stevenson in 1838 and sent to MPs. Her object was to obtain passage of the Custody of

Infants Bill, which had been introduced in 1836 and became law in 1839. It was a private member bill pushed through by her old friend Lord Lyndhurst, the former Lord Chancellor and law reformer. The act allowed a separated wife to petition the court and, upon proving good character, to gain access to her young children. It was a limited reform, but it set a precedent for the rights of women to their children and was a crack in the wall of nonpersonhood erected by the common law.

In the early 1850s she was pamphleteering again: *English Laws for Women in the Nineteenth Century* was published in 1854 under a pseudonym and distributed at her own expense. It outlined the inequalities in the law for married women.

Thus, when Caroline Norton sat frustrated at the intransigence of the Lords, she had already acquired a great deal of experience pressuring Parliament. Through her skill as a writer, she had been able to use her personal misfortunes to alert the public to the cause of women's rights. She had been friends for years with some of the most prominent leaders in government. In the 1850s some of them were still in Parliament, still moved by her descriptions of suffering under the law. Her style of direct personal influence was soon to become obsolete with the growth of the strong party government after 1867. But in the fragmented political climate of 1850-1857, a direct appeal to the Parliament could be successful.

In 1855 she published in her own name her most important pamphlet: *A Letter to the Queen on Lord Chancellor Cranworth's Marriage and Divorce Bill.* Her title was designed to point out the "anomaly" of the situation of married women who were nonexistent in a country governed by a woman. She, like many feminist writers, sought to promote the status of women by using Queen Victoria as a model of a woman who was not only wife and mother but head of state. Despite the fact that the Queen herself was not noted for her enthusiasm for women's rights, it was difficult for opponents to deny her accomplishments and abilities even though they preferred to emphasize her domestic roles.

Norton reviewed her own misfortunes, indicating that she had learned the English law piecemeal by suffering under it. She pointed out the absolute right of husbands to the control and guardianship of children and the injustice of her husband's rights, although separated from her, to own her copyrights, earnings, and inheritance. All she retained was her talent; even that was not her own, but the only means to seek a change in the laws. "I believe my gift of writing was meant for the noble purpose of rousing others to the gross injustices of the law."[33] If she were a man, she pointed out, she might have been able to do something about the unjust laws for women. "Since I am only a woman, absorbed into my husband, I will put on record in easy language, what the law for women is in this year 1855."[34] At the end of the pamphlet, she bitterly urged the Lord Chancellor to give this writing to her husband along with her other copyrights, since it is "only a woman's pamphlet."

Norton scolded the Lords for refusing to help women when many, including Brougham and commission members Campbell, St. Leonards, and Beaumont, had previously criticized the harshness and injustice of the common law. She likened the attitude of the Lords to "a party of miners who have given up the attempt to dig out persons buried in the superincumbent [sic] earth. They would be very glad to do something towards amending the laws for women but, really, 'the subject is so surrounded with difficulty.' "[35]

First, she clearly reviewed the position of married women under English law:

1. a married woman has no legal existence whether or not she is living with her husband;
2. her property is his property;
3. she cannot make a will, the law gives what she has to her husband despite her wishes or his behavior;
4. she may not keep her earnings;
5. he may sue for restitution of conjugal rights and thus force her, as if a slave, to return to his home;
6. she is not allowed to defend herself in divorce;
7. she cannot divorce him since the House of Lords in effect will not grant a divorce to her;
8. she cannot sue for libel;
9. she cannot sign a lease or transact business;
10. she cannot claim support from her husband, his only obligation is to make sure she doesn't land in the parish poorhouse if he has means;
11. she cannot bind her husband to any agreement.

In short, "as her husband, he has the right to all that is hers; as his wife she has no right to anything that is his."[36]

Then she criticized the government that refused to allow any relief for women. Despite the fact that members of both houses had denounced the laws as they affected married women, she noted, all their bill did was take power of divorce from ecclesiastical courts and give it to a civil court. The divorce law would allow a husband to divorce his wife, but not vice-versa, and the procedure would be expensive keeping divorce out of the reach of poor men as well.

The notion of equal grounds for divorce had been rejected by the powers that be despite the fact that, as Norton pointed out, the Scottish law had provided equal grounds for divorce for many years. The Lords seemed to be concerned with the effect on the morals of the community if a wife, like her husband, were able to sue for divorce on the grounds of a single act of adultery. She launched into a satirical account of the effects of equal grounds on morality in Scotland, intimating that the Lords were afraid of allowing divorce for women because men were so philandering that marriage would entirely crumble as an institution.

She saved her sharpest barbs for Lord Chancellor Cranworth, who had offered in the opening debate on the bill in 1854 his justification of unequal grounds for husband and wife, effectively restricting the right of divorce to husbands alone:

> If adultery on the part of the husband is to entitle him to a divorce, inasmuch as the husband—which may be bad morality, but it is the fact—suffers little on that account in the opinion of the world at large—for it is notorious that, while the wife who committed adultery loses her station in society the same punishment is not awarded to the husband who is guilty of the same crime—he may, without any sacrifice, on his part, but by merely being a little profligate, and multiplying his acts of adultery, be able to effect his object.[37]

Norton accused him of saying that with equal grounds, a husband could get rid of his wife by being only "a little profligate," that is, by committing simple adultery, and that a wife could easily condone such action in her husband, which, of course, was impossible for him to condone in her.

Ha! said Caroline Norton: starve or condone was the language of the law for women. Since she had no independence, she had to be forced to accept the sins of her husband or find herself friendless or penniless. Property was more protected in England than women were. A person could go to jail for stealing a shilling, but a man could spend his wife's income on his mistress and be considered only "a little profligate." "In brief, the legal axiom is that sin is not a sin in a man, if it be against a woman; and more especially against a woman he vowed at God's alter to cherish and protect." Norton continued: All men's sins were accepted socially as well. A wife had the choice of condoning his sins or living utterly alone, deprived of all, and married only to his name. "Either let men renounce the privilege of divorce, and the assertion that marriage is a dissoluble contract—or allow the weaker part that refuge from intolerable wrong, which they claim as a matter of necessity for themselves."[38]

A Letter to the Queen was widely read, and it appears to have had a substantial impact. A lively discussion in literary and legal journals ensued.[39] Although many agreed that something should be done to help women, few were willing to go as far as to agree with Norton that divorce and property rights should be completely equal for men and women. One who did was Barbara Leigh Smith, whose pamphlet *A Brief Summary in Plain Language of the Most Important Laws of England Concerning Women, Together with a Few Observations Thereon* had appeared anonymously the year before. After Norton's pamphlet was published, Smith gained the support of the LAS to launch a full attack on property rights of married women. The campaign of the Married Women's Property Committee is fully discussed in the next chapter.

Norton's opponents feared that equal rights would divide husband and wife and make antagonists in the home. Many could not agree that adultery of a husband should have the same legal status as that of the wife. Only the wife could bring "spurious children" into the marriage. What is important to the outcome of policy concerning divorce is not the public discussion engendered by Norton's pamphlet but its effect on the House of Lords, especially on two prominent ex-Chancellors: Brougham and Lyndhurst. Brougham, not always a Caroline Norton fan, said of *A Letter to the Queen:* "It is as clever a thing as ever was written and it has produced a great good. I feel certain that the law of divorce will be much amended and she has greatly contributed to it."[40] Lyndhurst, who had helped Norton with the custody of infants law reform in 1837, was apparently impressed once more with the lady's plight and her pamphlet.[41]

Lord Cranworth reintroduced the bill in May 1856 without a change. Although he referred to the Norton pamphlet, his position on women's rights was the same as two years earlier. As the secretary of the Lords reported his speech:

> It was the common feeling of mankind that, if a husband respected and treated his wife with kindness, the sin on the part of the husband was not necessarily an unpardonable offense. There were cases in which a wife might and ought to condone, but the common feeling of mankind told them that this must be on the part of the wife only.[42]

Although the views of Cranworth had not changed, the attendance at the House of Lords session had. Lyndhurst and Brougham came from their retirement to see to it that the new divorce law provided for more rights for women. Their biographies neglect to report on their participation in these proceedings, although Theodore Martin commented in *A Life of Lord Lyndhurst* that Lyndhurst "pushed through" the divorce reforms. Their careers are certainly not associated with the woman question. Their great contributions had been in an earlier time when they confronted each other over issues of constitutional and legal reform.

RESOLUTION OF THE CONFLICT

The debate and subsequent decision making unfolded in the mid-nineteenth-century English political and institutional context. This environment affected the way the conflict over divorce law reform and women's rights was resolved.

Between 1846 and 1867, the political parties in the House of Commons were unable to provide the basis for governments. For example, the general election of 1852 produced a loose array of liberal-conservatives and conservative-liberals, Whig families, Peelites, and protectionists.[43] The Tories, who had formed an electoral organization in 1833 and called themselves the Conservative party, held a plurality of 300. But the majority of the Commons was shared by liberal groups: 270 Whigs, 40 Peelites, and 40 Irish. None of them had any organization in Parliament itself, so the formation of Cabinets depended on informal negotiations among several strong leaders and the guidance of Queen Victoria and Prince Albert.

The Aberdeen coalition of Whigs and Conservatives governed from 1852 to 1855. It was, in a sense, an interim government between the rule of two rival political stars: Lord John Russell, Prime Minister from 1846 to 1852, and Viscount Palmerston, Prime Minister for nine years between 1855 and 1865. It was led by elderly politicians who tried to balance intense rivalries among Whig and Conservative factions. A younger group of leaders, including William Gladstone and Benjamin Disraeli were deeply involved in the intrigues surrounding the rise and fall of this coalition. Part of Aberdeen's agreement with Russell and the Whigs was that there be a Whig Lord Chancellor. They selected Lord Cranworth (Robert Monsey Rolfe) who had received his title in 1850 after a long career as a Whig lawyer. Thus he had little experience in the House of Lords when he became Lord Chancellor. Cranworth used his office to process law reform proposals, such as divorce, that had been initiated by his predecessors. He has been described as quiet, agreeable, and generally undistinguished. Probably owing to his unremarkable personality in a time of so many remarkable ones, he was able to stay in office until 1858.[44]

The Aberdeen government fell in a hail of criticism over the conduct of the Crimean War (1854-1856). The Queen tried in vain to persuade several others to form a government before turning to Palmerston.[45] He had been a popular foreign minister in the Aberdeen coalition and a fixture in English politics during most of the nineteenth century. The reconstituted coalition faced overwhelming opposition in the House of Commons, notably from Russell and Gladstone, Peelites and Radicals, and all of the Conservatives. But Palmerston was popular with the public and able to keep his first Cabinet in office for a year after the war ended.

In the spring of 1856, as soon as peace had returned, Cranworth brought his divorce bill back to the House of Lords. He was no doubt overwhelmed to discover that his distinguished predecessor, Lyndhurst, and his mentor, Brougham, took such an interest in the subject of married women's legal rights that they came out of retirement to participate in the proceedings. From the time Lyndhurst entered the chamber, he took control of the government's bill, and Cranworth receded into the background.

In the debate, Lyndhurst outlined the legal plight of married women, staying close to the catalog of complaints in *A Letter to the Queen.* First, he lamented the disabilities of coverture, which continued despite the fact that a married woman might be legally separated from her husband. Her property and earnings continued to go to her husband. A separated wife had no right to sue: she was "homeless, helpless, hopeless, and almost destitute of civil rights." For the first time, a member of Parliament suggested the need to improve the property and legal rights of married women in separation.

Second, he was critical of the law of criminal conversation, that quaint but destructive practice of suing the alleged lover of a wife for damages. He pointed to the unfairness of the practice to women. If the suit were successful, the wife would be ruined for life as an adulteress and lose all of her marriage rights, yet be unable to appear in court to defend herself. She would be denied all rights of the accused under English law. Even if the case were not proved, the woman suffered, for her reputation would be damaged just for having the issue brought up.

The third proposal made by Lyndhurst involved the unequal grounds for divorce contained in the government bill. He argued that divorce only on the grounds of a husband's incestuous adultery would be so rare as to be no right at all. Adultery by a spouse can be just as intolerable to the wife as to the husband:

> to live in a black state of desolution—all her prospects blasted—driven from her home, perhaps separated from her children, with no object on which to fix her affections, exposed to the designs of profligate men, and scarcely able by any care or caution to avoid calumny and slander—living on the brink of destruction.[46]

Lyndhurst sought control of a select committee to consider his amendments. His motion to refer the entire bill to such a committee was seconded by Brougham who, as president of the Law Amendment Society, pointed out that there was much interest in the society in the plight of married women (recorded by a House of Lords reporter):

> It would be not only superfluous but impertinent, after the statement of his noble and learned friend; to dwell longer upon these gross cases of injustice, cruelty, and inhumanity practiced upon married women by the present law; but he must say that unless something be done to change it—unless some redress be afforded—we must be content to continue to be held up to the rest of mankind as pretending to be a civilized country, while in reality living under a system more barbarous and more inconsistent with itself than existed in any other part of the world.[47]

The Lord Chancellor agreed to send the bill to a select committee after it passed Second Reading.

The committee was composed of the major proponents and opponents of the bill and held five meetings in May and June.[48] The changes in the area of women's rights recommended by the committee were:

1. A separated wife would have control of her earnings and property and might contract and be sued as if she were *feme sole.*
2. The grounds for divorce by a wife's petition would be expanded to include adultery by the husband plus extreme cruelty, incest, bigamy, or desertion for four years.

The committee considered a proposal to abolish suits of criminal conversation but rejected it. Lyndhurst's proposal for property rights for the separated or deserted wife was accepted readily.

Lord Campbell, chairman of the Royal Commission, expressed his support for the bill as amended in the select committee, including retention of criminal conversation suits and unequal although expanded grounds for divorce. With respect to the latter, he stated that the crime of adultery between husband and wife was the same, but the consequences were not. A wife might condone adultery by her husband, but "when adultery was committed by a woman all purposes of the marriage were forever annulled, there could be no condonation on the part of the husband."[49] Since the Lord Chancellor and the commission chairman accepted the committee's recommendations on women's rights, the bill passed after a brief Report stage and Third Reading. The House of Commons correctly anticipated a long debate on the measure. Since there was little time left in the session, the bill was deferred.

On 19 May 1857 Lord Cranworth launched the Second Reading debate for the third time. His arguments had changed little. Again he said on the subject of equality of grounds: "It was possible for a wife to pardon a husband who committed adultery; but it was hardly possible for a husband ever really to pardon the adultery of a wife.[50] Again he offered little explanation, assuming that any reasonable peer would certainly agree with what the Lord Chan cellor believed to be the overwhelming opinion of mankind.

Lyndhurst, now eighty-seven, was in the House to reiterate his arguments about equality of the sexes. He proposed a revision of the section on criminal conversation and was successful in getting the government to accept a substitute: "whoever shall commit adultery with a married woman shall be guilty of a misdemeanor" (later rejected by the House of Commons).

During 1856 and 1857 other opponents of the bill were active but not as successful in achieving changes as was Lyndhurst. Lord Redesdale was the sole dissenting member in the Royal Commission to oppose divorce of any kind. He found some allies among conservatives and bishops in the Lords. The Bishop of Oxford was a particularly staunch opponent of divorce. His amendments to prevent divorce were debated in July 1856. The arguments centered around interpretations of the Bible about whether divorce was permissible. The Bishop of Oxford rejected the government's argument that the bill merely extended the right of divorce to the poor by transferring jurisdiction from the Parliament to the civil court. There were no petitions from the poor demanding this right, the bishop said. Viscount Dungannon expressed concern that if the middle and lower classes found out about divorce, they would be in collusion to commit acts that would allow them to divorce, leading thus to a further deterioration of morals among a class already fearfully limited in respectability.

The Bishop of Oxford, seeing that his plea to eliminate divorce completely had limited chance against a determined government and aroused public opinion, proposed that to save the sacred nature of marriage found in scripture, the adulterous wife should not be allowed to marry her lover. This amendment was accepted in the House of Lords in 1856, but it raised such a furor in the Commons that it was omitted from the 1857 government bill. The opposition arguments among the Conservatives and bishops continued until the end, but they were not successful. The church was not united: the Bishop of London openly disagreed with the Bishop of Oxford by supporting the bill. The government asserted that it had the support of the Commons for the basic principles of the divorce proposal.

To summarize action by the House of Lords, the following is a list of policy proposals, their source, and their outcome in the legislative deliberations:

SOURCE	*PROPOSAL*	*ACTION*
Government	Divorce court	Revised in House of Lords
	Adultery for husband	Unchanged
	Adultery + incest—wife	Augmented by committee, House of Lords

SOURCE	*PROPOSAL*	*ACTION*
Lyndhurst	Separated wife property rights	Accepted, committee, House of Lords
	Equal grounds	Rejected, committee, House of Lords
	Abolish criminal conversation	Rejected, committee, House of Lords
		Accepted, House of Lords
		Rejected, House of Commons
Oxford	No divorce	Rejected, House of Lords
	No remarriage	Rejected, House of Lords

The bill passed the Third Reading on 23 June 1857. Lyndhurst and some colleagues filed a formal protest with the House after the bill had passed, recording their opposition to the unequal grounds for divorce. The reasons they cited were injustice and the contradiction with Christian principles: Adultery of the wife may lead to spurious offspring, but "so may adultery of the husband lead to other circumstances giving women equal claim to this remedy."[51]

At this point, however, Lyndhurst had done all he could in the cause of women's rights in divorce. He had wanted equal and expanded grounds, removal of criminal conversation damages, and property rights for separated women. He had been influenced in these matters directly by the Norton pamphlet and Mrs. Norton herself. The political climate was helpful to his effort. In 1855 the first women's rights organization was formed, and in 1856 the House of Commons received more than seventy petitions (one signed by 3,000 people including many women writers) for the improvement of laws affecting women. In 1857 a private member bill regarding married women's property was filed separately and passed the Second Reading in the Commons. The pressure was building. Lyndhurst was able to use his status and parliamentary ability to engineer the Lords' response to that pressure, but he could not achieve all he wanted—equal grounds for men and women in divorce. The government feared loss of support for the bill if the idea of equality was embodied therein.

After the bill passed the House of Lords, Palmerston decided to push it in the House of Commons. In those days, the Prime Minister had few procedural or political tools to have his way. The MPs guarded their power and independence. In 1840 they had reluctantly conceded more time to government bills and less to those of private members, but only after the threat of legislative immobility loomed. The government relied mainly on the goodwill of the members of both sides of the House to finish debates and allow a division.

Palmerston had no party organization to whip his supporters to the government's will. To add to his troubles, many opposed his Cabinet and were gathering forces to defeat him and bring about a general election. Waiting to trip him on the divorce bill was a formidable parliamentary opponent, Gladstone. Gladstone gathered opponents to defeat or at least test the Prime Minister, using the tactic of deliberately wasting parliamentary time, preventing any action on the bill at all.[52] Every stage of consideration provoked long hours of debate: there were several motions for postponement, each of which was defeated after a strong statement of support by one of the representatives of the government. Gladstone was called upon at one point to explain his role in the Lincoln divorce scandal eight years earlier.[53] The Prime Minister met Gladstone's challenge, keeping Parliament sitting through one of the hottest summers in decades, and threatened to stay sitting until the bill passed, no matter how long it took.

Many of the issues that were brought out in the Lords surfaced during the Commons debates on the bill in the summer of 1857. There were specific proposals to amend the bill to improve the status of women. The MP for Devonport proposed that married women be given separate property rights. This proposal was criticized by the government and withdrawn. Henry Drummond's amendment for "perfect equality" in grounds for husband and wife was defeated. The opposition argued for a separate moral standard for men and women. Buxton, for example, said: "the distinction drawn in this clause [unequal grounds] was consistent with the intuitive feeling of mankind. In all ages it has been felt that the adultery of the wife brought ruin on the married state, but not so simple unfaithfulness of the husband."[54]

Puller said that "if the same facility for divorce was extended to the woman as was given to the man, a power would be given to a selfish husband, by committing adultery, to drive the wife into divorce court."[55] *Punch,* commenting on the argument, suggested another purpose of the opponents: "Lastly Mr. Drummond, the Angel of the Church in Gordon Square, endeavored to place the husband and wife on a footing of equality as to the offenses for which divorce could be asked, and the Committee [of the House] being Men of the World, were mightily amused at so prepostrous a proposition, negatived it by 126-65 and doubtless have since made, in club windows, curious comments on the probable changes in London society which such an enactment might produce."[56]

In debate, Gladstone managed to straddle the major issues: he argued *against* divorce but *for* equality of grounds. It was not unusual at various steps in the bill's consideration for the proponents of equality and the opponents of divorce to vote together. Gladstone stands out as the only MP who combined both positions in his arguments.

He opposed divorce law as a retrograde step, "pregnant with the most dangerous consequences to our social interest."[57] It was not desired by the people and was against the teachings of Christianity. This argument was accompanied by a long interpretation and discussion of scripture. Attorney General Sir Richard Bethell pointed out that despite Gladstone's eloquent attack on divorce, he was a member of the Cabinet that introduced the same bill in 1854.

Scriptural authority was the basis of Gladstone's support of equal grounds:

> I believe that the evil of introducing this principle of inequality between men and women is far greater than the evil which would arise from additional cases of divorce *a vinculo;* . . . if it be assumed that the indissolubility of marriage has been the result of the operation of the Christian religion on earth, still more emphatically it may be assumed that the principle of the equality of the sexes has been the consequence of that religion.[58]

Equality of grounds would do a great deal to improve the status of married women as well: "By arming her with the right of divorce you would greatly increase her power over him, and would deter him from the commission of offenses which among husbands are infinitely more common than among wives."[59] This argument might have increased the fears of those who suspected that rights for women meant the undermining of male dominance in the respectable middle-class family.

During the committee of the whole and the Report stage, the debate continued on through August 7, 13, 14, 17, 18, and 19. Gladstone tried to talk the bill out, but the government persisted. On August 20 the Third Reading debate was capped by a supportive statement from Prime Minister Palmerston, his only formal statement on the subject. Lord Redesdale made a last attempt to table the bill when the Lords considered the Commons amendments; he was defeated by only two votes and the bill became law on August 28 with the Royal Assent.

Punch summed up the Divorce Act as a measure that (1) tried everyone's patience and eloquence, (2) consumed much time, and (3) was carried back and forth from one house to another: a long struggle for a measure that the government insisted did little to change the existing practice.[60]

Mr. Punch gave his own poetic analysis:

> The Divorce Bill Dissected
>
> *by Mr. Punch, 5 September 1857*
>
> He may get a Divorce—that's a grave and solemn thing;
> Annulling the marriage and melting the ring;
> And though actions like those which disgrace us are barred,
> He may claim from Lotharios what juries award.
>
> But you have no right for divorce Joan to stir
> (Save in cases so shocking they never occur.)
> Except he's so base as from virtue to draw
> One he may not espouse—say a sister-in-law.[61]

CONFLICT RESOLUTION AND FEMINIST INFLUENCE

The Divorce and Matrimonial Causes Act of 1857 changed the official definition of responsibilities and status of women and men in family law in England. Civil divorce *a vinculo* and separation were established. Unequal grounds for husband and wife, however, reinforced the double moral standard. A step was taken toward economic and legal rights for married women by guaranteeing separated women rights to property and earnings. The law did not affect property already in possession of the husband. These features were included in the new statute as a result of the particular pattern of interaction among various interests during the decision-making process. In characterizing this process, the influence of feminists on the policy outcome must be analyzed, since changes in the sex-role definitions in the law were, in part, due to the influence of feminists.

The two stages of conflict resolution were, first, to establish judicial separation and civil divorce and, second, to alter the status of married women in separation and divorce. The conflicts over whether or not to have civil divorce were settled by the Royal Commission on the Law of Divorce. Such commissions, which were originally instruments of the Crown, were very popular with governments of the period.[62] By their use, Cabinets kept control over the investigation of issues and the preparation of bills and avoided surrendering crucial decision-making power to the committees of the Commons. The government could be more certain of an outcome favorable to its own interests by appointing sympathetic commissioners, as well as prominent and distinguished public officials—in this case lawyers and judges—who gave the commission reports that added credibility with the public. In 1854 the government wrote the bill according to the commission's recommendations, and the law officers in the House of Lords and the House of Commons pushed the bill through, fending off amendments that would change its basic features. During the long legislative battle, the bill changed little with respect to establishment of a divorce procedure in civil courts based on ecclesiastic and legislative practice.

The policy changes concerning the status of married women in separation and divorce were enacted through a different process centering in the legislature rather than the administration. Proposals for equality for women originated among feminists outside the government and the legal community. The government and the Royal Commission considered suggestions for equal grounds and dismissed them. These demands were injected into the legislative discussion in the House of Lords by prominent nongovernmental members. The conflicts between proponents of women's rights, opponents, and the government were effectively settled in the Select Committee of the House of Lords in 1856 under the chairmanship of Lord Lyndhurst. The compromises worked out in that committee remained in the act.

The government was represented on the committee by the Lord Chancellor and Lord Campbell, the Chief Justice and chairman of the Royal Commission on Divorce. They wanted to solve the problem of civil divorce with as little departure from existing practice as possible. They were ready to accept only those amendments necessary to get the bill through the House of Commons, and they were not sympathetic to moral or ideological arguments about equality for women. The proponents of equal rights for women were led by the chairman of the committee, Lord Lyndhurst, and included the Marquess of Landsdowne, Lord St. Leonards, Lord Wynford, and Lord Somerhill (Brougham was not on the committee). They proposed equal grounds in divorce, property rights for legally separated or deserted married women, and an end to criminal conversation suits. Conservatives of religious, class, and moral bent constituted opposition on the committee, both to divorce and equal rights. They included Lord Redesdale and the Bishop of Oxford.

The government held the balance of power on the seventeen-member committee. It was prepared to accept only those changes that it believed had sufficient popular support to affect the bill's success in the House of Commons. The government accepted the proposal for property rights for married women who had been separated. It had to compromise on the issue of equal grounds by expanding grounds for women, but rejected complete equality. The proposal to eliminate suits for criminal conversation failed in the committee, with only the Marquess of Landsdowne, Lords Wynford, St. Leonards, and Somerhill voting with Lyndhurst to abolish it.

Lyndhurst and his supporters were not successful in getting the government to accept equal grounds for divorce or abolish suits for criminal conversation. The principle of the moral equality of men and women was contrary to the essential conservatism of many reformers. The double standard in the divorce law was complementary to middle-class notions of respectability and the separate spheres for men and women. Legislators had such widespread agreement on these points that proponents of inequality often merely asserted the differences in the adultery of the wife and husband without explaining or defending it. The politically active considered equality for women to be a revolutionary subject in the 1850s. Little outside pressure for equal grounds was evident, other than Norton's pamphlet. No one offered evidence that wives suffered due to the simple adultery of their husbands. Rather, legislators feared that husbands would force women into divorce, increasing the number of divorces drastically. It was thus agreed that severe restrictions on women's rights to divorce would protect both women and their families.

The major victory for the cause of women's rights was establishment of *feme sole* property rights for separated women. Property rights and the compromise on grounds were included in the act primarily due to the actions of Lyndhurst in proposing the changes and insisting on a select committee to amend the bill. Lyndhurst, in turn, was directly influenced by the writings of Caroline Norton. He quoted from her pamphlet *A Letter to the Queen* during debate. Norton's writings also stirred public opinion over the plight of married women who had been deserted by or separated from their husbands. Demands were coming to the House of Commons for a complete reform of married women's property law. Several petitions were sent to the Commons during the 1855 and 1856 sessions. A private member bill was introduced in 1857 for *feme sole* rights for all married women. Providing property rights in divorce gave the government the opportunity to alleviate the suffering of the hard cases without contemplating a major reform in married woman's rights.

The organized women's rights movement began in the 1850s over the issue of married women's property rights. The first group of women petitioned the House of Commons in 1855. Their activities contributed to the expression of public opinion in support of married women's rights and equality. However, they did not have a direct effect on the outcome through participation in decision making. Such improvements in the status of women that were achieved by the divorce bill were due to the influence of the writings of Caroline Norton on members of the select committee.

It follows, therefore, that feminists did have influence on divorce reform. To come to that conclusion, however, requires an examination of the allegation by Norton's biographers, Acland, Iremonger, and Moore, as well as Ray Strachey, that she did not believe in equality for women and was therefore not a feminist. They explain her political activities as nothing more than attempts to gain some relief for her personal problems. They have based their conclusions on two quotations from her writings.

In 1838 Norton wrote a letter to the *Examiner* denying she was the author of an anonymous article on women's rights in *Metropolitan Magazine.* She wrote: "I for one believe in the natural superiority of man, as I do in the existence of God. The natural position of woman is inferiority to man. Amen! That is a thing of God's appointing not of man's divising. I believe it sincerely as part of my religion. . . . I never pretended to the wild and ridiculous notion of equality."[63] This letter appeared at precisely the time Norton was seeking access to her children, then in her husband's control, through the pending Custody of Infants Bill. She professed opposition to equality and support for protection of women by men, all the while working for equalitarian reforms. This was no doubt a pragmatic move, for in the 1830s the people in power associated feminism with socialism. "Feminism attracted to its adherents a reputation for subversiveness in regard to the perceived notions about property and distinction between classes."[64] To be considered a feminist may have been proof of immoral character. Such a reputation could jeopardize her campaign to gain legal access to her children. To deny her egalitarian notions was politic, yet did not prohibit her from a future campaign for equality in the divorce law in the 1850s. By then her children were grown.

The other statement used to demonstrate her lack of conviction in women's equality is found in *A Letter to the Queen:* "So women are inferior to men. God has ordained it. I am inferior to Mr. Norton." From accounts of her life, it appears very unlikely that she *ever* believed she was inferior to George Norton in any way other than legally. Also, it is important to consider the statement in context. It is followed by this explanation:

> Put me then (my ambition extends no further) in the same position as all Mr. Norton's other inferiors—in that of his housekeeper whom he could not libel with impunity, of an apprentice whom he could not maltreat lawlessly, of a scullion whose wages he could not refuse, of a labourer with whom he would not argue that a signature to a contract is worthless.[65]

In other words, she asked the same legal rights as any person not married to Norton would receive at his hands. The notion of inferiority is used to make one of her points about the law most effectively.

These two statements, taken out of context, are unrepresentative of Norton's own views. Her many other statements advocate a feminist point of view, although there is no record that she labeled herself a feminist. She often wrote of the need for women to be protected by the law, since they were not protected by their husbands. But as can be seen in *A Letter to the Queen,* she was arguing that legal rights for women be guaranteed against the greed of husbands who might confiscate all their wives had earned. Such protection is not in the sense of special treatment for the "weaker sex," but rather, the equal protection of life and property that all citizens should expect from English law.

Recall her comment upon hearing the Second Reading debate on the Divorce Bill in 1854 that the Lords reminded her of "A party of miners who have given up the attempt to dig out persons in the superincumbent earth. They would be very glad to do something towards amending the laws for women but really 'the subject is so surrounded with difficulty.' " In *A Letter to the Queen* she asked: "Are the laws of England so surrounded with difficulty that they cannot possibly be remodeled to any pattern of equal justice, the laws between husband and wife?"[66]

Norton preferred to be evaluated as an individual in terms of her character and by the same standards as men: "That man is not my superior who has greater comeliness of appearance, or a quicker human intelligence; but he that is stronger hearted, and a more faithful servant to God."[67] Caroline Norton wrote on those subjects in which she had a personal interest, rather than the full gambit of the woman question. She concentrated on an area where law reform was crucial in order that most women might take full advantage of educational, employment, and political opportunities. Perhaps, at the time, she was even more daring than other writers who discussed conventional topics of education and employment, in that she challenged the legal foundation of the middle-class family based as it was on the dependence of women and the authority of men.

Caroline Norton became a feminist spokeswoman for the rights of married women and through her writing ability and political connections was influential in including her proposals in the Divorce Act. Why was she successful? She was talented at writing at a time when pamphlets were a major means of influencing public opinion. She wrote during a climate of reform when there was increasing interest in equal rights. She was able to take advantage of the aristocratic system through her personal connections in the House of Lords while that body still had the dominant role in law reform and before the increasing complexity of government required organization of interest groups. The government was not supported by strict party discipline and thus was more susceptible to make compromises in the legislature than if it had a solid party majority. Despite the fact that the Divorce Bill was sponsored by the government, through direct contacts with the legislature, an individual and a feminist was able to influence the policy outcome in favor of women.

CONCLUSION

The first Divorce Act in England was adopted at the end of a long period of reform that had begun in the 1820s in response to changes in the industrializing society. Law reform during this period was guided by utilitarian values of equality and happiness. Tensions between official values of marriage and the actual behavior in the families were reduced by easing restrictions on divorce, and the worst injustices of coverture property rights were alleviated by allowing a woman, separated from her husband, to have control of her earnings and property. The slight but important reforms in the legal rights of married women were made possible by the fact that the scope of conflict expanded from an administrative body to the legislature where the government did not have complete control. Weak party organization and the relative importance of personal connections made it possible for feminist views, expressed by one disenfranchised citizen, to be heard and incorporated, in part, into the law.

NOTES

1. Divorce and Matrimonial Causes Act of 1857, 20 & 21, *Vict.*, 85.

2. Of the 250 divorces granted by Parliament between 1658 and 1858, 200 were given after 1800. Four of the total were on application by women. R. H. Graveson, "The Background of the Century," in *A Century of Family Law, 1857-1957,* ed. R. H. Graveson and F. R. Crane (London: Sweet & Maxwell, 1957), 1-19.

3. There was a proposal in the House of Lords in 1844 to transfer authority for divorce to the Judicial Committee of the Privy Council.

4. John Osborne, *The Silent Revolution* (New York: Scribner's, 1970).

5. Neil J. Smelser, *Social Change in the Industrial Revolution* (Chicago: University of Chicago Press, 1959); S. G. Checkland, *The Rise of Industrial Society in England, 1815-1885* (New York: St. Martin's Press, 1964); J.F.P. Harrison, *The Early Victorians, 1832-1851* (New York: Praeger, 1971); Dorothy Marshall, *Industrial England, 1776-1851* (London: Routledge & Kegan Paul, 1973); Norman Gash, *Aristocracy and People: Britain, 1815-1865* (Cambridge, Mass.: Harvard University Press, 1979); Harold Perkin, *The Origins of Modern English Society, 1780-1880* (London: Routledge & Kegan Paul, 1969).

6. M. A. Crowther, *Church Embattled: Religious Controversy in Mid-Victorian England* (Newton Abbot, Devon: David and Charles, 1970).

7. Charles Dickens, *Hard Times* (1854; reprint ed., New York: Nathan Simon), 67-68.

8. R. G. Garnett, *Cooperation and the Owenite Socialist Communities in Britain, 1825-1845* (Manchester: Manchester University Press, 1972); John W. Derry, *The Radical Tradition* (London: Macmillan, 1967), 119-54.

9. Malcolm I. Thomis and Peter Holt, *Threats of Revolution in Britain, 1789-1848* (London: Macmillan, 1977), 100-116; Alex Wilson, "Chartism," in *Popular Movements, 1830-1850,* ed. J. T. Ward (London: Macmillan, 1970), 116-34.

10. M. H. James, ed., "Bentham and Legal Theory," *Northern Ireland Legal Quarterly* 24 (1973); W. Friedman, *Legal Theory* (New York: Columbia University Press, 1967); George L. Nesbitt, *Benthamite Reviewing: The First Twelve Years of the Westminster Review* (New York: Columbia University Press, 1934); David Roberts, "The Utilitarian Conscience," in *The Conscience of the Victorian State,* ed. Peter Marsh (Syracuse, N.Y.: Syracuse University Press, 1979), 39-72.

11. Margaret Hewitt, *Wives and Mothers in Victorian Industry* (London: Rockliff, 1958); Ivy Pinchbeck, *Women Workers and the Industrial Revolution* (London: Frank Cass, 1930).

12. Quoted by Sally Alexander, "Women's Work in Nineteenth Century London: A Study of the Years 1820-1850," in *Rights and Wrongs of Women,* ed. Juliet Mitchell and Ann Oakley (London: Penguin, 1976), 62.

13. Hewitt, *Wives and Mothers,* chap. 1.

14. Helene E. Roberts, "Marriage, Redundancy or Sin: The Painters' View of Women in the First Twenty-five Years of Victoria's Reign," in *Suffer and Be Still: Women in the Victorian Age,* ed. Martha Vicinus (Bloomington, Ind.: Indiana University Press, 1972), 45-76; Patricia Branca, *Silent Sisterhood* (Pittsburgh: Carnegie-Mellon Press, 1975).

15. Richard J. Evans, *The Feminists* (London: Croom Helm, 1977), 13-39.

16. Carol Bauer and Lawrence Ritt, *Free and Ennobled: Source Readings in the Development of Victorian Feminism* (Oxford: Pergamon, 1979);

Joseph and Olive Banks, "List of Relevant Books and Pamphlets on the Woman Question, Published in Britain, 1792-1880," in *Feminism and Family Planning in Victorian England,* (New York: Schocken Books, 1964), 135-40; John Killham, *Tennyson and the Princess: Reflections of an Age* (London: University of London Press, 1958), 4.

17. William Thompson, *Appeal of One Half of the Human Race, Women, Against the Pretensions of the Other Half, Men* (1828; reprint ed., New York: Source Book, 1970), vii, ix.

18. F. A. Hayek, ed., *John Stuart Mill and Harriet Taylor: Their Correspondence and Subsequent Marriage* (Chicago: University of Chicago Press, 1951), 60.

19. Ibid., 63-64.

20. Ibid., 74.

21. Parliamentary Debates, Official Report, III *Hansard* 24, c. 1268.

22. Quoted in Graveson, "The Background of the Century," 1-19.

23. Royal Commission, *First Report of Commissioners Appointed by Her Majesty to Inquire in the Law of Evidence, More Particularly into the Mode of Obtaining Divorce a Vinculo Matrimonii* (1604) XL 249, 1852-1853.

24. Ibid., 11.

25. Henry Peter Brougham, *The Life and Times of Henry Lord Brougham: Written by Himself* (Edinburgh: Blackwood, 1871); Arthur Aspinal, *Lord Brougham and the Whig Party* (1927; reprint ed., Hamden, Conn.: Shoe String Press, 1972).

26. Graham Wooten, *Pressure Groups in Britain, 1720-1970* (London: Allen Lane, 1975); Patricia Hollis, *Pressure From Without in Early Victorian England* (London: Edward Arnold, 1974).

27. Law Amendment Society, "Sixth Annual Report," *The Law Review* 10 (1849), 447.

28. Ibid., "Divorce," *The Law Review* 8 (1848), 349.

29. Ibid., "Divorce," *The Law Review* 1 (1845), 375.

30. III *Hansard* 134, c. 1.

31. Biographies: Alice Acland, *Caroline Norton* (London: Constable, 1948); Jane Gray Perkins, *The Life of Mrs. Norton* (London: Murray, Albemarle, 1910); Lucille Iremonger, *And His Charming Lady* (London: Seeker & Warburg, 1961); Katherine Moore, *Victorian Wives* (London: Allison & Busby, 1974). Caroline Norton was the model for George Meredith's heroine in *Diana of the Crossways,* 1885.

32. Killham, *Tennyson and the Princess,* 148.

33. Caroline Norton, *A Letter to the Queen on Lord Chancellor Cranworth's Marriage and Divorce Bill* (London, 1855), 151.

34. Ibid., 122.

35. Quoted in Perkins, *The Life of Mrs. Norton,* 244.

36. Norton, *A Letter to the Queen,* 29.
37. III *Hansard* 134, c. 7.
38. Norton, *A Letter to the Queen,* 58-59.
39. Law Amendment Society, "Review of C. Norton's A Letter to the Queen," *The Law Review* 23 (1855), 181-85.
40. Quoted in Perkins, *The Life of Mrs. Norton,* 248.
41. Sir Theodore Martin, *A Life of Lord Lyndhurst* (London: J. Murray, 1883).
42. III *Hansard* 134, c. 406.
43. Wilber Devereux Jones and Arvel B. Erickson, *The Peelites, 1846-1857* (Columbus: Ohio State University Press, 1972); Donald Southgate, *The Passing of the Whigs, 1832-1886* (London: Macmillan, 1962); Gash, *Aristocracy and People,* 250-82.
44. Southgate, *The Passing of the Whigs,* 229-59; J. B. Conacher, *The Aberdeen Coalition, 1852-55* (Cambridge: Cambridge University Press, 1968), 42.
45. Jasper Ridley, *Lord Palmerston* (London: Constable, 1970).
46. III *Hansard* 142, c. 413.
47. Ibid., c. 422.
48. Select Committee of the House of Lords on the Divorce and Matrimonial Causes and on the Law and Practice of Divorce, *Report* (1856).
49. III *Hansard* 142, c. 1978.
50. Ibid., 145, c. 490.
51. Ibid., 146, c. 230.
52. Ridley, *Lord Palmerston,* chap. 33.
53. The *Lincoln* divorce case involved Lady Lincoln's flight with her lover to the Continent in 1849. Gladstone followed her, found her pregnant, and reported the news to Lord Lincoln who sued for divorce.
54. III *Hansard* 147, c. 1280.
55. Ibid., c. 1270.
56. *Punch,* 15 August 1857, 61.
57. III *Hansard* 146, c. 855.
58. Ibid., 147, c. 1273.
59. Ibid., c. 1275.
60. *Punch,* 5 September 1857, 103.
61. Ibid.
62. Hugh M. Clokie and J. William Robinson, *Royal Commissions of Inquiry* (1937; reprint ed., New York: Octagon Books, 1969), 54-79.
63. Quoted in Iremonger, *And His Charming Lady,* 121-22.
64. Killham, *Tennyson and the Princess,* 147.
65. Norton, *A Letter to the Queen,* 99.
66. Ibid., 31.
67. Ibid., 123.

Married Women's Property Act, 1882 3

THE ACT

The long campaign to gain property rights for married women ended in August 1882 when a government bill quietly slipped through Parliament and received Royal Assent.[1] In a lead article on the Married Women's Property Act of 1882, the *Times* noted:

> It probably portends indirect social effects much greater than the disposition of property, and it may in the end pulverize some ideas which have been the basis of English life. Measures which affect the family economy are apt to be 'epoch making', and probably when the most talked about Bills of the Session are clean forgotten, this obscure measure may be bearing fruit.[2]

The act was hailed by its supporters as a long-awaited repeal of the common law doctrine of coverture and the establishment of economic rights for married women equal to those of single women (*feme sole*) and men. However, the act neither repealed coverture nor provided *feme sole* property rights for married women. It did remove some of their more glaring legal and economic disabilities and established the legal doctrine of separate property for married women. After 1882 married women remained unequal to their husbands with respect to their legal and economic status, although the gap between them had narrowed considerably.

The major provisions of the Married Women's Property Act of 1882 illustrate the concept of married women's separate property. The various categories of property that were considered to belong to the wife separately include: real and personal property in her possession before and after marriage; wages and earnings from trade, employment, and occupation or from the exercise of a literary, artistic, or scientific skill; savings deposits; stocks and bonds; and investments. The act stated that a married women had the right of acquiring, holding, selling, contracting, and suing and being sued *only with respect to her separate property.* This meant that a married woman could not be held personally liable in any suit against her but was liable to the extent of her existing separate property; "any damages or costs recovered by her in any such action or proceeding shall be her separate property; and any damages or costs recovered against her in any such action or proceeding shall be payable out of her separate property and not otherwise" (Section 2). Her husband need not have been joined in any action by or against her.[3] If she had no property at the time of the suit, no damages could be awarded, and any creditors were out of luck.

The act removed a married woman's disabilities with respect to standing in court for the protection of her separate property. It allowed for suits and contracts between husband and wife on matters of property and provided that the High Court of Justice should settle their disputes over the ownership of property. A married woman was made liable for the support of an indigent husband and her children, but only if she had separate property.

With the passage of the Married Women's Property Act, the British government changed its policy toward the legal and economic status of men and women in marriage. Married women attained the right to own their earnings and property that under coverture had belonged to their husbands. They achieved legal standing in court with respect to that property. The law noted a married woman's separate legal status by recognizing contracts between husband and wife. The gap between the legal status of men and women had been substantially reduced with the new act.

The status of married women, however, remained inferior to that of married men and single women. The statute restricted married women's legal rights and responsibilities. They were not themselves to be financially responsible; their property and earnings were set in a separate category for legal protection. They were not made personally liable for their financial dealings as were other citizens; their liability was proprietary. A married woman's capacity to contract was limited by a creditor's faith in the permanence of her property, not her personal responsibility. Her husband's relationship to her property had to be taken into account; no doubt her husband would be a better credit and contract risk than she, regardless of the extent of her wealth. Since married women were not fully responsible for their financial actions, their opportunities to achieve independent economic status were consequently limited.

It is curious that some advocates of equality for women believed the act had removed coverture disabilities and achieved equal rights when it, in fact, retained inequalities. The term *feme sole* was liberally sprinkled throughout the statute, but it was always modified by the limitations of separate property. Until the end, feminists believed the policy had given them equal property rights. Their confusion is understandable. The provisions of the act were very much a consequence of the tortured process of its enactment. The campaign for married women's property rights lasted twenty-seven years. Along the way, compromise was necessary and property rights were granted in a piecemeal fashion. The government finally took responsibility for the measure in 1882. The bill that became law was a collage of past successes, failures, demands, and compromises of the many individuals and groups that were active during the decades the issue was in the public arena.

THE DEMANDS

The 1857 Divorce Act permitted Victorian men of property to deal with some of the worst cases of women suffering under common law without disturbing their own dominance in their families and households. Only a woman who had been deserted could apply to the court for permission to keep her earnings, savings, and investments. If legally separated or divorced, she could resume her status as a single woman. It soon became clear that these small concessions won by Lord Lyndhurst would not be enough to answer even the worst hardship cases. The act did not affect wives living with their husbands. Many circumstances arose where husbands had moved out but not technically deserted and could legally confiscate their wives' earnings and household goods. The act did not protect the wife whose husband spent all of the money she had earned on gambling and drink rather than on the children, or the wife who ran away from a cruel husband. Furthermore, the social and economic conditions that gave rise to demands for equal rights for married women did not go away in the years after 1857, they intensified.

The number of women in the work force increased between 1851 and 1871, but with little improvement in real wages or in the kinds of work they did. Women remained in the textile mills at the looms, in urban workshops as needlewomen, and in domestic labor. The hardships of long hours, low pay, and hazardous conditions persisted. Beyond that, working women encountered more brutalities at home. Frequent news stories attested to wife torture among the working classes:

> The wife, a decent-looking woman who gave her evidence with manifest reluctance against her husband, said, she only wished to be parted from him; that the prisoner had lamed her with kicks, struck her in the face with his fist, and knocked her down. She had been married only eight years, but had been beaten and ill-used so many times, that she really could not say how often, but was seldom or never without black eyes and a bruised face. She sometimes earned as much as a pound per week at artificial flower-making, but what the prisoner earned she did not know, "as he never gave her anything but blows."[4]

Wife abuse was in part due to the poverty and lack of education among the workers. But women endured these "outrages," because they had little legal or economic independence:

> What is wanted, indeed, most of all is something that will make it less a necessity with women to unite themselves, legally or illegally with the other sex. In a large number of cases what a woman looks for, in matrimony or concubinage, is a bread-finder. The example is set by the "higher classes." Marriage is looked upon as the aim and end of a woman's life. What else, it is said, can she do? What but misery, it would be better to ask can result from such a system—what but wife beatings or slow-torturings can be the growth of such ill-sorted marriages as this fatal necessity involves? Let us make women more independent—let us open out to them sure sources of honest employment—and it will not be long before wife-beating and other outrages on women sensibly diminish.[5]

The interest of middle-class reformers in improving the savage behavior of the workers belied strains on the economics of marriage among the well-to-do themselves. The 1850s and 1860s were times of increasing wealth and prosperity for industrial society. Internal politics were free from disturbances that plagued Europe. The leaders of the propertied class congratulated themselves on the success of their social formula: a strict hierarchy based on principles of individual responsibility, self-help, family respectability, and "removable inequalities."[6]

At home, however, family patriarchs had to contend with challenges to their beliefs that marriage must serve to protect their newly won wealth and status. Daughters influenced by ideas of individualism insisted on choosing their own husbands. Like Edith Wharton in Anthony Trollope's *The Prime Minister,* many believed that to marry for love was the most important thing. Fathers, like Mr. Wharton, were themselves so affected by sentiment that they gave in to their children's fancies.[7]

Since marriages could no longer be relied upon, some other means had to be found to protect the family wealth. One solution would be to educate daughters, so they would be capable of managing their inherited property or, without inheritance, would be able to find suitable employment. Doubt over the ability of women to be so educated led to delays and disagreements.[8] Many families looked to law reform as a more immediate solution to their problems.

Since the fourteenth century, individual citizens mistreated by common law general rules had brought cases to equity courts. Equity developed as a body of legal principles and system of courts separate from regular law courts. In matters of marriage and property, wealthy families feared coverture would give complete control of a father's property to a son-in-law. Through a settlement made in equity court before marriage, the property of the daughter could be placed in trust. The trustee might be the husband, but it also could be the bank or a relative. The woman could enjoy the income from the property; all transactions would be carried out by the trustee, in accordance with her wishes or consistent with the terms of the settlement. Frequently, inherited property was further protected from the woman herself through a restraint on anticipation. Then she could not direct its sale or contract with respect to it.

Equity law established the principle of settled or separate property, a special category of property held only by married females and protected from husband and wife alike for use by future generations. However, to enjoy this protection a family had to go to court each time a daughter married. Even families with moderate fortunes were often unable to afford such an expense. Lawyers began to insist on more accessible procedures in the matter of marriage settlements as well as other areas of equity law. Increases in social complexity led to proposals for reform of the entire system of common law and equity, including a merging of courts, procedures, and principles of the two systems.[9] Since equity was considered more just, law reformers proposed that when law and equity were in conflict, equity principles be extended to all. These suggestions offered a solution to the marriage problems of fathers of middle-class daughters: extend the equity idea of separate but protected property to all married women.

Other reformers were intrigued by the idea of educating women. The economic plight of large numbers of incompetent and ignorant governesses had justified the establishment of Queen's College and Bedford College for Ladies in 1848 and 1849. These colleges attracted women who, through their families, had acquired more fragments of formal education than most women of their class. In a variety of courses, they exchanged ideas and enthusiasm for offering the chance to other middle-class girls to learn more than elementary reading and sums. During the 1850s and 1860s individuals and groups pioneered in women's secondary education: Mary Frances Buss at North London Collegiate; Dorothea Beale at Cheltenham College; Barbara Leigh Smith at London Secondary. Emily Davies took the next step and won the opportunity for women to sit for entrance examinations to Cambridge. This not only led to the eventual establishment of Girton College but alerted the government to serious deficiencies in women's education that were then substantiated by the report of the Royal Commission on Education in 1868. Although efforts to improve education affected the status of all women in the long run, the immediate effect was to bring together the best educated women in England, who had previously been isolated, to unite their efforts in the larger cause of women's rights.

A similar result came from women's participation in philanthropy. The commitment of middle-class reformers to the removal of social evils, aided by improved organizational techniques, intensified after 1850. At first, social convention prevented most women from venturing far from their own drawing rooms, despite the assurances from guardians of family morality that it was womanly to minister to the poor and suffering. However, some fathers educated their daughters as well as their sons to undertake good works. Tentatively at first, and then with missionary zeal, women saw for themselves the social evils and investigated causes and cures. Louisa Twining, for example, began to visit workhouses and brought her friends in the Workhouse Visiting Society.[10] When they attempted more than ministry by seeking governmental reforms, the women came face to face with the effects of their own powerlessness. From good works arose demands for women's rights.

These philanthropic circles in the 1850s nurtured Barbara Leigh Smith.[11] Through her father, Benjamin Smith, a Radical MP, and her first cousin, Florence Nightingale, she met many reformers. Her first cause was the drive for women's education, working with Mary Howitt and Anna Jameson, both prominent authors. In the early 1850s she helped establish the innovative London Secondary school. She was managing the school when she wrote her first pamphlet on women in 1854. Perhaps through discussions with her friends in the Law Amendment Society (LAS) or by the example of Caroline Norton, she selected legal rights as her subject. Unlike Norton, however, Barbara Smith and her friends saw that inequality in the laws was not an isolated issue, but intimately connected to women's inferior status in education, employment, and income.

The pamphlet *A Brief Summary in Plain Language of the Most Important Laws of England Concerning Women, Together with a Few Observations Thereon* was published anonymously in 1854 and later reprinted in 1869 under her married name, Bodichon, to assist in the campaign of that year. Smith argued for equal legal rights, including the vote, on the ground that "under a representative government, any class which is not represented is likely to be neglected." To illustrate this point, she made a strong case that "nothing is as barbourous or obsolete as the law as it pertains to married women and property."

At the request of Matthew Davenport Hill, a close friend of Smith's and a founding member of the LAS, the society held a public meeting to consider the law and married women. It was reported in the journal of the society that "a large number of ladies were present including Mrs. Jameson, Mrs. Howitt and many other lady authors."[12] Because of the interest shown, the LAS Committee on Personal Laws undertook a study of the issue in order to suggest possible reforms. The committee was chaired by Sir Thomas Erskine Perry, a member of Parliament and recently active in law reform in India.

Barbara Smith and her friends—James, Howitt, and Bessie Rayner Parks—formed the Married Women's Property Committee (MWPC), gathered evidence on the need for reform, and circulated petitions. They submitted 26,000 signatures in 1855, 30,000 in 1856, and 24,000 in 1857 from all over the country as well as a mass of information documenting, mostly through personal testimony, the wrongs suffered by women under the law. Through these efforts, the Married Women's Property Committee became the first organization of women to pressure Parliament for women's rights.

In 1856 Lord Brougham in the Lords and Perry in the Commons introduced the petitions and LAS resolutions for legal rights for married women. Brougham emphasized the need felt by large numbers of working women for legal protection. Perry urged the extension of the principle of equity "in accordance with the requirements of the age and in conformity with the opinions and usages of the wealthier and better classes of society."[13]

In the meantime, the LAS Committee worked on the assumption that married women needed special protection from the law. This approach was understandable, since so much of the publicity centered on the abuses that married women suffered from their husbands due to common law coverture. It was soon recognized, however, that married women didn't need special protection, but the same protection and rights that single women had of ownership of earnings and against the confiscation of property. In short, what was required was the abolition of the common law doctrine of coverture.

The report of the committee proposed six points:[14]

1. common law rules which make through marriage a gift of all personal property of the woman to her husband should be repealed;
2. married women should be allowed to hold property in common law as they can in equity;
3. a woman married without an ante-nuptual agreement should be able to hold property as if she were feme sole;
4. a married woman having separate property should be liable for her separate contracts, whether made before or after marriage;
5. the husband should not be liable for the wife's debts;
6. a married woman should have power to make a will;
7. rights of succession to real or personal estate or dower or curtesy should be in principles of equal justice.

A bill was drafted on the basis of this report.

Lord Brougham presented the LAS bill to the House of Lords,

but it was never considered. In 1857 Sir Erskine Perry and another LAS member, Monckton Milnes, introduced the bill in the Commons.[15] Perry said he had no expectation that the bill would pass but hoped he could get a discussion in the house on the issue. During the Second Reading debate Milnes stated that the purpose of the bill was not equality, but to make the contract law for the rich apply to all classes. Some opposition arguments were raised. Richard Spooner, a Conservative, opposed so drastic a change in the law. A reform should go only as far as to remedy the plight of the wife separated from her husband, and this would be provided in the new Divorce Act, he said. Sir William Fitzgerald pointed out that giving women all this independence would have bad effects on husbands and marriage: "the consequence might be that a gentleman who was strongly attached to an extravagant wife might find her arrested at his dinner table in respect of transactions of which he had no cognizance whatsoever."[16]

The Perry bill passed the Second Reading, 120-65, but it failed to keep a place on the public agenda. It was overshadowed during 1857 session by the Divorce Bill then in its final stages. Many MPs were satisfied that Lyndhurst's amendments to the divorce measure giving deserted and separated women some property rights took care of the worst evils of the common law. Sir Richard Bethell, the Attorney General, strongly opposed the bill for equality for fear it would place women in an independent position, quite unnatural to most "amiable women."

While Mrs. James and Mrs. Howitt continued the work of the MWPC for a time, Barbara Leigh Smith left the committee to launch a wider campaign for women's rights through the *Englishwoman's Journal (EJ),* which she founded with Bessie Rayner Parks in 1858. One of the first articles in *EJ* reported on the work of the MWPC and the Perry bill: "This bill, strongly supported in its first and second readings, was checked in the House of Commons by a promise from the government to take the subject into consideration during the recess and to bring forward a measure of its own; a promise yet unredeemed."[17] The article praised the work of the committee in translating public opinion for Parliament. When the Perry bill comes up again, said the writers in *EJ,* Commons will realize it has public support:

It should never be forgotten that all reform originates with the people, and that the sustained and organized expression of public opinion can alone lead to a successful issue. Lord Brougham and Sir Erskine Perry, with many other distinguished men, both in and out of the House, are warm advocates of this measure; but without the earnest and unflagging support of all interested in it we may never see it pass into the law of the land.[18]

In 1859 Palmerston formed his second government. His administration concentrated on foreign policy and gave little encouragement to domestic reforms. During this time, reform projects outside the legislature multiplied. Many private bills were drafted and submitted, but there was little action and frustrations grew. John Bright wrote of the Prime Minister in 1862: "As for Palmerston, he is the last link connecting us with a past generation, and when his time is out, we shall enter on a new and I believe better time."[19] Also hoping for a better time were Barbara Leigh Smith Bodichon, her father, and advocates of women's rights. They extended their studies beyond education to health, employment, and politics. Finally in 1865, two events changed the legislative future of women's rights: the death of Palmerston and the election of John Stuart Mill.

Palmerston's death removed the last of the old generation of Whig Ministers who believed reform had gone far enough. At last, Liberal and Radical MPs were able to work with outside reform pressure groups to clean up, once and for all, the loose ends of reform movements begun in the 1820s and 1830s. Top on the list was the extension of the suffrage, an issue that dominated political life until the passage of the Second Reform Act in 1867. The extension of the vote to urban workers brought about a favorable environment for change in many other areas, such as education, workers' rights, law, health, temperance, and disestablishment.[20]

The election of John Stuart Mill to the House of Commons in 1865 ensured that women's rights would be included in the agenda for reform. When he agreed to stand from Westminister, Mill made it clear that women's suffrage was a top priority. The feminists who had joined together a decade earlier to work for education, employment, and legal rights armed him with a petition of 1,500 signatures in favor of the vote. With the roll in hand, in 1866 Mill introduced the first debate in Parliament on the political emancipation of women.

Mill had long been a critic of the legal and economic status of women in marriage. When he married in 1851, he formally repudiated the legal aspects of marriage and declared his marriage to be based on individual freedom and equality. In his *Essay on the Sub-*

jection of Women, 1869, he discussed his philosophy of feminism and devoted a chapter to marriage. He described the status of the wife as worse than a slave—she was a twenty-four-hour slave, who not only must give her wealth and labor to her master but her love and sentiments as well. The only just and moral law must rest on complete equality of husband and wife, leaving each couple to divide the labor and income of a marriage according to their own wishes. In his essay Mill made one of the first arguments for equal partnership in marriage.

After the suffrage issue was settled (without giving women the vote), Liberals and Radicals mobilized to bring other long-neglected issues to the attention of the government and the public. Among them was a bill similar to the Perry bill of 1857 for married women's property. It was introduced in April 1868 by three prominent MPs: George Shaw Lefevre, a leader of Radicals in the Commons who would soon be a member of Gladstone's first Cabinet; Russell Gurney, a Conservative MP and Recorder of London; and Mill himself. The November general election brought Gladstone to power at the head of a strong, reform-minded Liberal government. Finally, the issue of married women's property would receive full parliamentary consideration.

THE CONFLICT

By the time the demands for rights for married women reached the public agenda, the complexity of pressure-group politics had increased substantially from the days of Caroline Norton and her pamphlets. Reformers still followed organizational forms and techniques that had been successful decades earlier in repealing corn laws and abolishing slavery, but the number and complexity of the organizations had changed dramatically. The basic pattern consisted of small groups of prominent citizens linked together by an executive committee of activists who coordinated efforts in the capitol. The goal of the group was to demonstrate to Parliament the extent of public support for the group's cause. Pressure was applied to individual MPs through letters, petitions, resolutions, pamphlets, public meetings, and news stories. Although party organization was also growing stronger, there was still a great deal of cross voting, what today is called "conscience voting." For each issue, a new association was born. By the 1860s reform politics had become a way of life for an enthusiastic circle of middle-class activists.

No clear boundary existed between Parliament and pressure groups. Inside the Commons, reformers used groups to develop support for their own proposals. Self-styled "tribunes of the people" such as Bright, Shaw Lefevre, and Mill participated in groups or invited their help in persuading fellow MPs to vote for their bills.[21] Therefore, a cooperative relationship developed between groups of Liberals and Radicals inside Parliament and dedicated reformers outside. A network of politicians and their families, friends, and allies worked together to bring bills successfully through legislative debates, committees, and divisions. Such a network gave women their first opportunity to participate in politics for feminist goals.

The seeds of the organized feminist movement had already been sown in the 1850s by Caroline Norton, Barbara Leigh Smith, Lord Brougham, and the Law Amendment Society. When the issue was temporarily put aside after the Divorce Act in 1857, Brougham sought to attract a larger number of people to all aspects of reform by forming an organization that focused on broad social change. He invited people to his home to present his ideas for the new organization. "A number of social reformers and philanthropists were contacted and they agreed to the need for a union of social reformers, to bring together all sorts of opinion."[22] They formed the National Association for the Promotion of Social Science (NAPSS or Social Science Association). Brougham announced that the association's role would be similar to that of the LAS. He insisted that the new group would not be political, but a service to Parliament, investigating important areas that Parliament and the government were too busy to study.

The NAPSS was patterned after the National Association for the Promotion of Science. Just as that organization had sought to apply the discoveries of science to the technological problems of the economy, so the NAPSS sought to apply the discoveries of social science to the social problems of the day. The goals of the association reveal the similarity to utilitarianism that marked Brougham's early career:[23]

1. application of a framework of society founded on certain ascertainable principles;
2. the best method of applying those principles for the production of human happiness;
3. a union of the moral and economic sciences;
4. the benefits of discussion among great men who had worked alone.

"Our professed function is to afford a centre for discussion in order to reconcile conflicting opinions, and pave the way for social improvement whether by legislative means or other."

The Social Science Association took up the issue of married women's property after it merged with the LAS in 1865. The Married Women's Property Committee came back to life with energetic leadership and a membership involved in other feminist causes. Most were active in the Manchester suffrage society: Ursula Bright, wife of Jacob Bright, Radical MP for Manchester; Elizabeth Wolstenholme, active in education and suffrage; Josephine Butler, leader of the movement for repeal of the Contagious Diseases Acts; Richard and Emmeline Pankhurst; Priscilla Bright M'Laren, sister of Jacob and John Bright and wife of Duncan M'Laren, Radical MP. Lydia Becker, who would lead the national suffrage movement in the 1870s and 1880s, was treasurer of the MWPC. Several MPs were also members, including George Shaw Lefevre, Russell Gurney, and Duncan M'Laren. The committee petitioned the NAPSS for affiliation.

On 5 December 1867 the Jurisprudence Committee of the association held a special meeting to consider the LAS's 1856 report and its bill on married women's property.[24] Arguments in support of the reform concentrated on the need to protect property and earnings of married women rather than on the demand for equality. The Jurisprudence Committee interpreted the proposal to be an extension of the principle of equity marriage settlements to all women. As such it was consistent with the NAPSS's general goal of a union of common law and equity. One member of the committee argued that it was unfair to require a husband to be solely responsible for support of his wife while she was able to keep her property and not have such an obligation. The dominant sentiment of the group that the wife had to be protected rather than treated as an equal was appropriate to such differences in responsibility. The committee resolved to have the bill reintroduced during the 1868 session.

Although the Social Science Association defined the issue as the extension of equity protection to all married women, the bill introduced by Shaw Lefevre, Gurney, and Mill in April 1868 in fact abolished coverture for married women, rendering the equal with single women:

A married woman would be given full *feme sole* rights to property.

A married woman would have standing to sue and be sued, with personal liability for debts and bankruptcy.

A husband would not be liable for his wife's debts, damages, or torts before or after marriage (unless he gets her property).

A wife would not be responsible for her husband's debts.

Conflicts between husband and wife over ownership of property are to be settled in court.

Shaw Lefevre opened the Second Reading debate.[25] He traced the history of the issue and its relation to the demands for women's suffrage. He noted that the 1861 census showed that 800,000 of 3,200,000 married women were employed (25 percent). They should have a right to their earnings, he said. The common law doctrine that justified giving the husbands the property of their wives, because husbands had a duty to support them, had been recently undercut by court decisions that demonstrated there was no way to force a husband to support his wife. Thus the law gave the husband the right to confiscate the wife's property without forcing him to support her. The MP "refrained from expressing his opinion whether women were or were not the equals of men."

John Bright summarized many of the arguments in favor of the bill: Men confiscate, legally, the property of their wives. Many women work and need the money they earn for their children. "With an increase of independence, such as the Bill would secure, there would be an increase of respect for women—of real respect which is a thousand times more valuable than the conventional politeness which is always so easy to pay."[26]

An extended debate did not take place, but the opposition had a chance to forecast the problems faced by the bill. Some argued it was not needed, since marriage settlements were available for the few who had property, and the Divorce Act of 1857 provided for the worst abuses—cases of deserted or separated wives. Others argued that the bill was too revolutionary, since it would not, in fact, establish equity principles of protection but give the wife absolute control of her own property and far too much independence.

Sir Gabriel Goldney began his long campaign against the bill with the following arguments: a woman's right to sue and be sued would encourage irresponsible behavior on the part of the husband;

marriage would become a common partnership; in fact, the wife would be enjoying all of the advantages (being supported) but none of the risks; the measure would lead to immorality, "because it would so free a woman from restraint that in any quarrel she might have with her husband she would be enabled to say 'I have my own property, and if you don't like me I can go live with somebody who does.' "[27]

With this sort of opposition, Shaw Lefevre was further drawn away from the issue of equality toward the notion of protection in justifying his bill. He brought in the testimony of an American lawyer, Dudley Field, whom he had asked to comment on the effects of the Married Women's Property Act in New York, to allay fears about the effects of such a "revolutionary" measure described by the opposition. Since Field could not enter the Commons debate, Shaw Lefevre asked the *Times* to print his letter, which appeared five days after Goldney's remarks.[28] Field pointed out that married women had had control of property and earnings in New York since 1860. No dissension in families had been noted as a consequence. The motive of the law was to give poor women the same protection as rich ones get through marriage settlements, to give mothers the means to supply children's needs when husbands neglect them, and "the belief that the mutual affection of husbands and wives would be more promoted by their standing up in equality than by their being made inferior to the other except where it was absolutely necessary." Field mentioned equality, but it was in the context of contributing to the maintenance of the family, not for its own sake. In later testimony before the House of Commons Committee on the bill, Field commented on one of those areas of necessary inequality: where the husband was required to support his family. "I have never heard any change in the law in this respect proposed. It would be offensive to the pride which all men among us have in assuming responsibility for their families." This argument appealed to Liberals who defined self-sufficiency and responsibility in terms of a man's ability to provide for his family. He also implied that women's earnings were unlikely to be substantial enough to matter.

The bill passed the Second Reading and was sent to a select committee in July. In the autumn of 1868 at the annual Social Science Congress, Arthur Hobhouse presented a major paper entitled "Property of Married Women." The paper concentrated on further responses to the opponents of the Married Women's Property Bill in the 1868 session. Hobhouse based his arguments on the importance of the law in achieving justice. Critics had argued that common law was not bad, but that some husbands abused their rights. The paper emphasized the importance of freedom and justice for women and that they should be legally responsible like everyone else. In fact, Hobhouse argued that property rights for women would have a beneficial effect on all society:

> . . . the effect of satisfaction proved by all laws founded on justice and enlarging freedom; the effect produced on all human beings by the possession and ownership of property; the effect, namely, of enlarging the minds and strengthening the characters of women, and, as a necessary consequence, of further civilizing and elevating the community to which they belong.[29]

The major proposal to reform married women's property law in the form of a bill sponsored by the NAPSS was to guarantee equal property rights to married women through the repeal of coverture disabilities. Proponents of the bill chose to define the issues less in terms of equality and more on points such as the extension of equity protection from rich to poor and the needs that mothers have for earnings to support their children when the husbands failed to do so. Some offered married women's rights as a safeguard against women's suffrage. To avoid giving women political rights, it was argued, their grievances should be heeded. Only occa sionally was the notion of equality mentioned; most advocates stayed clear of that controversial issue despite the fact that it had been the basis of arguments of feminists such as Barbara Leigh Smith, Caroline Norton, and John Stuart Mill.

A second proposal was put forward during legislative consideration of the Shaw Lefevre bill. It completely eschewed the notion of legal equality in property and centered on the protection of property, with as little change in the law as possible. This counterdemand to protect women's property would literally have extended the equity idea of the marriage settlement to all marriages by statute. A letter to the editor of the *Times,* 15 June 1868, the same day the Dudley Field letter was published, suggested that as part of the marriage contract, all of the wife's property should automatically be put in trust at the time of the marriage, thus giving the poor what the rich already have (of course, the poor rarely had any property). A year later, the *Times* itself agreed that no major changes in legal principles should be undertaken by the married women's property reform, but that "injustices for poor women" should be eliminated. It definitely opposed the notion of an equal partnership in marriage, because it was too radical. In fact, according to the editor, subordination in marriage was the essence of the marriage state.[30]

The demand to take care of injustices against poor women with the least possible change in the law found expression in the form of a bill, introduced by Conservative Henry Cecil Raikes in the House of Commons in 1870. Although it received only a First Reading, it provided the basis for those in the Commons and the Lords who criticized the Shaw Lefevre proposal. The bill would protect the property of married women as follows: the husband automatically would become the trustee of the wife's property upon marriage; the wife could petition for a court-appointed trustee, not the husband; if a wife proved that she had earned more than half of the family expenses for six months, the judge could grant her a protection order; a married woman holding a protection order had *feme sole* rights to earnings and would be liable for her own acts and contracts.

In other words, only the poor could achieve control of earnings (with court supervision); for the rest, property would remain in trust for, but not in control of, the married woman. This, it was argued, would embody the true fusion of law and equity supported by law reformers. Such a reform would still be consistent with the husband's responsibility to support his family and would not disturb the security of the family, which to Conservatives was dependent on the unity of husband and wife under the control of the husband. The only concession would be to give the wife the right to her earnings if she were not adequately supported. Social reformers in the Lords expected that this provision would apply only to the poorer classes whom they viewed to be beyond the pale of middle-class, Victorian family life. The protectionist proposal for married women's property law reform was supported by Conservative lawyers, leaders in the Lords, and the *Times*. The Shaw Lefevre proposal for equal rights was supported by Liberals in the Commons, the NAPSS, and the feminists.

RESOLUTION OF THE CONFLICT

The committee stage is an important hurdle in the slow-moving parliamentary process. Many a bill, the principle having received support at a Second Reading, passes away for want of leadership on a committee. In 1868 the married women's property bill had supporters capable of forming a select committee, taking testimony, and making a report to the full House of Commons. The leading witness was G. W. Hastings, secretary of the NAPSS and former secretary of the LAS. Others included a female textile worker, a priest in a laboring parish, the owner of a factory, and the American Dudley Field. They presented evidence of the abuses that married women received under the law and about the serious and responsible nature of working married women. The only solution, they argued, was to give the woman legal control over her earnings. The committee was in favor of the reform:

> Looking therefore to the result of this experience and to the general tendency of the provisions of equity, so far as they have been made available to the wealthy classes only in this country, your committee is strongly of the opinion that the common law of this country which gives the wife's property to the husband should be repealed, and that the wife should have control over her property and earnings, and that her disability to contract and to sue and be sued in respect of them should be removed.[31]

The resignation of the government and the general election in November and December 1868 prevented further immediate action on the bill. The proponents had to wait for the outcome of the first election after the Second Reform Act. Before the legislative odyssey of the Married Women's Property Bill resumed, important changes occurred in the political base of the government, the cohesiveness of the majority party, and the attitudes of the leadership in the House of Commons.

By 1868 the party system was becoming stronger, able once again, as in the 1830s, to provide the political basis for the executive. The new leaders of the two main parties, Disraeli and Gladstone, led the campaign. The Conservatives had better electoral organization, but the Liberals benefited from the recent expansion of the suffrage in the cities and won a majority of 112. Inside Parliament, the Prime Minister still had few procedural resources to maintain party discipline. The new majority relied on the personal leadership of Gladstone to attract a group of leaders who shared his belief in the need for party unity.[32] His administration appealed to the factions of his party: the conservative Whig families, nonconformists, reformers, and Radicals. However, a majority of the Cabinet came from the House of Commons, and many of them were new Liberals from the middle class, committed to change and strong executive leadership.

Despite the emphasis on unity, MPs still retained their independence. The issues that dominated Gladstone dominated the Cabinet. Intense controversy over the question of disestablishment and land reform in Ireland occupied the government. Meanwhile middle-level leaders and backbenchers brought many reform issues to Parliament as private member bills. Most MPs still owed their election as much to principle and local interest as to party affiliation and organization. They were susceptible to influence from interest groups as well as the Cabinet. Thus while the government struggled with one or two major policies, the House of Commons deliberated on a wide range of reforms, proposed by various informal coalitions. At the same time, the parliamentary leadership had enough influence and resources to block or change unwanted proposals, so reformers often sought support from Cabinet officers.

After the election, only one of the originators of the Married Women's Property Bill, Russell Gurney, the Conservative, was left on the back benches. Mill was defeated for reelection and Shaw Lefevre joined the Gladstone government. Gurney introduced his measure again in 1869 and won Liberal backing and a Second Reading. Another Commons committee considered the bill and included some amendments in its report:[33]

BILL BY SHAW LEFEVRE, 1868, AND GURNEY, 1869	*BILL AS AMENDED BY THE SECOND HOUSE OF COMMONS COMMITTEE*
1. Married woman has *feme sole* right to property and personal estate.	1. Retained.
2. Married woman has standing to sue and be sued; personal liability.	2. Married woman has proprietary not personal liability in contracts.

BILL BY SHAW LEFEVRE, 1868, AND GURNEY, 1869	*BILL AS AMENDED BY THE SECOND HOUSE OF COMMONS COMMITTEE*
3. Husband not responsible for wife's debts, nor damage and torts before marriage.	3. Retained; added: no suit between husband and wife for tort.
4. Wife not liable for husband's debts.	4. Retained.
5. Marriage settlements to continue.	5. Retained.
6. Conflicts between husband and wife over property resolved in court.	6. Retained.
	7. Added: wife liable to support children and indigent husband if she has the property.

The main change brought about by the second committee was to introduce the notion of proprietary as opposed to personal liability with respect to contracts. This turned out to be a crucial concession to the protectionists, for it would make married women less legally responsible for payment of debts than other citizens. If a married woman had no property, her creditors could not be satisfied, and they were forbidden from suing the husband.

During 1869 and 1870 members of the NAPSS who were interested in the issue of married women's property were active in the Married Women's Property Committee. Some of them such as Gurney and Duncan M'Laren were MPs and could speak for the bill. Others, including the Pankhursts, Elizabeth Wolstenholme, Lydia Becker, Josephine Butler, Ursula Bright, and Priscilla M'Laren, mobilized public support. The committee circulated 250 petitions against the Raikes bill and in favor of its own bill and submitted 46,199 signatures. It was successful: the Raikes bill was defeated in the Second Reading, 208-46.

The proponents accepted changes made in the bill by the Commons committees, and parliamentary members of the MWPC introduced the amended bill in 1870. It passed a Second Reading without a division. The Solicitor General, John Duke Coleridge, favored the bill on its successful Third Reading, although at no time did the Gladstone government become officially involved in this reform. Ultimately, the reform was supported by the House of Commons on the ground that it would merely extend the rights of the rich to the poor and would have little effect on the family. Opponents, like Raikes, tried to link the change to the drive for equal rights for women, arguing that it would destroy the family. He had little success in the Commons, but his argument found a warm reception among the peers.

The climate in the House of Lords was generally unfavorable to reform and especially chilly to women's rights. The upper house was suspicious of the effects of the Second Reform Act, which had brought large numbers of new voters to the polls. The Gladstone Cabinet turned to these new constituencies for support, weakening the dominance of the noblemen. Several old Whig peers along with the Tories opposed the Liberal government as too radical, too democratic. All reform proposals originating in "the other place" were suspect; the Lords were convinced that their usual modifyng amendments would not be enough to save Queen and property. They threatened to rewrite Commons bills completely. The peers got plenty of practice in carving up the government's Irish land and church bills. Only through negotiation could the Ministers fend off these attacks. The married women's property proposal was a threat to property law that had, through centuries of equity marriage settlements, preserved large landholdings intact for the peers and their families to enjoy. As a final insult, here was a bill coming from private members in the lower house, daring to supplant the traditional prerogatives of the lawyers and judges in the upper house over matters of law and law reform.

The Second Reading debate in the House of Lords in June 1870 on the amended Gurney bill was dominated by the six Law Lords who were themselves divided on the issue. Quietly supporting the bill were Lord Cairns, a Tory lawyer, Lord Romilly, Master of the Rolls, and Whig Lord Chancellor Hatherly. The opposition was formidable. Lord Penzance, a Whig, had sat for many years on the divorce court. Lord Westbury, Lord Chancellor from 1861 to 1865, had attacked the Perry property bill in 1857, as had Attorney General Richard Bethell. He was also among the Whig peers who actively opposed Gladstone's Liberals. Finally, Lord Shaftesbury, the former Tory MP and philanthropist, had long feared the social and moral effects of women working outside the home.

These three made it clear from the beginning that they saw *feme sole* property rights as a threat to the integrity of property and the dominance of men over the family. Lord Penzance stated: "The Bill invoked the question whether the husband should rule his own household, for if the wife had coequal power over the property she would obviously have considerable share in its management."[34]

The opponents agreed that there was some justification for women keeping their own earnings. Shaftesbury asserted that earnings should be protected for women by law, but that this would mostly apply to the lower class. He pointed out that the women of that class were generally of better character and industry than the men. The peers were quite concerned, however, that if women got hold of their real property or inheritance, they would squander it selfishly, since they had no legal obligation to support their husbands and children. The right to sue and to contract, argued Penzance, would certainly break up families, with wives suing their husbands or going to business with men who were *not* their husbands.

Penzance, Shaftesbury, and Westbury controlled the select committee assigned to review the bill. Although the MWPC asked to testify, the committee refused. When it made its report on 21 July 1870, noting that finally the bill was "workable," the opposition had carried the day. Entire sections on ownership of property, contracts, torts, and bankruptcy (1-5, 7-11, 14-17) were eliminated, and two new sections were substituted giving married women control only of their earnings and certain other categories of separate property, including savings and investments. In those areas, married women were to have separate use of such property, could sue and be sued, and were liable to support children and indigent husbands to the extent of such separate property. The husband remained responsible for all torts. The committee eliminated references to real property, except to guarantee a married woman the right to £200 of her inheritance.

To appreciate the extent of the changes in the bill, compare the first clause of the Commons bill with that amended by the peers:

Commons bill: Married woman shall be capable of holding, acquiring, alienating, devising and bequeathing Real and Personal Estate, of contracting, and of suing and being sued as if she were feme sole.

Lords bill: The wages and earnings of any married woman acquired or gained by her after the passage of this Act in any employment, occupation, or trade in which she is engaged or which she carries on separately from her husband, and also any money or property so acquired by her through the exercise of any literary, artistic, or scientific skill, and all investments such as wages, earnings, money and property shall be deemed and taken to be property held and settled to her separate use, independent of any husband to whom she may be married; and her receipts alone shall be a good discharge for such wages, earnings, money, and property.

The Gladstone government did not take a stand on the bill, and although the Lord Chancellor was on the select committee, he did not figure prominently in its business. Gladstone needed all of his political resources to keep the substance of his Irish reform bills. Tacit government support on married women's property might have been of little use in fending off the Lords' revisions.

The Married Women's Property Committee was distressed at the Lords' committee report. It presented a petition of objections to Lord Shaftesbury urging the House of Lords to reject the bill and restore the *feme sole* principle that the Commons had accepted. Nevertheless, the changes wrought by the committee quietly passed a Third Reading in 1870.

An emergency meeting of the supporters of the bill was held July 27; attending were Hobhouse, Gurney, Lord Houghton, Lydia Becker, and Priscilla M'Laren. They decided not to urge the Commons to reject the much-altered bill. In the face of imminent European war, they settled for the limited changes allowed by the House of Lords: "The attention of Parliament might be so fully engaged in providing the most effectual methods of making widows that it would be utterly hopeless to claim any attention for the wrongs of wives."[35] They resolved, at the same time, not to let the matter drop.

In the debate in the Commons on the Lords' amendments, 3 August 1870, Gurney, the bill's sponsor, acknowledged great alterations made in the bill. He noted that instead of repealing the common law marital property regulations, the House of Lords had applied specific remedies to specific evils. He urged the house to accept the bill and vowed to work for further reform. It received Royal Assent in August 1870.

The Married Women's Property Act of 1870 provided married women with a limited right to earnings and set forth the idea of their property for "separate use." This statute was quite different from the bill for equality proposed by the Married Women's Property Committee and introduced in the House of Commons. The policy outcome was the result of the domination of the House of Lords over the decision-making process.

The conflict over reform of common law coverture was between those who advocated *feme sole* equality for married women and those who wanted to extend equity rights in a limited way to protect property. The conflicts were resolved in the House of Commons Select Committee of 1869 and in the House of Lords Select Committee in 1870. In the Commons, the advocates of *feme sole* equality were successful in passing a bill that, for the most part, established a new principle of married women's property. The Lords committee rejected any new principles and sought to make only the most limited change necessary to remedy some of the suffering of women workers. Due to the outbreak of war and the pending end of the session, equalitarians in the Commons had to accept the Lords' protectionist amendments. They realized that even such a limited reform as the right of a married woman to her own earnings was better than no reform. The alternative would likely have been to delay any reform for several more years.

The role of feminists was very important in the policy process in the Commons. The bill that was passed there had been drafted and promoted by the Married Women's Property Committee under the auspices of the NAPSS. The executive committee of the MWPC included many feminists. Often Helen Downing would attend MWPC meetings to lend official support from the National Society for Women's Suffrage and the women's movement in general.

The feminists had little influence in the House of Lords. Lyndhurst and Brougham had died, and the Law Lords were no longer personally connected with the Liberal circles of the feminists. Nor were they susceptible to the influence of pamphleteering and pressure. Politics was getting too complicated for the pen of a Caroline Norton to have a direct effect on outcome of policy as it had fifteen years earlier.

Lydia Becker, treasurer of the MWPC, wrote two letters of protest to the *Times.* Commenting on the Lords' amendments on August 4, she stated that they removed the simple concept of *feme sole* status for married women that had been in the House of Commons bill and substituted the concept of property for "separate use'' by married women, borrowed from upper-class marriage settlements. Separate ownership is not equal to separate use. ''Married men are allowed to own their own property without this ugly condition. We ask the same for married women.'' A second letter on August 25 from Becker and Secretary Wolstenholme repeated arguments objecting to the act, because it failed to establish once and for all a woman's right to property. They vowed to keep up the struggle.

CONFLICT—AGAIN

The most immediate problem with the 1870 act resulted from confusion over the liability for a wife's antenuptual debts. Under the common law, because the husband received his wife's property, he became liable for her debts contracted before marriage. The House of Commons bill gave the wife the right to her own property and removed the husband's liabilities. When the Lords swept away the *feme sole* provisions, they neglected to deal with the debt provisions. Section 12 of the act provided that a husband was not liable for his wife's debts before marriage. The wife would be liable to the extent of her separate property. However, under the preceding sections of the act, if a woman married without a marriage settlement, her property went to her husband. Her creditors were unable to sue for payment, since she had no separate property and her husband was not liable. Judges, lawyers, and creditors were very critical of the act, which they claimed was contradictory and unclear.

The strongest critics were in the Married Women's Property Committee, which had become so active during the previous legislative struggle. After the disaster in the House of Lords with its bill, the committee resolved to fight on to get an act that would give married women equal rights. In the 1870s the MWPC stepped up its activities, increased its membership and budget, and published an annual report and numerous pamphlets.

During this time the committee consolidated its position. In the 1860s some confusion had arisen between the equal rights provided for in the bill the committee was supporting and the justification in terms of protection offered by the committee spokesmen on its behalf. By the 1870s the supporters of reform concentrated on the demand for equal rights, and little reference was made to protecting poor women or combining rules of law and equity. The following are some representative views of the committee members from pamphlets and reports of the second policy-making phase:

The Law relating to the property of Married Women has been amended, not in the spirit of justice but with a grudging sense of expediency which has left it more full of anomalies than before. . . . No amendment of the law has touched her status; she is now non existent as she was before Mrs. Norton was born; she may be libeled with impunity; she cannot sue or be sued; all her personal property passes to her husband at the day of her marriage, and his by the same process is her rental property.

Arthur Arnold 1878

The Act [1870] passed in the shape which we well know and I venture to say that it is an act quite disgraceful to the Legislature—a more confused, illogical and absurd piece of work does not exist on the statute book of our country.

Shaw Lefevre 1879

The confiscation of a man's property is associated in our minds with felony or high treason; the confiscation of a woman's property with marriage.

Amelia (Mrs. Arthur) Arnold 1879

No question of social or domestic concern can surpass this in importance, that no interest can transcend this in magnitude and it is of supreme moment to the well-being of society that the most intimate and sacred of human relationships should rest on those broad foundations of equality and justice of which the recognition of the property rights and responsibilities of a married woman may be held to be the cornerstone.

1876, Report of the
Executive Committee

All those paltry cobblings and piecings, these miserable mendings of ancient laws borrowed from ignorant heathens 2000 years ago, so unutterably demoralizing to men, so cruelly oppressive to women, will continue until we become brave enough and honest enough to declare in the face of day, the great truth that all human beings are born free and should be equal before law. . . .

Amelia (Mrs. Arthur) Arnold 1878

Perhaps the most telling criticism of the act pointed out the effects on the opportunities of married women. Upholding protectionist principles while allowing low-salaried women to keep their earnings impeded independent business opportunities for married women. "This legislative blunder had cruel consequences for women traders, who could obtain no credit when there was ground for suspicion that by accepting the non-existence of married women they might defraud a creditor."[36]

A woman in business separate from her husband was a poor credit risk, since she was not in total control of her property. A single woman was a risk too, since she might marry to avoid her debts. All women were prevented from achieving economic wealth on an independent basis. These issues of equality for women and the economic consequences of inequality became the major concern of the MWPC during the 1870s.

After the continental war was over, the MWPC urged the MPs to take up their bill again. There were other proposals to amend the 1870 act. In 1872 Stavely Hill, MP, introduced an amendment to the Married Women's Property Act. It sought to remedy the problem of liability for a wife's antenuptual debts. It provided that husband and wife could be sued jointly for such debts, and the husband would be liable to the extent he had taken possession of the wife's property as a result of the marriage. The bill did nothing to change the rights of wives, but merely gave relief to the wife's creditors.

The MWPC opposed the Stavely Hill bill. It argued that the logical remedy to the problem of the wife's debts was to give to her her own property to pay them. At the annual general meeting, the committee urged the postponement of the Hill bill and sent a resolution to Gladstone to give the issue of repeal of common law marital property disabilities the attention of the government:

> As a great question of social justice the subject is worthy of attention of the Government at any time . . . the present moment, when the mind of the nation seems rather on social reforms than purely political reforms, [is] preeminently favorable for the impartial consideration and just settlement of a question which vitally concerns the interest of all women of the nation and hardly less vitally, if less directly, the interests of all the men.[37]

The resolution was submitted to the Prime Minister, but the committee received no reply. It went ahead with its private member bill, finding John Hinde Palmer, MP, to sponsor it during the 1873 session. The bill was similar to that originally drafted by the LAS and introduced in 1857, 1868, and 1869.

A brief debate on the Palmer bill took place in February.[38] Palmer, George Osborne Morgan, and Shaw Lefevre, all MWPC members, spoke in favor. They pointed out the defects in the 1870 act, which Palmer described as "mutilated." They noted that the Commons had already accepted their bill in 1869. Now there was even more need to treat women fairly. Women had been denied the vote in 1867 based on the belief that their interests could be properly taken care of by men. The opposition charged that the bill would destroy the family and was also unfair: it would deprive a husband of the means required to support his family. Sir John Duke Coleridge, the Attorney General, favored the bill, although the government as a whole was not committed. "He did not see why if a woman had property, she should not enjoy rights of property like everybody else, or why even a husband should take away from his wife that which was her own."[39] The bill passed the Second Reading but died from lack of time and interest. The Married Women's Property Executive Committee reported at the general meeting in 1873 that the bill was postponed six times for insufficient attendance in the House. This situation illustrated the difficulty, it noted, of getting legislative action on matters affecting a group that had no vote.

In 1874 the Parliament passed the Stavely Hill bill. The MWPC, which had actively opposed it and had succeeded in getting it postponed in 1872, did not oppose it this time. The measure remedied the contradiction over the wife's antenuptual debts, making the husband responsible only to the extent of his control over his wife's property. Therefore in 1874, when the first Gladstone government passed away, it had taken neither action nor official notice of the issue of equal property rights of married women. The elections of 1874, the first after the Ballot Act of 1872, turned out the Liberals and established a Conservative government under Disraeli. Two of the major advocates of married women's rights, Hinde Palmer and Jacob Bright, lost their seats. Coleridge was elevated to the House of Lords in 1874. The committee held little hope that the new House of Commons would be any more sympathetic to its demands than the old. In fact, it expected a good deal more apathy.

After 1873 the membership and tactics of the Married Women's Property Committee changed. Some of the feminists dispersed to concentrate their efforts on one of the other women's rights campaigns: Josephine Butler to the struggle for the repeal of the Contagious Diseases Acts; Pankhursts and Lydia Becker to the suffrage; Frances Power Cobbe to relief for victims of wife torture. Ursula Bright and Elizabeth Wolstenholme Elmy became the main leaders. They urged prominent men such as George Osborne Morgan and Arthur Arnold to work for equality. Bright gradually changed the focus of their campaign. They kept up their efforts at demonstrating public support to individual MPs through annual meetings, resolutions, pamphlets, petitions, and private member bills. However, their goal was no longer to persuade a majority of MPs through pressure from outside.

The events of 1870 convinced the MWPC that it needed government sponsorship to assure success. This meant it must convince the law officers—the Lord Chancellor, Attorney General, and Solicitor General—to include its bill for equality for married women as part of the government's program. Its best hope for success would be under a Liberal government. While the MWPC was waiting for a change of party in power, Ursula Bright and her friends entertained prominent and influential lawyers to intercede with Liberal leaders. This shift in tactics reflected the growing centralization of the political parties and dominance of the executive over the legislature. In the 1870s the era of pressure group politics and independent MPs free to vote their consciences was drawing to a close.

After the Conservatives won the majority in the House of Commons, the MWPC, vowing to keep the issue in the public arena, turned its attention to the House of Lords. Lord Coleridge, the former Attorney General, introduced its bill in 1877. In his speech he argued that the House of Lords was better able than any other assembly to deal with the issue of married women's property. Quoting Lord Lyndhurst, he reiterated the arguments put forth by sponsors of the bill in the Commons: married women should control their property to avoid abuses by husbands. He noted that the bill would leave marriages unaffected. Despite Coleridge's prominence and reassurances, the bill was rejected. Lord Cairns had offered his lukewarm support in 1870; now as Lord Chancellor, he led the official opposition of the Disraeli government to further reform in the law affecting married women.

In 1878 the committee persuaded Sir John Hibbert, a Liberal, to introduce its bill in the House of Commons once again. Although committee members circulated petitions and wrote letters to MPs, the bill got nowhere in the 1878 session. They called for people to report specific cases of injustice under the 1870 act. The *McCarthy* case, publicized during 1878 and 1879, involved a decision in magistrate's court. A wife had obtained a legal separation from her husband, a protection order, and a marriage settlement for control of her property. The husband then came to her house and took a valuable watch belonging to her. She sued for the theft. The court ruled that a wife could not prosecute a husband for such stolen property. The committee used the *McCarthy* case to show that even though some safeguards were in the 1870 act, they did not effectively protect property from the clutches of a husband even when the couple were legally separated and the wife's property was under the protection of the court.

In 1879 Hibbert won permission by ballot to introduce his bill again. The major problem was securing a quorum. The Commons had never had enough attendance for a division on the married women's property issue under the Disraeli government. This time the MWPC distributed circulars and pressured MPs to attend. The Second Reading had a good turnout, including some Ministers. The Chancellor of the Exchequer then asked Hibbert for his time to consider the government's Army Discipline Bill. Hibbert agreed but asked the government for help with his bill during the next session. Ursula Bright followed with a letter to the Attorney General. This time the government replied. The law officer said he had no plans for the issue. It appeared unlikely at that point that the government would ever follow up on Hibbert's request. At the 1880 general meeting, the MWPC resolved once again to introduce its bill for equal rights in the next session of Parliament.[40]

RESOLUTION OF THE CONFLICT—AT LAST

The composition of the House of Commons had changed by the time it again considered married women's rights, and the feminists were optimistic about their chances for final success. In the 1880 campaign, Gladstone once again led the Liberal cause. He asked the women to help, and they stumped for Liberal candidates. Many sympathetic men, including the MWPC's own members Hinde Palmer and Osborne Morgan, defeated opponents of women's rights. The election brought the Liberals back to power with 350 seats and an absolute majority of 48 over the 238 Conservatives and 64 Irish Home Rulers. Osborne Morgan became Judge Advocate General in the new government.

Once again the Gladstone Cabinet was seriously divided over foreign policy and Irish reforms. As a result of these pressures, the Prime Minister had to rely heavily on his Ministers for executive tasks and for monitoring pertinent legislation in Parliament. Matters such as the married women's property issue and other law reforms were rarely the subject of his or the Cabinet's concern. The new Lord Chancellor and Attorney General were left on their own to make decisions about necessary law reform.

From 1868 to 1885 the country had only three governments and two Prime Ministers. This executive stability coincided with increasing strength of political parties and party leadership in the Commons. By 1880 many of the Liberal MPs owed their election to affiliation with the national organization and Gladstone's leadership. Strong parties allowed the institutionalization of government control over the operation of the Commons. One rule adopted during the second Gladstone ministry was the closure or "guillotine." It had always been possible for members to tie up debate until the House ran out of time to consider a measure. Gladstone had used the technique himself in the 1857 debate on the Divorce Bill and was defeated only by the sheer force of the personalities of government ministers. By the 1870s and 1880s the press of business coincided with the representation of recalcitrant Irish Home Rulers to bring the problem of obstruction to a head. In early 1881 the Irish kept the House in session for forty-one and one-half hours. The House rules were amended in 1882 to allow closure of debate by vote of 200 members or 100 if 40 or fewer opposed. These rules were made permanent in 1887. Thus the government had resources that pressure groups sorely needed. It became important that advocates of equality for married women persuade Lord Chancellor Selborne and the Attorney General, Sir Henry James, to sponsor their bill.

Hinde Palmer introduced, on 9 June 1880, "A Bill to Consolidate and Amend the Married Women's Property Acts of 1870 and 1874." The bill was put together by combining the proposal of 1873 (the same as in 1857 and 1868) of the MWPC with provisions of the 1870 and 1874 Married Women's Property Acts. It provided for *feme sole* rights to property and earnings for married women and responsibility for torts with two additions already part of the law: the right of the wife to effect an insurance policy and the requirement that she be responsible for maintaining her indigent husband and children to the extent of her separate property. This last provision was from the 1870 Married Women's Property Act.

It introduced the concept of separate property for the first time into a bill proposed by the MWPC; it was only the beginning.[41]

Hinde Palmer pointed out in the Second Reading debate on his bill that it was a modest reform. Whereas earlier amendments in 1874 had solved the problem of a wife's creditors, this bill, he said, would be an advantage to married women as well as tradesmen and society in general by allowing women to sue, be sued, and contract. It would restore that section of Gurney's 1870 bill that had been eliminated by the House of Lords: "That a married woman shall be capable of acquiring, holding, alienating and bequeathing her property and of contracting, suing and being sued, as if she were unmarried."[42]

During the Second Reading debate, the Attorney General, Sir Henry James, stated that the government agreed "in principle" and then introduced its objections to the measure. He disagreed with Hinde Palmer's presentation of the bill as constituting a limited reform: "The bill . . . would effect a great revolution in matters not merely within but outside the household of every married man."[43] For example, it provided no limitation to the wife's power to contract. "She was allowed to contract, not merely in reference to her own property but generally." This, he reluctantly pointed out, may have some political effects. She might be liable to pay rates on a home, thus strengthening her claim to the vote. She would also be liable to bankruptcy.

Others picked up the theme introduced by the Attorney General: they supported the principle of property ownership but objected to the contracting powers it conferred. Morgan Lloyd suggested a modification:

> It was proposed that a married woman should have the right to enter any contract the same as if she were unmarried. If her right to contract were limited to contracts binding her separate property both at law and in equity, he should agree to that alteration of the law.[44]

As the bill stood, it would have the effect of rendering a husband liable for all of his wife's debts, he said—not legally liable, but morally liable; no husband could stand by and let his wife go to prison or into bankruptcy. On the other hand, if only her property were liable, the husband would be protected. MPs were also critical of the provisions allowing suits between a husband and wife on property matters, because they would lead to domestic disharmony. Support existed for a bill for married women to own property, but many, including the government, wanted to see some limits on their economic and legal rights that would recognize the special status of women in marriage.

The bill passed a Second Reading without a division, since both public opinion and the Liberal majority favored extending property rights for married women. Not enough time was left in the shortened 1880 session to complete all steps on the bill. Hinde Palmer introduced the same bill again in 1881 with one change. The 1880 bill referred to new rights for married women as *feme sole* rights. The 1881 version referred to married women's property also as *separate property* but continued to give them *feme sole* rights to that property. Hinde Palmer described the bill on the First Reading, 10 January 1881, mentioning the wife's separate property but claiming that this was the same bill he had introduced in the last session.

The bill passed the Second Reading on January 13 and was submitted to a House of Commons committee. The Attorney General chaired the committee. It met for two weeks and reported on March 8. The committee reorganized sections of the bill. A proposal by Edward Gibson to make a woman liable for contracts "in respect of her separate property" was defeated on a committee division, 7-5. However, the Attorney General, who favored such a revision, was not present. Later a new third clause was added without a division providing that a married woman entering into a contract would be assumed to be binding her separate property unless it was shown to the contrary. The committee also inserted the clause that a husband "need not be joined" in any suit against her. Other changes in the bill included adding sections regarding stocks and investments from the 1870 Married Women's Property Act. Steps were thus taken in the House of Commons committee to undermine further the contract liability of married women. After the report, no action on the bill was taken in 1881.

During 1881 the MWPC continued to attract the interest of public opinion on the issue but concentrated on persuading the Lord Chancellor to sponsor the bill. In January Jacob Bright, Arthur Arnold, Arthur Hobhouse, and John Hinde Palmer met with Lord Chancellor Selborne. The *Times* reported that Lord Selborne agreed only to study the matter further. Also in January the *Times* reported on the paper by Charles B. B. M'Laren, MP, son of Duncan and Priscilla M'Laren, given at a meeting of the NAPSS. According to the younger M'Laren, the major principle of the bill of 1881 was that "the labour of each of the partners in matrimony should be for the use of both, and that neither partner should be responsible for the acts of the other. [The bill would secure] in the case of a happy marriage the enjoyment of this property to both while in the case of domestic discord it gave to each the complete dominion over his or her separate estate."[45]

The purpose of the meeting, according to the NAPSS, was to generate public discussion and arouse opinion on the subject at the time the Lord Chancellor was studying the matter. It was attended by MPs and members of the MWPC, and discussion was held before passing a resolution in favor of "establishing for women the same rights and liabilities with regard to property and contract as appertain by law to men."[46] The MWPC and its parent organization had little further activity on the bill.

Sometime during 1881 the law officers of the government agreed to sponsor the "Married Women's Property Bill for England and Wales" as it had been amended by the House of Commons Select Committee. In March 1882 the Lord Chancellor introduced the bill in the House of Lords. Little is recorded on how this decision came about, but it was probably made among the law officers themselves.

From the beginning, the officers of the second Gladstone government had shown more interest in the issue of married women's property than had any previous government. The Attorney General voted in support of the 1880 and 1881 Hinde Palmer bills and chaired the House of Commons Select Committee on the issue. In 1881 the Married Women's Property Bill (Scotland) was sponsored by the Lord Chancellor after a private member bill had passed in the Commons. Previous reforms of the Scottish law had paralleled the English: in 1861 women gained property rights when separated, and after 1877 married women could keep their earnings. The 1881 act dealt with married woman's property, making her personal property during marriage her "separate estate," but stopped short of guaranteeing her equal rights. The Attorney General and the Solicitor General were pleased with the measure, noting it was more moderate that the bill proposed for England.

Lord Chancellor Selborne had been an equity lawyer, and during his tenure as Lord Chancellor in the first Gladstone government, he was largely responsible for the passage of the Judicature Act of 1873, which combined law and equity in one court system.[47] Selborne was conservative, a staunch supporter of the church, and seventy years old when he took over the Married Women's Property Bill. He was, no doubt, reluctant to support any radical change, such as equal status for women, in the law. The measure he introduced for England retained the notion of married women's separate and special status as the Scottish reform had done and as MPs had requested during debate in 1880 and 1881.

This time proponents had little reason to fear that the bill would be mutilated as it had been in 1870. The conflict between the Lords and Gladstone's Liberals persisted, but the balance between old property and new democracy had shifted in Gladstone's favor. A drastic decline in agricultural profits had beset landowners since the mid-1870s. The weakened productive status of large-scale family lands encouraged radicals and socialists to step up attacks on property and privilege. Some of this conflict focused on Irish land tenure and compensation bills that occupied much of the government's time at the beginning of the administration. Successful policy-making required bargaining between the Prime Minister and prominent leaders of the upper house. Since the constitutional power of the House of Lords itself was vulnerable to increasing attack by radicals, most peers, as the Queen advised, were careful not to unduly antagonize the lower house.

In 1881 the Married Women's Property Bill came to the House of Lords as a government bill, with support of prominent lawyers and judges. Led by the Lord Chancellor, the legal establishment had removed the threatening idea of legal and economic equality and guaranteed that the reform would do nothing more than combine law and equity, extending equity guarantees to all. On 7 March 1882, during the Second Reading debate in the House of Lords, the Lord Chancellor said: "it was the result, with merely trifling alterations, of the deliberations of the select committee of the House of Commons which sat last session when the bill was referred to that Committee."[48] The bill passed through the parliamentary steps quickly and passed a Third Reading on June 8.

These "trifling alterations" completed the destruction of the concept of economic and legal equality and substituted limited rights of married women to separate property in the bill. Married women would be able to acquire and sell property on the same basis as men and single women; their right to use and be responsible for that property would be different. Compare section two of the committee version with the government's version:

Committee: A married woman shall be capable of entering into and rendering herself liable on any contract, and of suing and being sued, either in contract or in tort, or otherwise, in all respects as if she were *feme sole,* and her husband need not be joined with her as plaintiff or defendant or be made a party to any action or other legal proceeding.

Government bill: A married woman shall be capable of entering into and rendering herself liable in respect of and to the extent of her separate property on any contract, and of suing and being sued, either in contract or in tort, or otherwise, in all respects as if she were *feme sole,* and her husband need not be joined with her as plaintiff or defendant, or be made a party to any action or other legal proceeding brought by or taken against her; and any damages or costs recovered by her in any such action or proceeding shall be her separate property; and any damages or costs recovered against her in any such action or proceeding shall be payable out of her separate property and not otherwise.

The government bill established proprietary liability for contracts rather than personal liability enjoyed by other citizens. The government bill also eliminated Section 9, which would have made a married woman liable for her own torts.

The Second Reading debate in the House of Commons revealed little concern over the changes in the bill made by the government. Osborne Morgan represented the MWPC in helping push the bill quickly through the House. He said that inasmuch as the bill was virtually identical to that which was settled by a select committee and inasmuch as it had received the sanction of Lord Cairns and that the House had discussed it over and over, he expected a quick Second Reading.[49] An opponent of the bill protested that the members had only received the bill a day before the debate, and they hadn't had time to study it, but the proponents viewed these comments as little more than delaying tactics. Campbell complained of the kind of response he got to his intention to give the bill a full discussion as reported by the scribe: "he was free to confess that the current was running the other way—that the 'women's righters' were exceedingly energetic whilst the friends of the poor married man were indolent so that the case of the poor married man was hopeless. . . . Those who proposed this bill desired that the woman should have all the privileges of the man, the control of her own property and none of the man's liabilities."[50] It was clear from the brief discussion during the report stage that opponents and proponents were discussing a bill that was different from the one the government had actually introduced: no one commented that it included the very provisions demanded by the Attorney General in the Second Reading debate a year earlier.

The Married Women's Property Committee met one final time in November to congratulate itself and to explain the act, since it had passed parliament with such little public discussion. Shaw Lefevre chaired the meeting and credited the passage of the act after the twenty-five-year struggle to George Osborne Morgan. Osborne Morgan replied, "he had merely put the coping-stone upon an edifice reared by others; and gratitude was due to the devoted band of earnest minded women, who, with very slender resources at their back and in the face of determined opposition were resolved to secure for the poor women of this country that control over their own property which their richer sisters enjoyed."[51] That, rather than equality, is precisely what they got.

In that statement, Osborne Morgan summed up two major points about the decision-making process surrounding the MWPA of 1882. First, the MWPC derived its energy from the women; especially Elizabeth Wolstenholme Elmy, Ursula Bright, and Lydia Becker. Second, it kept the pressure up and assisted Jacob Bright, Hinde Palmer, Shaw Lefevre, and others in promoting the campaign in the Commons until the government could feel comfortable in sponsoring it. Yet at the same time, women received rights less like those of men and more like the rights given to women through marriage settlements under equity law: ownership of property and earnings that had previously gone to their husbands, but limited responsibility as economic actors. They did not retain personal rights to contract and sue and consequent responsibilities and credit that men enjoyed, and their husbands remained liable for any tort committed by them.

CONFLICT RESOLUTION AND FEMINIST INFLUENCE

The Married Women's Property Act of 1882 altered the common law doctrine of coverture to include the wife's right to own, buy, and sell her separate property. It made her property liable for damages in any suit against her and held her only partially responsible for her contracts and torts in that her husband might be sued with her. This act was the product of legislative action on a private member bill from the Married Women's Property Committee that would have provided *feme sole* rights for married women—equality rather than special treatment. The bill was altered gradually, as has been seen in the preceding description of the policy process.

The major controversy over married women's economic rights centered on two assumptions about married women's property and legal status. The issue was whether married women should be treated as a special category, as they had been under both common and equity law, or the same as all other citizens. If they remained in a special status, law reform would simply remove injustices. If they were to be equal with other citizens, law reform would involve a major overhaul of common law and equity. The outcome in the Married Women's Property Act represented a compromise between the equalitarians and the protectionists. Proponents of equality achieved their demand for a married woman's right to her earnings and to buy, own, and sell real and personal property. The proponents of a separate protected status for married women were successful in limiting their liability in contract and tort and in establishing for the next fifty years the concept of married women's separate property in English family law.

Conflicts between equality and protection for married women in the ownership of earnings, ownership of property, separate property, and contract and tort were resolved in four stages before the final enactment in the Married Women's Property Act of 1882:

First, the right of a married woman to her own earnings was provided for by the Married Women's Property Act of 1870. Proposed by the MWPC and included in the bill passed by the House of Commons and its committees in 1868 and 1869, it was accepted in the final draft of the bill by the Select Committee of the House of Lords. The provision was repeated in the MWPC bills of 1880 and 1881 and retained by the government law officers in their draft in 1882.

Second, the right to acquire, own, and sell real and personal property was proposed by every MWPC bill but not enacted until 1882. It was included in the draft approved by the House of Commons Select Committee in 1881 and remained in the government bill.

Third, the notion of a married woman's "separate property" first appeared in a clause of the bill recommended by the House of Commons Select Committee in 1869 and was mentioned in the 1870 act. The phrase was liberally distributed throughout the MWPC bill of 1881 and fused into the heart of the 1882 government bill taking priority over the phrase *"feme sole."*

Fourth, a wife's limited liability for contracts and the consequent responsibility of the husband for his wife was in the draft bill approved by the Commons Select Committees of 1869 and 1881. That a married woman's liability for both contracts and torts was only to the extent of her separate property was specifically and clearly stated in the act by the government law officers.

The process of conflict resolution in passing the Married Womem's Property Act involved a combination of legislative and administrative structures. Those aspects of the Married Women's Property Act that gave equal status in ownership of earnings and property were placed there by agreement of legislative committees and accepted by the government. Those provisions that made married women's property rights less than equal, placing them in a protected separate status, were written into the act by the law officers in the administration.

The Married Women's Property Act fell short of achieving legal equality for married women because of the government's control of the decision-making process during the final stages of the policy process. Proponents of equality, the Married Women's Property Committee and its MPs, wanted the government to take over the bill. Government assistance was essential at the time to push the measure, which had been dangling for twenty-five years, past parliamentary obstacles and toward Royal Assent. The government, led by strong party leadership, was consolidating its control over the business of the House of Commons. The Lord Chancellor could help smooth things in the House of Lords. However, the very government involvement in sponsoring the bill placed it in a key position to determine policy outcomes. It used this opportunity to resolve conflicts in favor of a separate and unequal legal status for married women.

The MWPC was the main organization of feminists campaigning to reform the law of married women. A number of prominent feminists in the women's rights movement were associated with the committee as were MPs and liberal reformers of the LAS and NAPSS. The committee drafted the bill based on proposals of feminist Barbara Leigh Smith. Between 1868 and 1882 the MWPC kept the issue in the public eye through annual meetings, papers, and pamphlets. It circularized MPs and brought in petitions. It worked to persuade prominent lawyers and MPs through personal contacts. It had close connections with MPs and peers who repeatedly introduced its bills.

The committee had direct representation on various Commons' committees that considered its issue. These committees achieved resolutions to conflicts on issues of ownership of earnings and ownership of property. Therefore, feminists were influential in securing those aspects of the act that provided equality for married women. They were not represented among law officers of the government who had the final say on matters of separate property and liability for contract and tort. The feminist influence with the government was indirect: the MWPC asked the Lord Chancellor to take up the issue and then ran a publicity campaign designed to convince him of the support its proposal enjoyed and the need for it. The government, by assuming responsibility, ensured the passage of the reform. However, the MWPC had no say about government changes in the bill that limited married women's rights. Credit is due to the feminists for the reform of married women's property law coming to the fore as a public issue and for the policy outcome that removed married women's disabilities with respect to ownership of earnings and property. That they did not achieve their full goal of legal and economic equality is due to their absence during the final stages of conflict resolution among government law officers.

CONCLUSION

The process of enacting the Married Women's Property Act of 1882 illustrates the changes in the political system in Britain in the second half of the nineteenth century. The pattern of legislative-executive conflict resolution reflects both the increasing sophistication of interest groups in lobbying Parliament and the concentration of power in the centralized leadership. Married women's property reform was associated by both proponents and opponents with feminist goals of equality. It attracted supporters from among middle- and upper-class feminists, but at the same time, those who feared the effects of equality for women on society and their own place in it were moved to dilute demands for married women's property rights.

NOTES

1. Married Women's Property Act of 1882, 45, 46 *Vict.,* 75.

2. *Times,* 17 August 1882, 9.

3. Courts interpreted this section to be permissive, allowing but not requiring the husband to be sued with the wife. Scott v. Morley, 1887, 20 QBD 120; Edwards v. Porter, 1925, A.C. 1.

4. Quoted from the *Times* by J. W. Kaye, "Outrages on Women," *North British Review* 25 (May 1856), 234.

5. Ibid., 256.

6. John Roach, "The Mid Victorian Social Structure," in Roach, *Social Reform in England, 1780-1880* (London: Batsford, 1978), 153-73; Geoffrey Best, *Mid Victorian Britain, 1851-1875* (London: Weidenfeld & Nicolson, 1971), 228-81.

7. First published in eight monthly parts, 1875-1876.

8. Herbert Spencer, *Social Statics* (1851; reprint ed., New York: Kelley, 1969).

9. A. V. Dicey, *Law and Opinion in England during the Nineteenth Century* (London: Macmillan, 1905); Anthony Babington, *The Rule of Law in Britain* (Chichester: Barry Rose, 1978), 217-56; Sir William Holdsworth, *A History of English Law, Vol. XIV* (London: Sweet & Maxwell, 1966).

10. Ray Strachey, *The Cause* (1928; reprint ed., Bath: Cedric Chives, 1974), 80-83.

11. Barbara Leigh Smith married Eugene Bodichon, 1857. See Hester Burton, *Barbara Bodichon, 1827-1891* (London: J. Murray, 1949).

12. Quoted by Burton, *Barbara Bodichon.*

13. Quoted by Lee Holcombe, "Victorian Wives and Property: Reform of the Married Women's Property Law, 1857-1882," in *A Widening Sphere,* ed., Martha Vicinus (Bloomington, Ind.: Indiana University Press, 1977), 11.

14. As reported by Mary Taylor, "On the Conditions of Women as Affected by the Law," *The Englishwoman's Journal* 10 (October 1862), 124-27.

15. Parliamentary Debates, Official Report, III *Hansard* 146, c. 155.

16. Ibid., c. 1522.

17. "Property of Married Women," *The Englishwomen's Journal* 1 (March 1858), 58.

18. Ibid., 59.

19. Quoted in H. Ausubel, *In Hard Times: Reformers Among the Late Victorians* (New York: Columbia University Press, 1960), 8.

20. Roach, *Social Reform in England,* 153-248.

21. John Vincent, *The Formation of the British Liberal Party* (New York: Charles Scribner's, 1966), 141-238.

22. National Association for the Promotion of Social Science, "Introduction," *Transactions* 1 (1857).
23. G. W. Hastings, *The History and Objects of the National Association for the Promotion of Social Science* (London, 1861), 11-12.
24. "The Proposed Measures for Improving the Laws Relating to the Property of Married Women," *The Englishwoman's Review* (April 1868), 418-29.
25. III *Hansard* 192, c. 1352.
26. Ibid., c. 1363.
27. Ibid., c. 1360.
28. *Times,* 15 June 1868, 6.
29. National Association for the Promotion of Social Science, *Transactions* (1868), 249.
30. *Times,* 15 April 1869; 31 July 1869.
31. Special Report of the Select Committee on the Married Women's Property Bill, *Parliamentary Papers,* VII, 1867-1868 (17 July 1868), xiii.
32. David Southgate, *The Passing of the Whigs* (London: Macmillan, 1962), 324-55; Philip Magnus, *Gladstone: A Biography* (New York: Dutton, 1954), 167-223; E. J. Feuchtwanger, *Gladstone* (London: Allen Lane, 1975); Sir Ivor Jennings, *Party Politics, Vol. II: The Growth of Parties* (Cambridge: Cambridge University Press, 1961), 83-164.
33. Special Report of the Select Committee on the Married Women's Property Bill, *Parliamentary Papers,* III, 1868-1869 (13 May 1869).
34. III *Hansard* 202, c. 604.
35. Married Women's Property Committee, *Third Annual Report of the Executive Committee for Promoting the Married Women's Property Committee* (23 September 1870), Fawcett Library, London, 11.
36. Ibid.
37. Married Women's Property Committee, *Fifth Annual Report of the Executive Committee for Amending the Law with Respect to the Property of Married Women* (13 September 1872), Fawcett Library, London, 7.
38. III *Hansard* 214, c. 667.
39. Ibid., c. 688.
40. Married Women's Property Committee, *Tenth Annual Report of the Married Women's Property Committee* (4 February 1880), Fawcett Library, London.
41. Another bill, identical to the MWPC bill of 1873 without the consolidation features, introduced by M'Laren, Anderson, Leon Playfair, and others, did not go beyond a First Reading.
42. III *Hansard* 252, c. 1533.
43. Ibid., c. 1537.
44. Ibid., c. 1539.
45. *Times,* 24 January 1881.

46. Charles M'Laren, "The Married Women's Property Bill, 1881," in National Association for the Promotion of Social Science, Sessional Proceedings, 31 January 1881, Fawcett Library, London.

47. Holdsworth, *A History of English Law,* 97-104.

48. III *Hansard* 267, c. 316.

49. III *Hansard* 268, c. 615.

50. III *Hansard* 273, c. 1604.

51. *Times,* 21 November 1881.

Legal Equality Achieved, 1923-1937 4

THE ACTS

In the decades after World War I, Parliament adopted three statutes reforming divorce and matrimonial property laws. Women achieved equal and expanded grounds for divorce. Clarification of property law removed legal disabilities that lingered after the Married Women's Property Act of 1882. These acts also affected public policy with respect to sex roles. Two of the statutes gave equal legal status to husband and wife. The third reinforced official views of the separate and distinctly different spheres of husband and wife in marriage.

The Matrimonial Causes Act of 1923 was enacted to make the grounds for divorce equal for men and women.[1] It did not specifically guarantee equal rights. The wording of the statute allowed a wife to sue for divorce on grounds of simple adultery, which at the time was also the only ground for a husband's suit. The act was considered a means of enforcing an equal moral standard between the sexes. Proponents of this reform attacked the Victorian double standard that made married women the sole guardians of purity and faithfulness in the society. The act established a new official standard of morality: adultery by a husband was just as much a violation of marriage vows and just as destructive of family stability as unfaithfulness by a wife.

The Matrimonial Causes Act of 1937 expanded the grounds for divorce for both men and women.[2] Courts could grant divorce on grounds of desertion, cruelty, and insanity as well as adultery. The act increased grounds for nullity to include refusal to consummate the marriage, mental unsoundness, venereal disease, and pregnancy at the time of the marriage by another person. This divorce reform continued and reinforced the official view that marriage involved separate spheres of activity for husband and wife.

Although the wording of the act applied equally to husband and wife, it is clear from debates and discussion surrounding the reform that the legislators expanded the grounds for divorce largely to accommodate the special needs and circumstances of women in marriage. They expected the husband to be more likely to desert his children and the home, and the wife to be more attentive to the needs of her children and the home. Being able to sue for divorce on the grounds of desertion would be a relief for the wife, rather than the husband. Similarly, since husbands were more likely to mistreat their spouses and children physically than wives were, cruelty would also be of benefit to women. These conclusions were supported by the fact that women, far more than men, used cruelty and desertion as grounds for legal separation. The 1937 act transferred these grounds from the magistrates court to the divorce court largely for use by women. Legislators expected that husbands would continue to sue on grounds of adultery, the offense wives were most likely to commit. Insanity, a nonoffense ground for divorce, was expected to apply to very few cases.

Married women finally achieved equal rights to own and use property and equal personal responsibility for their financial actions with the enactment of the Law Reform (Married Women and Tortfeasors) Act of 1935.[3] It provided that all property of married women "shall belong to her in all respects as if she were a *feme sole* and may be disposed of accordingly." It made a married woman responsible for her own torts and contracts and the husband definitely *not* liable for antenuptual or postnuptual debts and contracts of the wife simply because of his status as husband. It retained one feature of equity notions of protection of married women's property: restraint on anticipation in marriage settlements made before 1936 would stand, but all limitations on marriage settlements were removed for marriages after 1936.

The law reforms in the 1920s and 1930s completed the initial steps toward equal status for married women taken over fifty years before. Officially, the statutes treated married men and women as having equal moral responsibilities in marriage and separate and equal economic and legal rights outside of marriage. Divorce policy continued to be based on official norms that marriage separated men and women into different spheres by sex—the wife to the children and the home and the husband to economic and personal interests outside the home. Matrimonial offenses committed by husband and wife would therefore be different. Although both were susceptible to adultery and insanity, the wife would be more likely to be aggrieved by desertion or cruelty than the husband.

Proposals to change divorce laws were much more controversial than those about property. The various steps toward divorce reform originated many decades before enactment of the statutes. The subject made its way to the public agenda several times before final resolution of the conflicts. The property reform, however, was settled quickly. Parliament used this reform to clear up some loose ends of the law rather than make a major change in women's rights. In this chapter processes leading to changes in divorce policy are considered separately from those affecting married women's property.

DIVORCE: THE DEMANDS

The Royal Commission on Marriage and Divorce had considered demands for equal and liberal divorce grounds for men and women in 1850. The Divorce Act of 1857, however, failed to incorporate these proposals. Equal grounds remained among the unachieved goals of feminists. Some believed in the value of equality under the law for its own sake. Others argued that equal grounds would mean moral equality and have the effect of raising the standards of males to those of females. The idea of an equal moral standard had inspired Josephine Butler to campaign successfully for repeal of the Contagious Diseases Act in the 1870s and 1880s.[4] Later it was a demand voiced most frequently by middle-class feminists who believed women deserved equality because of their superior qualities. If men were required to adhere to women's standards, a general improvement in society would result. If a wife could sue for divorce because of one act of adultery by her husband, he would be as reluctant as she to commit even one immoral act.

Suggestions for reform of the divorce law came almost as soon as the courts applied the 1857 act. Lawyers and their clients found that the law was not consistent with the realities of marriage in that it did not provide relief for spouses, especially women, trapped in unhappy marriages. Divorces were expensive and only one court in the entire country could grant them. Limited grounds made it difficult for all but the most determined to end their marriages. Despite these barriers, the number of divorces grew steadily. Increases included both simple adultery and adultery plus other offenses, the only ground available to women (see table 1). Lawyers found that adultery, being the sole grounds for divorce, was unnecessarily restrictive. Pressure for divorce often forced couples into perjury or collusion to avoid the suffering and anguish of a well-publicized divorce trial.

Table 1
Average Number of Divorces Granted in England and Wales

YEARS	*TOTAL*	*ADULTERY*	*ADULTERY + OTHER OFFENSE*
1867-1869	149		
1870-1874	232		
1875-1879	318		
1880-1884	337		
1885-1889	368		
1890-1894	374		
1895-1899	500	230[a]	208[a]
1900-1904	590	306	229
1905-1909	645	357	287
1910-1914	699	376	322

Source: Appendix, *Royal Commission on Marriage and Divorce, Evidence and Report,* 1956 (Cmnd. 9678).
a. Figures available only from 1896.

During 1897-1906 when 5,700 divorces were granted, over 87,000 orders for separation and maintenance, the poor man's or more often the poor woman's divorce, were made.[5] Many couples wanted to end their marriages, but most could not afford the costly procedures of the central court.[6] Since separation did not allow legal remarriage, the unhappily married had to choose between being alone and establishing illegimate consensual families. By the beginning of the twentieth century, most of the legal profession considered the Divorce Act of 1857 to be out of touch with the realities of marriage.

In 1906 the Divorce Law Reform Union (DLRU) was organized by

M. L. Seaton-Tiedemann. It was composed of lawyers and others concerned that the divorce laws were unrealistic and caused a great deal of suffering. Many wives and some husbands were left desolate by being bound to drunken, criminal, insane, or excessively cruel spouses and could not be free to remarry under the current law. The DLRU advocated that grounds be expanded to include insanity, cruelty, desertion, drunkenness, and penal servitude. The union was a small interest group dedicated to increasing public awareness and pressuring Parliament.

The major opposition to divorce reform came from the Church of England and the Roman Catholics. During the early 1900s the church was united in its support of the indissolubility of Christian marriage. The clergy rejected any attempt to expand grounds or otherwise make divorce more accessible to people as a threat to the Christian family. They reiterated their stand by refusing to marry divorced persons in the church; even a spouse who was innocent of matrimonial offense was denied remarriage. The church did not object to equal grounds for men and women; however, a few ultra-conservatives considered this too to be liberalization and opposed the proposal on that basis.

The need for divorce reform was brought up for public discussion by Lord Gorell, who, as Sir John Barnes, had presided over the Divorce and Admiralty Court from 1892 to 1906. He considered the law to be unjust for women and was concerned that the poor were being denied divorce due to concentration of court activities in London. In *Dodd v. Dodd,* 1906, Gorell denied a woman a divorce, because her adulterous husband had not technically deserted her. In that decision, he asserted that it was time for Parliament to consider a reform of the law.

In 1909 Gorell brought the matter to the official attention of Parliament through a motion in the House of Lords to extend jurisdiction in divorce matters to county courts. Ostensibly a procedural motion, it gave him an opportunity to make a speech on the issue of divorce and test the waters of parliamentary and public opinion. During the debate, many peers agreed that the entire area of divorce law was a mess and that it required investigation by a Royal Commission. The Liberal Lord Chancellor Loreburn, seeing the interest in the subject, agreed to take up the matter with the Asquith government. The opposition was quiet during the debate and belied its entrenched nature. The Archbishop of Canterbury made a ritual statement reflecting the church's opposition to any extension of the grounds for divorce or its administration. The archbishop did not say anything about the issue of equal grounds.

In 1909 Prime Minister Asquith appointed the Royal Commission on Marriage and Divorce to be chaired by Lord Gorell. He charged the Gorell commission to consider the extension of the jurisdiction of the county courts to include divorce, the position of women in divorce in relation to men, the extension of grounds for divorce, and the publication of reports of divorce proceedings. The commission included representatives of the church, the law profession, Parliament, and the women's movement. It received testimony for two years and issued its report in 1912. Testimony from a large number of women's organizations and individuals was overwhelmingly in favor of establishing equal grounds in divorce. The most popular argument was that different divorce grounds for men and women established two standards of morality. Since adultery by men was not a grounds for divorce, the law sanctioned adultery by men while making it a serious offense if committed by women. Thus, it was argued, equal grounds would elevate the moral standards of men. As Millicent Fawcett testified: "The law sanctions a lower standard for men and I think this has an injurious effect upon them."[7] She reasoned that if a threat of divorce arising from adultery existed, men would be less likely to commit adultery.

The Women's Cooperative Guild polled its members and submitted evidence of strong support for equal grounds as well as for additional grounds such as cruelty, desertion, insanity, and separation. The members also wanted more accessible divorce procedures through county courts. The Guild even found some members who believed in divorce by mutual consent and incompatibility. Marriage should rest on consent, not compulsion, they said.

The commission issued a majority report recommending several major reforms in the law:

1. Expand the grounds for divorce to include adultery, desertion for three years, cruelty, incurable insanity, habitual drunkenness, imprisonment under a commuted death sentence.
2. Guarantee equal grounds for husband and wife to sue for divorce.
3. Expand provisions for nullity (failure to consummate, insanity, venereal disease, pregnancy).
4. Limit publication of details of divorce cases.
5. Reduce cost for divorce procedures.

Three members of the fourteen-member commission—Cosmo Gordon, Bishop of York; Sir William Anson, MP; and Sir Lewis Dibdin, MP—dissented from the majority over the expansion of the grounds for divorce. They cited the strong opposition of a 278,000-member church group, the Mothers' Union, to any liberalization of the divorce laws. They did, however, agree with the majority on equal grounds, nullity provisions, publication, and cost recommendations.

The Gorell Commission Report very likely reflected public demand for divorce, but it failed to take adequate account of the strength of the church's opposition to expansion of divorce grounds. Whereas in 1853 the government quickly introduced a bill on the basis of the previous Royal Commission report, no government would touch the 1912 recommendations. Gorell died shortly after the report was published. His son introduced a bill in the House of Lords in 1914 to add desertion as a grounds for divorce and extend jurisdiction over divorce to county courts. It passed a Second Reading but was dropped because of the war. It was reintroduced in 1918 in the Lords but failed the Second Reading.

The problem for advocates of divorce reform was to get their issue on the public agenda, so Parliament could make a decision. The House of Lords led by the Law Lords was more receptive to the proposals of the Gorell commission than was the lower house. Since the Parliament Act of 1911, however, the House of Commons was the dominant chamber. To capture its attention required first capturing the attention of the government. Opponents of liberalization were vigilent to prevent that from happening. Meanwhile, feminists saw that their demand for equal grounds, although facing little opposition, would be kept away from Parliament, too, unless it could be relieved of the intense controversy surrounding expansion of grounds. It was not until the feminists drafted their own bill for equal grounds in 1923 that their demand was accepted by the legislature for action. Proponents of expanded grounds, later joined by feminists, had to wait until the mid-1930s to surmount the formidable barrier of opposition erected by the churches.

THE CONFLICT: EQUAL GROUNDS

By the time women were permitted to vote in 1918, feminist pressure groups had lost ground. Until the 1880s small organizations such as the Married Women's Property Committee gathered around single issues and presented bills through friends and family to influential MPs directly. The expansion of the suffrage and the centralization of political parties changed all that. Each party needed a great coalition of supporters to gain a majority of the seats in the House of Commons. They appealed to class, occupation, and region. Individual MPs depended on the overall popularity of their party for their own election. Single-issue pressure groups were of little help at the polls.[8] The interest groups that could exert pressure on the leaders of the Liberal and Conservative parties were those that had strong central organizations and large numbers of constituents. These so-called peak organizations spoke, by and large, for economic interests such as trade unions, professional organizations, and employers' associations.

Feminists, frustrated at their lack of influence, began to focus on a single issue, the vote. Three main groups were in the suffrage battle: militants, constitutionalists, and socialists. Each used different types of organizations and tactics. Both militants and constitutionalists formed peak organizations, but they refused to work with the political parties. The constitutionalists, through general lobbying, tried to convince MPs one at a time. The militants spoke directly to the government, leader to leader. The socialists did not form a separate suffrage organization but worked among the trade unions and the new Labour party.

The militants of the Women's Social and Political Union (WSPU), led by the Pankhursts, used violence, disruption, and martyrdom, enduring prison and force feeding, to gain the attention of the government. The militants brought publicity to the campaign but at the same time provided an excuse for its discreditation by those who found it popular to denounce violence. Emmeline Pankhurst believed, however, that no people had ever achieved political rights and freedom from others without violence.[9] She considered votes for women to be crucial to their overall social, economic, and political emancipation.

The moderates were led by Millicent Garrett Fawcett in the National Union of Women's Suffrage Societies (NUWSS). The NUWSS concentrated on gaining favorable public support and pressured the government and Parliament through personal contacts, letters, petitions, and deputations. Its newspaper, *Common Cause,* was devoted entirely to the suffrage issue. During the long struggle, the national Executive Committee of the NUWSS gained experience and established channels for influencing Parliament.

Working women hoped the vote would be a means to improve the status of women workers, the chief victims of sweated conditions and low pay. Between 1895 and 1906 the Labour party came to life from a coalition of trade union and socialist organizations. They were deeply divided on the issue of suffrage. Many, such as Henry Quelch in the Social Democratic Federation, demanded votes for all men before any women were given the franchise. Others such as Kier Hardie were ardent feminists, active in the national campaign for votes for women. It wasn't until 1912 that the Labour party passed a weak resolution for women's suffrage. However, socialist women failed to establish a strong organization of working-class women for women's rights. Some stayed to work from inside the Labour party. Others joined the constitutionalists or the militants to work full time for the suffrage.

None of the suffrage groups was very successful. The constitutionalists were the only players left in the game when the dislocations and upheavals of World War I forced the government finally to review the election laws. The WSPU and the working women were involved in war work and had set aside the suffrage campaign. The NUWSS learned of the planned revision in the suffrage and demanded justice for women: the war had brought many women into the work force and they had proved to be indispensable. No justification could be found for the old opposition arguments about protecting women from the rigors of politics and keeping them in the home. Modern politics was proving to be as important to women as it was to men. The Representation of the People Act was passed in 1918 and gave women over age thirty the vote, while extending male suffrage to those over age twenty-one. Although equality had not been attained, votes for women had, and the long campaign was at last victorious. The militants did not survive the victory. The Pankhursts organized the Women's party in 1918, but it lasted only one year. None of its members achieved formal political power.

Trade union women opposed feminism and worked to promote the Labour party. There, feminist ideas were buried under the rhetoric of the labour movement. In 1908 Ethel Snowden had written in *The Woman Socialist* that women's equality was basic to all other social change.[10] Granting votes even for a few women on the same basis as men would remove the stigma of inferior birth from all women. Then they could expect equal status in marriage and divorce, education, work, and pay. By 1917 the Oxford essays in feminism presented a far different view of the place of women in socialism.[11] In his introduction, Victor Gollancz argued that by getting the vote, women had received just about all of the equality they should get. They had special needs as wives and mothers. Once the Labour party was installed at Westminster, women, like everyone else, would receive the special services they needed from the state.

In 1918 the NUWSS was all that was left of the organized feminist movement that had been formed in the 1860s. The National Council of Women was strong, but not primarily a feminist organization. Other groups such as the Six Point Group were just forming. The NUWSS realized that its goal of equal suffrage had not been entirely achieved but expected it would be forthcoming. What it was concerned about was that women not get complacent now that the suffrage issue had been won. Some may have found it difficult to remember what other issues there were, since the suffrage campaign had been so long and intense. Votes were not an end in themselves but a means of achieving equality for women in all areas of society through their influence on elected representatives. Now they could begin to concentrate on these goals.

Millicent Fawcett, the link with the origins of the movement, stepped down as president in 1918, and the association was reorganized and renamed the National Union of Societies for Equal Citizenship (NUSEC), a name consistent with its expanded interests. It retained its basic organizational form: local societies were organized to gain membership support, raise money, and educate women and their communities on women's issues. The national office with a parliamentary secretary and staff was to take responsibility for lobbying at the national level. "Organization is necessary, and women, irrespective of differences in politics, religion, or education must unite to form a solid body of opinion on the great moral issues for which they as women have a special responsibility."[12]

In 1919 the NUSEC expanded its program and elected Eleanor Rathbone president. At this point the program emphasized legal equality: suffrage on an equal basis; an equal moral standard (which included equal grounds for divorce and equal control of men and women in prostitution); equal nationality rights; equal guardianship of children; equal access to political and professional jobs; equal education; equal training and trade union membership; state pensions for widows with dependent children; more women in Parliament. Parliamentary secretary Eva Hubback launched an extensive effort to accomplish these goals through law reform. In most cases, this activity involved monitoring bills, publicizing the support or opposition of the NUSEC, and using channels to pressure Parliament, such as personal contacts, letters, formal visits. Only in a few cases did the NUSEC actually propose specific legislation.

The years immediately following 1918 were successful for the NUSEC. It was unified in seeking equality in many areas of law. Statutes that seemed to be achieving its goals were enacted:

1. Parliament (Qualification of Women) Act 1918: women eligible for the House of Commons.
2. Sex Disqualification (Removal) Act 1919: women eligible for law profession, some civil service jobs.
3. Law of Property Act 1922: women and men equal in intestacy.

Defeats occurred, of course, such as the Emancipation Bill of 1919, introduced by a private member of the Labour party in the Commons, a bill that would have removed all legal inequalities at once. It passed the House of Commons but was defeated in the House of Lords with the assistance of the government.

In 1920 Lord Buckmaster, former Liberal Lord Chancellor, introduced a new bill based entirely on the majority recommendations of the Gorell Commission, expanding grounds to include desertion, insanity, drunkenness, and life sentence, providing equal grounds for men and women, and extending the jurisdiction of the county courts. The bill received strong support among the Law Lords, especially Lord Birkenhead, the Lord Chancellor. The Divorce Law Reform Union, of which Birkenhead had been honorary president, assisted in promoting the bill. The Lord Chancellor during debate reported that a petition with 100,000 signatures in favor of the bill had been received. He argued that a reasonable divorce law based on human needs would raise the standard of morality, not break up homes.[13] Divorce law is not a disease, he noted, but a remedy for a disease. The bishops opposed the expansion of grounds for divorce, because then the state policy would contradict the moral teachings of the church. They argued that marriage was a sacrament and should not be dissoluble. The bill passed a Third Reading but was dropped in the House of Commons.

In response to the Buckmaster bill, the NUSEC adopted the following principles of divorce reform: causes of divorce should be the same for men and women; divorce should be available in local courts; alimony granted to wives should be adequate; press reports should not include details. The union came down solidly in agreement with the minority report of the Gorell Commission. The Equal Moral Standards Committee of the NUSEC publicly supported the part of the Buckmaster bill dealing with equal grounds. The committee did not make a special effort, however, to campaign for the bill because of differences of opinion among its members over the expansion of the grounds for divorce. Members could agree on equality, but some feared the extension of grounds might hurt women by lessening their security in marriage.

The same year Athelston Randall introduced a motion in the House of Commons in support of the Gorell Commission's majority report. Randall's motion lost due to opposition of the church, lack of interest in the issue, and poor attendance. Advocates and opponents alike agreed on the desirability of equality in the law, however.

Thus encouraged, the second Lord Gorell introduced another bill in the 1921 parliamentary session. This bill was based on those areas of agreement between the majority and minority of the commission: equal grounds and expansion of grounds for nullity. *Women's Leader and Common Cause,* the NUSEC publication, called it "a reform for which all those interested in the status of the married woman and the establishment of an equal moral standard have been working for years."[14]

The Archbishop of Canterbury supported this bill, because it did not change the principle of limited divorce but answered grievances over the working of the law. This support from the church changed when the Lords accepted an amendment by Lord Buckmaster to expand grounds for divorce to include desertion. Gorell feared the amendment would endanger the chances of the bill's passage in the Commons. He was right; although the bill passed the Third Reading in the Lords, no action was taken in the Commons.

Meanwhile, Randall prepared to urge a resolution by the House of Commons in support of the widely accepted minority report of the commission. Again, he failed, he claimed, because opponents in the Commons thought it was the same motion as before, and they were dead set against any extension of grounds. At that point proponents of divorce reform decided to wait until the new election was held in November 1922.

The NUSEC sought to extract pledges from candidates during the campaign. Most publicized was the response it received from Andrew Bonar Law, Conservative Leader and the next Prime Minister. He was not an ardent supporter of equality and pointed out difficulties he had in supporting equal suffrage or equal economic opportunity. But he found the issue of equal grounds in divorce less controversial and pledged his support: "The question of making the existing grounds for divorce the same for women and men appears to be a matter of right and wrong, and I am in favor of equality in this respect."[15]

At this point the issue of divorce reform had been divided into two distinct parts: equality and liberalization. Both demands were considered by the Gorell Commission and incorporated into their final recommendations. Parliament had several chances to consider them together. It was evident that widespread support for equal grounds existed; yet when the proposal was connected to the issue of increased grounds, it was repeatedly defeated. The feminists under the leadership of the NUSEC vowed to separate the two issues and to campaign for equality only, rather than the complete package of divorce reform proposals. From 1922 on, the reforms followed different legislative paths: equality to immediate success in 1923, liberalization to a grueling fifteen-year test.

CONFLICT RESOLVED: EQUAL GROUNDS

The NUSEC was confident that the narrow issue of equal grounds in divorce faced little opposition either in the Parliament or in the country. However, the postwar political scene was chaotic with conflicts over the personality and style of the Prime Minister, power struggles among the leaders, and divisions in the party system. The feminists had to be vigilent to prevent their simple bill from becoming the pawn in someone else's power game.

The 1918 election, despite an expanded suffrage, continued the war-time coalition Cabinet of Conservatives and Liberals with David Lloyd George as Prime Minister. Lord Birkenhead, a Conservative, was Lord Chancellor. The government enjoyed a majority of 230 with the backing of 335 Conservatives, 133 Liberals, and 10 Labour members. However, controversy over Lloyd George's heavy-handed leadership grew. The Liberal party itself was becoming less and less popular as more workers joined the Labour movement. Conservatives were reluctant to continue participation in a coalition under a Liberal Prime Minister. Andrew Bonar Law, the Conservative Leader of the Commons, resigned from the government in 1921. In October 1922 Conservative backbenchers withdrew their support from the coalition, forcing Lloyd George's government to resign. The general election in November returned 345 Conservatives, 116 Liberals, and 142 members of the Labour party. Bonar Law formed the government, and Viscount Cave, who had been at the Home Office until 1919, became Lord Chancellor. Despite its majority, the new government was plagued by great conflicts in the Parliament over foreign policy, Ireland, labor rights, and free trade.

Many divisions were evident in the political parties in both houses. Conservative leaders, such as Lord Birkenhead, who had supported the Lloyd George coalition to the end, were defeated or excluded from participation in the new government. The Liberals lost seats in 1922, and those that were left formed two factions, followers and opponents of Lloyd George. The Labour party was growing rapidly but had little internal cohesion.

In the face of all this, the feminists were united and well organized. After the 1922 election, the Executive Committee of the NUSEC drafted a simple bill providing for nothing more than equal divorce grounds for men and women. "In view of the fact that practically all schools of thought are united in the need for this particular reform and that the Prime Minister in his letter to the National Union at the time of the General Election intimated his opinion that the need for such a reform was urgent, this bill should become law during the next session."[16]

Constituency societies of the NUSEC were assigned to pressure their MPs to attend sessions and vote for the bill. The bill had the support of a number of women's organizations, most notably the National Council of Women, whose president, Lady Frances Balfour, had been on the Gorell Commission as well as the NUSEC Executive Committee. They all agreed to concentrate on the equality issue and not endanger the bill's chances by expanding it.

Eva Hubback, the parliamentary secretary of the NUSEC, took responsibility for finding an MP to sponsor the bill. She persuaded Major Cyril Entwistle, who got second place in the private member ballot, to undertake it. In the 1920s for the first time, feminists had sympathetic women to sponsor their bills and speak for their issues on the House floor. Lady Nancy Astor had been elected in 1919;

Margaret Wintringham joined her in 1921. Now Astor, Conservative, and Wintringham, a Liberal, along with another Liberal, Sir John Simon, cosponsored the bill for equal grounds.

During the Second Reading debate Major Entwistle emphasized the need for an equal moral standard.[17] The issue the bill raised was that of justice and equality and was "practically universally demanded by the women of this country." He pointed out that divorce reform itself was too controversial. "I don't regard this as a divorce reform but rather a measure for equality of the sexes." The opponents of Entwistle's bill were few but articulate. Some opposed any change in the divorce law; others argued that acts of adultery by the two sexes were different. As Henry Craik noted:

> Chastity in women is a star that has guided human nature since the world began, that points far higher and teaches us of the other sex things which we otherwise would not know. . . . But I do not think that any mere man would thank us for enshrining him in such a halo.[18]

The bill safely made it through a Second Reading and the committee Report stages without change. Opponents monopolized debate during the Third Reading, although the passage of the bill was never in trouble. The drawn-out debate turned out to be a tactic used by the opponents of the next private member bill on the schedule, Lady Astor's proposal for prohibiting sale of intoxicating liquor to those under age eighteen. When the division was finally called, Major Entwistle's bill passed, 257-26.

The NUSEC feared that Lord Birkenhead, a zealous and unpredictable advocate of liberalization of the divorce law and enemy of the Bonar Law government, might ruin the bill's chances by attaching expanded grounds to it. Lord Buckmaster agreed to sponsor the bill in the upper house and to ward off such attempts. Most advocates of the bill were convinced at that point that the Conservatives in Commons would not accept any tampering with the divorce grounds. The simplicity of the bill guaranteed its passage in the wake of the acceptance of the principle of legal equality for women and the almost unanimous support by the newly enfranchised women's groups. The coalition would have crumbled in the face of proposals for liberalizing divorce laws.

The bill thus went peacefully and quickly through the Lords with Buckmaster, Birkenhead, Gorell, and the Archbishop of Canterbury all in support. It received the Royal Assent on 20 July 1923. In the meantime, Bonar Law had resigned, and Baldwin had become Prime Minister. That momentous event seems to have had little effect on the steady passage of Major Entwistle's and Buckmaster's private member bill.

THE CONFLICT OVER EXPANDED GROUNDS

The step-by-step removal of legal inequalities continued with the passage of the Guardianship of Infants Act in 1926, making husband and wife equal as guardians of their children. While the feminists applauded this reform, a controversy was building in their ranks over the goals of the women's movement as a whole. As a result, after 1923 issues of family law were of little immediate interest as the NUSEC tried to keep the ideological divisions from destroying the organization. The old feminists who had dominated the NUSEC before 1918 believed in absolute equality of men and women under law. As long as legal barriers were removed, they believed, women would be able to achieve in all areas that men could. The new feminists, on the other hand, argued that women were different from men, that their roles as mothers left them at a disadvantage when competing with men, and that they needed special assistance and protection to be able to gain anything from the economy.

Eleanor Rathbone, in her second inaugural address as president of the NUSEC in 1923, proposed that the union begin to adopt programs consistent with the new feminism. "I want women to build up their own status, liberties and opportunities free from men's restrictions, but not necessarily identical with those of men."[19] New feminism looked beyond legal equality to the actual situation of married women in the home and proposed special programs to help them. Rathbone feared that when the middle-class women had achieved their goals of access to politics, education, and the professions, they would become complacent and cease to help the majority of women who were economically dependent wives and mothers.

In March 1925 the NUSEC added two new goals to its program: family allowances and birth control. Rathbone stated that family allowances, payments from the state to mothers to aid in support of children, was the sort of policy that recognized that homemaking and childrearing were socially valuable occupations. Governments would thus recognize the importance of women's work instead of forcing women to be like men to get any benefits. Birth control services would assist women in maintaining control of their family responsibilities.

The conflicts in the NUSEC between the new and old feminists intensified. In 1926 Dame Millicent Fawcett, the union's founder and guiding light, resigned over the issue of family allowances. In 1927 Socialist members advocated protective legislation for women workers. The problems of working-class women were fundamentally different from middle- and upper-class women, they argued, and required different solutions. The old feminists opposed different treatment for different classes of women. Lady Balfour proposed that the NUSEC declare that family allowances, birth control, and protective legislation were of secondary importance to issues of equality, such as married women's right to work, equal pay, and equal divorce. When she was defeated, Lady Balfour and nine members of the Executive Committee resigned, thus leaving the field to the new feminists and social reformers. After 1927 the NUSEC continued its legislative program and tried to combine equal rights with the goals of the new feminism.

The NUSEC and its parliamentary secretary Hubback occasionally discussed divorce reform, but it was not one of the primary goals of the organization. In 1931 the feminists of the NUSEC finally agreed to support expansion of divorce grounds. At the annual general meeting, the Executive Committee adopted the following resolution:

> This council holds that, as divorce cannot be obtained unless adultery be proved, the present law both encourages immorality and leads to much individual hardship. This council therefore urges the government to carry out the recommendations of the Royal Commission on Divorce Laws and to introduce or to support legislation based on Lord Buckmaster's Bill twice passed in the House of Lords, by which the grounds for a divorce for both husband and wife shall include adultery, desertion, persistent cruelty, persistent drunkenness, prolonged insanity, or imprisonment under life sentence.[20]

This resolution illustrates the approach to divorce reform taken by many of its proponents. They did not consider divorce as a woman's right to free herself from a restrictive institution. Rather, they viewed reform as a means of promoting morality, respect for the law, and marriage itself. Abuses of the law led people to absurd lengths to obtain divorces and, in some cases, where adultery was not present or could not be proved, forced people to endure impossible marital conditions without being able to obtain a divorce.

Only the Divorce Law Reform Union actively lobbied Parliament to liberalize divorce laws. As a small single-issue pressure group, it had limited political resources. An important resource was the energy and life-long commitment of its leader Mrs. M. L. Seaton-Tiedemann. Through her personal connections with a few peers and MPs, a bill was brought before six sessions of Parliament between 1924 and 1934. The DLRU convinced Lord Buckmaster to try in 1924 to get his bill on the pathway to Royal Assent. It received a Second Reading in the House of Lords. Buckmaster said he would not push the matter further unless he got assurances of help from the Prime Minister. The bill was not brought up again until 1930.

The DLRU then persuaded Holford Knight, MP, to make divorce his issue. In 1930 he moved that "leave be given to bring in a bill to amend the law relating to matrimonial causes."[21] He sought to add one additional ground—insanity. The proposal was opposed, because it would constitute divorce at the instigation of one spouse without the respondent, probably a woman, being able to defend herself. Reverend G. Lang (Labour) said:

> One of the most difficult cases is that of the insanity of women at a certain age and it seems a terrible thing if it is going to be possible at that time, after the man has had a full life, for the woman to be haunted with the fear of being permanently insane while the man will be free to marry again.[22]

The motion passed, 210-102, but no further action was taken that session. Another bill along those lines was introduced in 1931 by J. C. Ede but did not come up for a Second Reading. Knight brought his bill again in 1932. He explained that it would be a test of sentiment of the house if it passed; then the government could feel secure in introducing a reform embodying all the recommendations of the Gorell commission. His motion to introduce the bill passed, 96-42; the bill itself stopped at the First Reading.

In 1933 the Knight bill was debated for a Second Reading vote but was talked out by Dr. W. J. O'Donovan, a Roman Catholic.

He discussed insane asylums, effects of the bill on family responsibility, the expenses to the state of housing divorced lunatics, and so on until fewer than forty members remained on the floor. Finally, in 1934 Knight, noting the government's failure to take responsibility for a needed reform, introduced a complete revision of the divorce law, expanding the grounds. He reported that he had the support of the Labour women, the Women's Liberal Federation, and the Law Society. Again O'Donovan talked the bill out until adjournment, and the divorce reform was dead for another session.

The issue of divorce reform as defined by the NUSEC, the DLRU, and the law profession in the 1930s was the same as Gorell derived from his 1890s divorce court. The Church of England and the Roman Catholics remained opposed to any liberalization. The government's refusal to assist in the consideration of such a controversial issue had stymied the considerable efforts at change for nearly twenty-five years. The situation remained unresolvable until the 1935 election. Two things occurred in the 1935 election that changed the fate of divorce reform. First, a strong Conservative majority was returned under the leadership of Baldwin, who formed a new coalition National government. Sir John Simon, a prominent Liberal and feminist, was made Home Secretary and Deputy Leader of the Commons. He had cosponsored the Entwistle equality of grounds bill in 1923 and had been a member of the NUSEC in the 1920s and 1930s. Secondly, the newly elected Independent member for Oxford University was Alan P. Herbert. Herbert, a writer, humorist, and journalist, was personally interested in the issue of divorce reform.

Herbert's recent novel *Holy Deadlock* had been widely read and was very popular. In it he used his wit to point out the absurdities of the divorce business. Mary Eve and John Adam, married several years and separated for two, want a divorce. Both realize their marriage is dead and have plans and partners to remarry. Neither has committed adultery and will not involve a prospective fiance in a sordid divorce trial. John resolves to "behave like a gentleman." This means he hires a woman to help him set up all of the court evidence for proof of adultery in a hotel in Brighton. This plan fails miserably as do all later attempts to dispose of the marriage. At the end they remain hopelessly tied to each other in name only.

In Herbert's election campaign, he had discussed divorce reform to the effect that if the government wouldn't take up the issue as it should, he would. His district was strongly conservative and a bastion of the Church of England; yet he was elected with the support of some clergy despite his honest and forthright intention to pursue a liberalization of the divorce law against official church policy.

He was no doubt encouraged in his quest by what appeared to be a crack in the church's solid opposition. The Upper House of the Convocation of Canterbury composed of the Anglican bishops had recently passed a resolution indicating its acceptance of the need and demand for reform in the divorce law. It called for the church to make sure that whatever reform was adopted would not make marriage a temporary alliance. It also condemned the operation of the current law for encouraging perjury and collusion.

In any case, Herbert immediately declared his mission and in the process broke many of the conventions of the House of Commons. His sense of humor and his very audacity put the divorce issue in a new light. It lost the image of a hopeless cause or a hardy perennial. As an Independent, Herbert could offer a truly nonpartisan bill and seek his supporters on both sides of the House.

The bill he introduced in early 1936 was based mainly on the recommendations of the Royal Commission of 1912: "the Report has stood the test of time. It provided the flesh, bones, blood of the present Act. All we have done is to give the picture a new frame, hang it in a better light and sell it."[23] Specifically, Herbert cast the reform as a means of saving marriage: he entitled it the Marriage Bill. The first clause prohibited a divorce decree during the first five years of marriage. Clause 2 extended the grounds for divorce to include the Gorell-Buckmaster-Knight grounds: adultery, desertion, cruelty, drunkenness, insanity, and penal servitude. The commission recommendations had some embellishments: clauses to extend the powers of magistrates courts, to allow members of the clergy to refuse to marry divorced persons, and to permit divorce after a two-year legal separation.

Herbert reported that, although he consulted with two or three friends, the bill was his own work. One of these friends was Claud Mullins, a London magistrate. In his book *Wife v. Husband in the Courts,* he advocated extending the practice of legal separation to the full divorce court. Magistrates, who handled legal separation, often were involved in conciliation between husband and wife, trying to save marriages. Such conciliation was not possible in divorce court, which required an adversary situation between the spouses. At his suggestion, Herbert included legal separation as a ground for divorce and extended the jurisdiction of magistrates courts to include divorce.

Interest groups were wary of the bill at first. In 1932 the NUSEC had divided into two separate organizations: the National Council for Equal Citizenship (NCEC), which was to concentrate on parliamentary activities, and the Townswomen's Guilds, which were to educate women about relevant public issues in the local communities. During the 1930s the NCEC was led by Eva Hubback, Helena Normanton, and Marjory Corbett Ashby. Normanton thought the Herbert bill was too liberal: "We must have a better bill than this awful thing put forward by Mr. A. P. Herbert MP."[24] Mrs. Seaton-Tiedemann of the DLRU criticized the bill, because it contained additional provisions not found in the DLRU bills. The basic idea of the bill received support of reformers and especially women's rights groups including the National Council for Women and the NCEC. MPs who sponsored the bill included two women: Eleanor Rathbone, an Independent, former president of the NUSEC, who was working for her own bill on family allowances; and Maud Tate, a Conservative, who took an active interest in the Herbert bill, debated it, and helped marshall the necessary support. The Marriage bill was printed in 1936 but did not receive time for a Second Reading during that session.

RESOLUTION OF CONFLICT: EXPANDED GROUNDS

A proposal for liberalization of the divorce law finally found a place on the public agenda in 1936. As a private member bill, it faced enormous obstacles to final passage. Since the middle of the nineteenth century, the government had monopolized parliamentary time. Many leaders would have been happy to do away with private bills completely, but backbenchers persisted in introducing them. For the most part, they viewed these bills as a way of airing issues not of interest or too controversial for majority party leaders.

The biggest enemy of the private member bill was time. Since 1902 Fridays had been allotted for debates and motions, but the government frequently confiscated whole years of Fridays: during World War I, 1921, 1928-1929, 1931-1932, 1934-1935.[25] Even when

Fridays were left undisturbed, there were problems. The order of the Second Reading debate was assigned by ballot. The debate and vote had to be completed by 4 p.m. Since, typically, there were six Fridays for debates, only six bills would be assured of consideration. If a bill were in second or third place on a Friday, the opponents could easily "talk it out." That meant they would monopolize and extend the debate to 4 o'clock, as O'Donovan had done with the Knight bills. Unless the proponents could close debate and force a vote, the bill would die for that session. To keep control of the bill meant keeping 100 MPs favorable to the bill on hand for closure votes. This was a problem when many MPs deserted Westminister on Fridays. Even after a successful Second Reading, a tremendous effort was needed to keep the bill on the agenda of a committee and fend off destructive amendments. Promoters of private member bills needed several kinds of help: an MP with a number from one to six on the ballot, pressure groups to lobby MPs and generate public support, and gifts of parliamentary time from the government (or at least a guarantee against confiscation.) A. P. Herbert found a sponsor for his bill, Rupert de la Bère, who had number two on the ballot. He had help from the DLRU, lawyers, and feminists. What he needed was a guarantee from the government.

From 1931 to 1935 Great Britain had been governed by the National government, a coalition of leaders from the main parties and party factions. Ramsay MacDonald was Prime Minister (Labour); Stanley Baldwin, First Lord of the Council (Conservative); Sir J. Gilmour, Home Secretary (Conservative); and Viscount John Sankey, Lord Chancellor (Labour).

In 1935 Baldwin and MacDonald exchanged places and called for a new election. This last election before World War II brought back 432 Conservatives, 158 Labourites, 21 Liberals, 1 Communist, and 4 Independents, including A. P. Herbert. The National government coalition continued by reshuffling Cabinet positions. Sir John Simon (Liberal) moved to the Home Office, and a Conservative, Lord Hailsham, became Lord Chancellor. As Prime Minister, Baldwin continued the tentative leadership style of the previous government. He retreated from controversial legislation and preferred to fulfill the symbolic and constitutional roles of his office. He became heavily involved in the abdication crisis of 1936. Matters such as the divorce issue were left to appropriate Ministers. Little hope existed that Herbert could persuade the Cabinet to introduce his bill. What he wanted was their help or, at least, their neutrality.

The subject of divorce brought opposition from the churches, which could have been unpleasant for any of the parties. The Roman Catholics were opposed to the bill, and MPs and the government alike were impressed by the Catholics' ability to communicate forcefully their horror at an extension of the laws of divorce. The Church of England had opponents as well. The bill was so complex and controversial that the extensive parliamentary discussion it would have required would have been extremely divisive and unnecessarily painful to the government leaders. Unless the government could be persuaded to allot time for consideration, the bill, like the Knight bill before it, would become a hardy perennial or, worse, a hopeless cause.

In May 1936 Herbert asked the Prime Minister directly for help on the divorce bill. When Baldwin took the matter to the Cabinet, he found his law officers divided. Lord Hailsham, the Lord Chancellor, opposed liberalization of divorce, despite advice from the president of the Divorce Court and his colleagues: "We are convinced that if an attempt is to be made to stop the rot it must be now."[26] The Lord Chancellor's office recommended that the Cabinet ignore the Herbert bill, since it had little chance of passing. On 17 November 1936 Claud Schuster, the Permanent Secretary, wrote: "I do not believe myself, however, that it has any chance." Later on 20 November he added: "It is not improbable that the bill may receive a Second Reading though I do not think there is a substantial risk that it will get through all of its stages."[27]

On the other side, Donald Somervell, the Conservative Attorney General, and Sir John Simon, the Liberal Home Secretary, favored expanding the ground for divorce. They advised the Cabinet that the Herbert bill had widespread support and would pass a Second Reading. They argued that the government could not afford to ignore it.

On November 18, in the absence of the Lord Chancellor who was ill, the Cabinet agreed to the following plan:

1. The Attorney General was to watch the progress of the bill and represent the government's position of neutrality.

2. The government would offer assistance of law officers and parliamentary counsel during the committee stage of the bill.
3. The Cabinet ministers were not to vote on the Second Reading but would not be bound in a later vote.

This decision meant that the government had accepted the idea of divorce reform and the high probability that it would pass. They assumed some responsibility for making sure that the bill was correctly written and embodied workable principles. They did not want to commit the majority to the bill through the Whip and left the problem of gaining the necessary votes to the backbenchers.

Government law officers opposed some of the provisions that went beyond the recommendations of the Gorell commission. They disapproved of Clause 1 that prohibited divorce in the first five years of marriage but considered it necessary to dilute opposition from the church. The Solicitor of the Treasury objected to the extension of divorce powers to magistrates courts and the possibility of divorce after two years separation. He suspected these radical proposals were due to Claud Mullins's influence; the legal profession viewed him as a renegade. Parliamentary support for those sections of the Herbert bill that were not from the Gorell commission was untried. They became matters for bargaining between Herbert and the government. The government offered to assist in providing time in later stages of the bill if its sponsors would strike the objectionable features. Negotiations in January 1937 were successful. Herbert agreed to drop the clauses, and in return the government removed obstacles from the path to Royal Assent for his bill.

Meanwhile, the Second Reading debate in the House of Commons in November had gone smoothly. De la Bère, the bill's chief sponsor, and Herbert introduced the debate. They brought out the points that would remain the basis of arguments in favor of reform during the consideration by Parliament.[28] First, they criticized the present law as "ineffective and farcical." To obtain a divorce, said Herbert, one had to commit adultery or perjury. The law forced many couples to live in sin. Those who had bad legal marriages, but were reluctant to commit either perjury or adultery, were forced to suffer alone. If they formed new unions, these unions were illegal, and the children were illegitimate. Second, they discussed the desirable aspects of their reform. The intent was not to destroy but to preserve the church, the law, and marriage. These institutions were being threatened by lack of respect for antequated divorce procedures. The reform would increase respect for marriage and the law, since it would be more realistic. The church's support for some reform would improve its own image as well.

Rev. R. W. Sorenson embellished on the theme of respect for marriage and the law by arguing that marriage should be based on the "desire to dwell together out of sheer affection and respect for each other."

> There is no other real basis for matrimony. Any institution, any legislation, any tradition or prejudice that props up matrimony on any other basis and that tries to hide the real difficulties of our existing matrimonial institutions, is doing no real service to humanity, to matrimony, to religion or to the State. In the end the rottenness eats its way out; like a cancer it grows, and drains away the life and well-being out of the body politic.[29]

Little opposition appeared during the Second Reading debate. W. P. Spens pointed out that any liberalization of the law could increase the number of divorces, and this would do more harm than good. Children are always the ones to suffer in any divorce, he argued. Although proponents were ready to counteract all religious opposition arguments, none was brought up in the debate. Just before the division, the Attorney General announced that the government would assist during the committee stages on the bill.

The division was favorable: 78-12. Herbert attributed the low turnout to the unexpected early ending of debate. The vote was taken during the lunch hour. It was the first time in eighty years that the House of Commons had given a Second Reading to the expansion of grounds for divorce. Herbert credited his success to the moderate nature of the bill and the fact that it was presented not as a threat to marriage, but as its salvation. Another reason for its success was the support of the Attorney General and Home Secretary. Simon congratulated the bill's sponsors after the debate and again offered the assistance of the government.

The Commons committee met right through the abdication crisis of December 1936 and into February 1937. Herbert, with de la Bère's help, tried to keep the issue of divorce reform separate from the scandal of "a certain divorce case" brought by Mrs. Wallis Simpson. Committee proceedings were especially delicate during the final week leading to the abdication. On Tuesday, December 8, the committee was to meet to insert "persistent" before "adultery" to prevent hotel divorce. Members were milling around in the hall reluctant to debate this particular amendment. "It would be impossible, they said, to avoid indiscretions." They delayed proceedings again on the 10th. Herbert suspected this upset was a tactic to delay the bill: "Also, now that after twenty-three years, we had at last got the subject onto the political map I resented bitterly the suggestion that the affairs of any individual should be considered sufficient to put it in the dark again. I said that I had not, so far, made any reference to particular cases, and did not intend to do so; and that others could presumably avoid any indiscreet details as well."[30]

The crisis over, business resumed in January with little further delay. Adultery remained undefined in the act. The bill that emerged was largely what the Royal Commission had proposed with the addition of a five-year waiting period. A judge of the Divorce Court wrote that the bill had been accepted inside and outside the House "as a serious attempt to solve a difficult social question and in particular to put an end to the mischiefs which are said to arise out of the present law."[31]

Opposition to the bill surfaced in the committee from two sources: conservative lawyers who feared any expansion of the law would increase divorce and church opponents who questioned divorce on any other grounds than adultery. During the committee's meetings, several compromises between antagonists of the bill, with the silent acceptance of government law officers, were accomplished:

1. Two of the six original proposed grounds were dropped—habitual drunkenness and penal servitude.
2. The clause allowing immediate divorce after separation was rewritten to let separations granted on grounds also leading to divorce to suffice as proof when petition for divorce was ultimately sought.
3. The clause extending divorces to magistrates courts was eliminated.

The committee adjourned on February 9, but the Commons did not take up the report until April 9. During the intervening two months, pressure groups took their stands and wrote to their representatives. The National Council of Women (NCW) had supported divorce reform at its 1934 annual conference. It backed the Herbert bill but regretted the changes it had undergone in the committee.

In early 1937 the NCW reaffirmed its support. The NCEC actively supported the bill as well, and Hubback used her parliamentary organization to lobby for it.

The most vocal opposition came from the leadership of the Mother's Union, an Anglican organization of married women. (It would not allow any divorced members.) The union viewed divorce with horror and opposed any liberalization of the law whatsoever. Leaders of the Mother's Union had testified at the Gorell commission in opposition to any reform. They preferred to see the laws of the state as close as possible to the laws of the church. Herbert discounted what he termed the "postal barrage" from the Mother's Union as representative even of its own members. It was mechanical and well organized, rather than spontaneous. He noted that many of the bishops of the church were prepared for the reform.

On March 18, the Cabinet again took up the issue. The Lord Chancellor, still opposed to reform, advised them that the expanded grounds, if adopted, would increase the load on the courts and would require additional judges for the Probate, Divorce, and Admirality Division. The Home Secretary, Sir John Simon, advised the government to continue its position of benevolent non-intervention and await the exhaustion of private member time in the report stage before offering government assistance. "I imagine that we should not be prepared to star the bill and take it over, but, on the other hand, I feel strongly that the government should not let the bill lapse merely for want of a little more time if that is all that is needed to get it through a substantial majority in the House."[32] The Cabinet agreed to express the hope that there would be enough time on Fridays and to be prepared to give a little extra time if the bill got in trouble in its final stages. The Cabinet also recognized the need to strengthen the judicial bench if the measure passed. The government would remain neutral during its consideration in both Houses.

Opposition that had been absent in the Second Reading debate surfaced during the Report stage. Debate was especially drawn out over proposals to drop desertion as a divorce grounds. Herbert, frustrated at the delays, berated the critics for attacking the bill when they had been silent during earlier debates. Viscount Wolmer said the desertion clause would make divorce too easy: "We do not want to make it easier for people to get a divorce. It is better, in the long run, to have hard cases than to lower the standard of marriage or encourage people to enter into matrimony lightly."[33] The motion removing desertion grounds failed, 118-39.

The debates were lengthy, and de la Bère and Herbert had to request additional time from the government. Baldwin, in accordance with the Cabinet policy, agreed to assist the divorce reform because of the "advanced stage" of the bill. The Third Reading was held on 28 May 1937. The opposition stepped up its arguments against the bill, describing it as striking "at the very root of the highest conception of the religious and social obligations which have regulated family life for many generations."[34] Maud Tate countered that reform of a law that is the laughing stock of the country should increase support for democratic government. Herbert closed the debate by predicting that his bill would increase the sum of human happiness. It passed the Third Reading, 190-37.

The church leaders in the House of Lords were divided on the bill.[35] Some agreed with Viscount Fitzalan of Derwent that it was a step further down the "slippery slope" to moral oblivion. Others agreed with the Bishop of Birmingham that the time for reform of divorce law had come. The Archbishop of Canterbury straddled the fence. He agreed that many evils in the law needed change. People treated adultery not as a sin but as a means to divorce. Couples would actually fake adultery just to satisfy the law. He went on to note that as head of the church that opposes divorce and remarriage, he could not vote for the legislation, but he didn't vote against it either. (The archbishop was Cosmo Gordon who as a Bishop of York had dissented from the Gorell Commission Report twenty-five years earlier). Bishops Durham and St. Edmondsbury and Ipswich voted for the bill, St. Albans voted against it, and the archbishop abstained.

Although thirty-five amendments were added to the bill during its sojourn in the House of Lords, only one was of contention: reducing the time before a divorce could be sought from five to three years. This clause turned out to be the source of conflict between law reformers and the church. The church, not happy about any liberalization of divorce, was pleased with a provision that prevented early divorce, viewing it as a way of letting marriages work and requiring people to be responsible by preventing them from getting divorced on a whim. The reformers viewed the clause as inconsistent with social norms and too restrictive. The compromise on the matter was hammered out in the House of Lords and accepted under protest by the House of Commons as the price for the expansion of divorce grounds.

On 30 July 1937 the bill received the Royal Assent. Between the extension of time on May 6 and the Assent, the government changed. Baldwin retired, and Neville Chamberlain became Prime Minister. Sir John Simon became Chancellor of the Exchequer, and Sir Simon Hoare went to the Home Office. The government continued to provide time for the bill's final stages. The Lord Chancellor's Permanent Secretary with over fifteen years of experience, had confidently predicted in 1936 that the Divorce Reform Bill would never pass. He was mistaken.

Why did Herbert's bill pass in 1937 after so many rejections by the Commons of bills with identical features? The war and the Depression led to changes in the status of women and other strains on traditional marriages. Demands for divorce could not be met under restrictive laws. The law was forced to bend and finally break by collusion, perjury, and sham. A coalition of supporters, concerned about the tension between the law and behavior, united to push divorce reform over the top. Judges wanted reform to limit the perversion of the law brought about by increased demands. Many religious leaders saw the need for law change and accepted the fact that public policy need not be the same as church policy. In 1935 the government was confident and had strong party support in the Commons. It could afford to show positive interest in the divorce law, especially when it realized the House of Commons was in favor.

The social and political conditions being favorable, a catalyst appeared in the form of Alan P. Herbert. He was an Independent, bright, famous, and personally committed to the reform of divorce law. He was more convincing than other MPs who presented bills given to them by special-interest groups. Divorce reform might have been put off again because of economic programs and foreign policy issues had it not been for Herbert. He presented the bill in a way that undercut opposition: "The success of the bill is, without doubt, in large part due to the distinction it has drawn, implicitly and explicitly, between the Christian ideal of marriage upheld by the Churches and the provision which, *ex hypothesi,* the State is compelled to make for marriages which have attained that ideal and have foundered."[36]

The policy process changing the divorce law to include equal and expanded grounds for divorce was remarkable in its extreme length: over thirty years. After World War I the reform issue of equal and expanded grounds for divorce had to be separated, and equal grounds alone received easy acceptance. The two acts that eventually resulted from the Gorell commission recommendations followed different paths to acceptance, equal grounds being the work of a feminist interest group that wrote the bill, got the sponsor, and lobbied for parliamentary support and the 1937 act being promoted by a maverick MP who, with the help of groups, wrote the bill, pressured the government, and sought public support. The 1923 act for equal grounds stands out from all other reforms as the only one specifically designed to achieve equality for women under law.

MARRIED WOMEN'S PROPERTY: THE DEMANDS

The Married Women's Property Act of 1882 was viewed as "an ill conceived and ill drawn Act, sanctioned by the ignorance and stupidity of Parliament and rendered more complicated by the subtlety of judicial interpretation."[37] Dissatisfaction with three aspects of the married women's property law led to demands for its reform.

The first problem was the interpretation of the extent of married women's liability for debts, contracts, and torts. The language of the act led to two possible interpretations. One interpretation was that since the married woman was guaranteed the use of her property as if she were *feme sole,* she had the same rights as single women. However, reference in the act to married women's separate property implied a second interpretation that liability was limited to property as it was in equity law. A Queen's Bench decision in 1887 selected the second interpretation. In *Scott v. Morley* (1887, 20 QBD 120), the court agreed that a married woman could be sued for a debt only to the extent of her separate property and no more. The judges considered the law to be a protection for married women's property through the extension of equity law to all, rather than a guarantee of *femme sole* rights to married women making them subject to the Debtor's Act.

A second problem arose with respect to the husband's liability. If a wife was liable only to the extent of her property, could the husband be sued for her contracts, debts, and torts? *Scott v. Morley* was unclear on the husband's liability. In that case, Lord Esher pointed out that before 1882 the common law provided that a husband could be sued for his wife's torts and that married women had no legal liability: "It seems to me that the Act of 1882 does not alter legal liability of married women at all. It does not prevent the bringing of an action against a husband and wife in respect of contract made before marriage and does not affect the case of a wrongful act committed by a wife during marriage."

Any questions involving the husband's liability for tort under the 1882 act were resolved by a controversial 3-2 decision in the House of Lords in 1925, in the case of *Edwards v. Porter* (1925, A.C. 1). The Law Lords ruled that a husband was still liable to be sued with his wife for tort committed by her during coverture. The majority pointed out that the act did not say the husband was *not* liable. Rather, the language that the husband "need not be joined" with the wife in a suit against her was permissive rather than prohibitory. Lord Sumner: "it seems to me to preserve the liability for her torts committed during marriage for the benefit of those who would otherwise have no remedy if she has no sufficient separate estate." Viscount Cave (Lord Chancellor) and Lord Birkenhead (former Lord Chancellor) dissented, claiming that the intent of the Married Women's Property Act was to give married women equal property rights and that it did so by saying that a married woman could sue and be sued as if she were *feme sole:* "In short, the previously existing legal unity between husband and wife has been dissolved and with it has gone the whole foundation for the old rule as to the husband's liability."

A third problem of the law of married women's property was the retention of "restraint on anticipation" from the practice of marriage settlements in equity law. Under this provision, a married woman could be legally prevented from using her property beyond disposing of the income from it. Such property was not liable for her debts under the Married Women's Property Act and could not be used to raise capital. The purpose of the provision was, first, to protect family property from being exploited by the husband; second, to protect property from the wife's creditors; and third, to protect property from the married woman herself. There was no way, while married, that a woman could remove this restraint. It was such "protection" that resulted in the limited economic independence and responsibility of married women.

Several groups were dissatisfied with the Married Women's Property Act of 1882 and its interpretation. Creditors of married women found that they were often denied relief, since according to the law, married woman had all of the rights but none of the liabilities of independence. A second dissatisfied group was the lawyers. They were concerned with the injustice of holding a married man liable in a suit for his wife's torts and contracts, especially when he had no claim to any of her property or income and no legal control over her behavior. She could act irresponsibly, and he would be liable. The third group, feminists, pointed out that married women were handicapped by their limited liability, since they were poor credit risks. The philosophy behind the law was that a woman, due to the fact of her marriage alone, was less capable of handling her economic affairs than before marriage.

At this time married women were experiencing real setbacks in work status. After the war women were fired to make room for returning veterans. Trade unions that had let women in during the war closed ranks and pushed them out. Married women were often prohibited from certain jobs, regardless of their economic circumstances. Some who had achieved token success in professions of law, medicine, and teaching saw the training institutions begin to exclude women. In every area of work, pay was grossly unequal and the discrimination was justified on the grounds that only men had families to suppoort.

That the so-called emancipation of women was more a matter of style than economics became absolutely clear in the wake of the economic Depression of the 1930s. Unemployment rates began to soar to the three-million mark. With many men unemployed, no woman's job was safe. Workers resented women working and argued that a married woman was needlessly depriving a man of employment. In some families, then, the father was unable to find work, and the mother was denied a job, because she was married. Women did not have a right to work and were considered a reserve labor force to be used at times of labor shortage.

As a result of little sympathy for the working married woman, the remaining inequalities in family property law were considered by many to be injurious to men, not women. The first issue to get to Parliament was the husband's liability for the wife's debt. The Lord Chancellor in the Bonar Law government, Lord Cave, declined to review the law with respect to the extent of the husbands' liability; his Permanent Secretary noted there was "no popular demand for a change in the law or any reason to suppose that the law is not both reasonably clear and equitable."[38] In 1925 Cave delivered the minority opinion in the *Edwards* case and had presumably learned that, indeed, inequalities did exist. In May 1925 Lord Danesfort asked the Lord Chancellor to appoint a select committee to review the law dealing with a husband's liability. He pointed out the inconsistency of the law in light of recent acts reflecting sweeping changes in the status of women. "As a matter of fact, all the organized associations of women, some of which have communicated with me, are entirely in favor of this change in the law."[39]

Lord Darling saw this change as giving equal rights to benefit men, and he wholeheartedly endorsed the notion. He recalled that under coverture, a husband could punish his wife, because he was responsible for her torts, but since he was no longer able to give such punishment, he should no longer be responsible. "I wish to put the woman's point of view. I am sure, regarding themselves as perfectly independent and affranchised, they would desire not to be joined with their husbands any more than is absolutely necessary."[40]

Viscount Cave picked up the spirit of the argument. "We have heard about the rights of wives for some years, but in this case we ought to consider the rights of husbands. The matter seems to me to lie in so small a compass that really no committee is needed to pronounce on the matter." Thus the Lord Chancellor pledged to introduce appropriate remedial legislation. A bill was drafted in his office and introduced three weeks later. The Second Reading debate produced little opposition to the measure, although Lord Buckmaster expressed some dissatisfaction at the piecemeal way the law was reformed. He suggested that the government might undertake a complete examination of all marriage law, indeed, of all law affecting relations between men and women. The bill, which was one short clause stating that the husband of a married woman shall not be liable to be joined in any suit for tort committed by her, received a Third Reading and was sent to the House of Commons where it was withdrawn at the end of the session without debate. The government did not find time to consider it but promised to bring it up in the next session. It was not heard from again.

The NUSEC established a subcommittee during the 1920s to review the law respecting married women. Specifically, the Executive

Committee wanted to eliminate forever all provisions of coverture from the law. In 1925 the committee sent a draft of the "Bill to Remove Couverture Disabilities" to the Executive Committee of NUSEC. It provided husband and wife with equal rights with respect to torts and contracts, the right to sue and be sued, and the right to bankruptcy. It would abolish restraint on anticipation and the concept of "separate property" and substitute just plain "property." The wife would be guaranteed a share in her husband's income to back up her legal liability if she had no income of her own. Thus women would not be punished because of their inferior position in the economy.

In July the government bill on a husband's liability for tort was making its way through the House of Lords, and the NUSEC agreed to support it, while circulating copies of its coverture removal proposal. Hubback asked Lord Buckmaster to introduce the NUSEC bill, an appropriate request, since he had suggested a massive overhaul of the law relating to marriage. After some prompting and an intervention by the formidable Lady Balfour, he agreed that if the bill were properly drafted, he would introduce it. The task was thus put off, and the Removal of Coverture Bill was not heard of again. The following year, 1927, the drastic split in the NUSEC between the old and new feminists occurred, and the new feminists were not as eager to consider the problems of married women as were Lady Balfour and her supporters.

The legal profession continued to be interested in the problem. The Law Society, which had been a bit skeptical of Lord Cave's 1925 bill, passed a resolution in 1933 urging the Lord Chancellor, now Viscount Sankey, a Labour party leader, to introduce it again. The *Law Times* noted increasing interest in the problems created for husbands by existing law: judicial utterances and the press were full of concern for the oppressive treatment of husbands. All who commented agreed that the law should be revised.

Pressure on the Lord Chancellor's office was appropriate, for he was considering the establishment of a committee to review specific problems in the law and to advise him with respect to change. This was not the first such legal advisory group, but it was the first to deal with the law relating to married women. The Law Revision Committee was appointed in January 1934 and was charged with reviewing the law with respect to tortfeasors, civil injury, liability of husband for wife's torts, and right of recovery in civil proceedings. The committee was chaired by Lord Wright and was made up of male judges and lawyers.

THE CONFLICT

In the 1870s and 1880s law reform had been guided by liberal and utilitarian philosophies. In the 1930s new and revolutionary ideologies were challenging the entire system of British democracy. Although at one time the idea of economic independence for married women had frightened respectable middle-class men of property, socialists, communists, and fascists now had plans to destroy the entire society to eliminate its evils. Law reform was odious to them; the new law would come about only with an entirely new society.

In the midst of these ideological storms, a few lawyers and legal scholars, in the utilitarian tradition, were still interested in law reform. Much of their concern was with jurisdiction and administration of the courts. Some advocated a program of legal aid to the poor. Others wanted the courts and legal profession to be consolidated into a Ministry of Justice, along the lines of the European ministries, that would take responsibility for appointment, administration, and accountability as well as for any needed reforms. As far as the Lord Chancellor was concerned, decision making about married women's property rights involved little more than clearing up the loose ends of a nineteenth-century issue.

In general, however, the twenties and thirties were not a political climate especially favorable to systematic law reform. In Parliament Conservatives were in a mood to consolidate, left-wing Labourites wanted to destroy the property class system and completely redo the law, and Liberals were fighting for their very existence. Only the moderates among Labour leaders showed any interest in law reform issues. Viscount Sankey, the Labour Lord Chancellor in the 1931-1935 National government, on his own initiative, appointed the Law Revision Committee to advise his office on any area of law he wished. The committee's work attracted little attention.

Among the feminists, only a few middle-class equalitarian groups took an interest in further reform of the law affecting married women. Many of the politically active women were involved in the Labour movement. There, they placed demands of the working class above those of women. As Susan Lawrence, MP and chair of the National Conference on Labour Women, stated in describing the former chair Dr. Marian Phillips:

> She was alive, as few people were, to the especial wrongs and hardships which women suffer; but she was very far away from the spirit of that narrow thing called feminism. She was too good a Socialist not to know that, in politics, the class division is greater than the sex division. . . .[41]

Often there was ambivalence over the rights and status of married women in the labour movement itself. Single women demanded equal pay; married women, who were often the first to be fired to make room for a man, wanted protective laws, family allowances, and maternity services. Each group considered the other a threat to its own job security. The women in the Labour party and trade unions were occupied with conflicts with each other and with working-class men. They were skeptical of proposals supported by middle-class feminists with ties to the Liberal or Conservative parties. Furthermore, they did not agree that financial problems of married women were the concern of all women.

Several small feminist groups remained in the field to advocate married women's rights before the Law Revision Committee. The NCEC took the opportunity to ask for more than a tidying up of the 1882 act and put forth its 1924 resolution for repeal of coverture. A letter for repeal was sent to the committee from the Open Door Council, the Six Point Group, St. Joan's Political and Social Alliance, the National Union of Women Teachers, and the Edinburgh Society for Equal Citizenship: "We see in the responsibility of a husband for his wife's torts and acceptance of the doctrine that the personality of the wife is merged with the husband—a doctrine we repudiate."[42]

A similar argument was put forth by Viscountess Rhondda, journalist and peeress in her own right, on behalf of the Equal Rights Committee. She pointed out that the problems of the law of married women were the result of piecemeal reform. The law of coverture had been modified without being abolished. Her committee made the following requests: that a husband no longer be liable for his wife's torts, since such a law was unfair to husbands and treated the wife as if she were a horse or dog; that recovery of debts from married women without funds be the same as from any poor person; that restraint on anticipation be abolished as a disadvantage to women as well as creditors. Restraint on anticipation made it impossible even for a rich woman to make contracts and go into business: she was a poor person to do business with—a poor credit risk.

Another group that was interested in the reform were creditors represented by the National Chamber of Trade and the National Association of Trade Protection Societies. These interests recognized the problem with the current law. For a husband to be liable for a wife's torts and contracts was unfair when he had none of her property and no legal control over her actions. However, the creditors had needs too, and they found it impossible to get money from a married woman with no funds. According to the National Association of Trade Protection Societies, a possible solution might be for the husband to be viewed as the wife's employer and that he pay her for being his housekeeper. Then either the husband could be joined in the debt or could have his earnings attached to pay the wife's debts. This novel suggestion of placing an economic value on a wife's housekeeping duties arrived at the committee in December after the report had been completed. It is unlikely that the suggestion would have been seriously considered at this point, since the motive behind the reform was to relieve husbands of an unfair burden and leave creditors to their own devices in their dealings with married women.

The Fourth Interim Report of the Law Revision Committee appeared in December 1934. It was apparent then that the committee did not define its task as being as dramatic as the removal of coverture. The charge was to determine whether a husband should be liable for his wife's torts and other liabilities, and whether a married woman's liability to answer for damages in contract or tort or otherwise should be personal as in the case of a man or an unmarried woman (*feme sole*) or whether any judgment against her should be proprietary, that is, limited to her separate property.

In tracing the development in law of husband and wife, the committee pointed out that at one time in the nineteenth century, the law could have given married women equal rights, if the 1882 act had been based on the provision of the 1857 divorce law that gave women separated from their husbands full *feme sole* rights with respect to property. Instead, the equity concept became the dominant part of the 1882 act. The key provisions, Sections 1, 2, and 5, mention *feme sole* but concentrate on concepts and phrases such as women's rights over "separate property," "without the intervention of any trustee," liability "to the extent of her separate property," and "her husband need not be joined as defendant."

In commenting on the decision in *Edwards v. Porter,* the committee agreed with the minority that it was not the intent of the law to make husbands liable for wives' torts and that any basis for interpretation to the contrary should be abolished. The committee recommended that the law be revised to make it clear that husbands were not liable for the wives' debts and torts and that married women should have personal liability:

> Women, nowadays, whether married or single engage in almost all professions, trades and businesses, and are eligible to hold and do in general hold every sort of public and official post and exercise every right and franchise, just as much as men. There seems no reason, once it is established that they are no longer debarred by the law from holding property independently of their husbands, why they should not do so with all the corresponding rights and liabilities like everybody else.[43]

The committee also recommended that the equity provision of restraint on anticipation be abolished, as suggested by Lady Rhondda. The purpose of the practice was to protect a married woman's property not only from her husband and her creditors, but most significantly from herself: "from her own extravagance, generosity, speculation, or national desire to comply with her husband's suggestions for its use." The effect was to prevent a woman from raising capital on her own property. The committee recommended that restraint on anticipation be abolished and that if parents wanted to protect such property, they should use protective trusts as are used for men, since a separate provision, such as restraint on anticipation, was "no longer consistent with the present position of married women."

The committee's report was favorably received. Most people had thought that married women already had received equal rights in 1882. The *Times* published a lead article on the report and pointed out that the Married Women's Property Acts of 1870 and 1882 were not sweeping and simple revisions as was thought at the time, but that they were piecemeal extensions of equity notions of separate property.[44] The article emphasized the disadvantages that men, not women, suffered under the law. The husbands were at the mercy of their wives. The *Times* sounded the chord that became the basis of parliamentary rhetoric in support of the measure: the reform was basically for the benefit of men, not women. "Indeed there is almost no limit to the loss that a vindictive wife equipped with a modicum of law might inflict on an unoffending and helpless consort." The reporter went on to admit that such abuses happen rarely, because either there are few vindictive wives or many ignorant ones.

Despite the growing view that this was a men's rights issue, Hubback expressed the support of the NCEC for the report. She emphasized the effects of equity provisions on women's opportunities in the business world: "what is not often realized is that [the lack of responsibility of married women] is unfair also to married women themselves if they are in business, in that many people are unwilling to enter into contracts with a married woman when there are so many methods open to her to escape her obligations."[45] The NCEC criticized the committee for not going far enough in abolishing limitations of coverture. At the annual general meeting in March, it passed a resolution supporting the report but also asking that income tax laws that made the husband responsible for his wife's taxes be repealed. This law has its origins in the effect of coverture on the Income Tax Law of 1819, whereby profits of the wife living with the husband were deemed to be profits of the husband and assessed in his name.

RESOLUTION OF THE CONFLICT

The report of 1934 corrected the effects of piecemeal reform in the past but did not suggest major revisions in the law of husband and wife. As such, it was in keeping with previous approaches to law reform in divorce and married women's property: correcting the law to bring it in line with practice, in a limited way, rather than full-scale change to achieve the goal of equality. In the case of this issue, it was argued that there was an equalitarian spirit of the age and that the reforms were merely in keeping with changes in lifestyles that had already occurred.

Lord Sankey was not in a position to push for a more substantive reform of the law. The report of the Law Revision Committee came after Sankey had been in office for five turbulent years. As a Labour party member, he clung to the top legal job in a government becoming more and more conservative. Sankey had joined the minority Labour government of Ramsey MacDonald as Lord Chancellor in 1929. The election of 1931 was a major defeat for Labour: 473 Conservatives and 52 Labour members were returned. Of them, only twelve supported the National government of MacDonald and Baldwin. Nevertheless MacDonald insisted on keeping Sankey as Lord Chancellor, despite efforts by Neville Chamberlain, the Chancellor of the Exchequer, to replace him with a Conservative.

As Lord Chancellor, Sankey was an activist. He welcomed his political role in advocating reform legislation and showed little interest in the litigation work of the other Law Lords. His belief that law reform should be a continuing commitment of the government had led to his assembling the Law Revision Committee in the first place. Now its report was ready, and it was his responsibility to make sure the necessary legislation was passed. MacDonald had liked Sankey's activist approach, but by 1934 the Prime Minister's position had been weakened due to ill health and lack of Labour support. More and more, Baldwin and Chamberlain took over the leadership of the government. Before final deliberation on the law reform proposals, MacDonald and Sankey were replaced, during June 1935, by Baldwin and Lord Hailsham.

January to May 1935 was taken up with the preparation of a bill for the Lord Chancellor that would accomplish the recommendations of the Law Revision Committee. This process indicates some of the changes from the nineteenth century in the role of parliamentary counsel. Such counsel had been used by the Ministers of the government since the 1800s, but their roles assumed importance as legislation became more complex. It is their responsibility to put legislative proposals in the proper form to be acceptable to the lawyers in and out of Parliament and to indicate exactly what sections of which statutes already on the books will be affected by the reform. Individual MPs without benefit of counsel are at a disadvantage in introducing acceptable legislation.

Before going ahead with a bill, the Lord Chancellor wanted to make sure that no significant opposition existed. Since this was a women's issue, in part, he arranged to have a meeting with women members of Parliament. Only since the equal suffrage act of 1928 had enough women been in the House to *have* a meeting on a woman's issue. Fourteen had been elected in 1929 and fifteen in 1931. In 1935 women MPs numbered thirteen Conservatives, one Labourite, and one Independent. Eleanor Rathbone, the Independent, had long been involved with feminist issues in the NCEC. Several of the Conservatives—Lady Astor, the Duchess of Atholl, Maud Tate, Thelma Cazalet-Keir, and Norah Runge—were advocates of women's legal equality.

The Lord Chancellor dispatched his Permanent Secretary to consult with a moderate Conservative MP, Marjorie Graves. He wanted to convince the women that proposals for abolishing the effects of coverture entirely were outside the scope of the proposed reform and that they should not try to amend it. Graves "realized and other members with the exception of Lady Astor and Miss Rathbone would also realize that some of the matters put forward by the Advanced Women were outside the scope of the Report and that others, though possible within the scope, were best left alone since it would be impossible to obtain unity on them," reported the Permanent Secretary.[46] Graves recommended that only a few supporters among the women be invited: Lady Iveagh, Florence Horsburgh, Irene Ward, Megan Lloyd George (Lib). Other women in Parliament should be omitted: Runge, Tate, Cazalet-Keir, Rathbone, Astor, and Atholl.

The Lord Chancellor rejected such a partial meeting. The Whips would agree to push a bill only if they were convinced it was noncontroversial. If a meeting were held excluding some women, they would raise embarrassing questions. When the meeting of all women MPs was held in February, Lady Astor was unable to attend. She wrote, however, urging reform of married women's income tax laws. The Permanent Secretary replied that a tax reform was outside the scope of the Lord Chancellor's responsibilities. He repeated this to the meeting of women: income tax reform was not a matter of law but a matter of taxes, thus within the scope of the Chancellor of the Exchequer. At the meeting Rathbone questioned the fact that restraint on anticipation was not to be abolished retroactively. The Lord Chancellor's response did not pertain to her point, but she accepted his explanations that changes in the bill at that time would entail difficulties and postpone consideration.

The Lord Chancellor had to wait until April 1935 before the parliamentary counsel got around to drafting a bill. Copies of the draft were distributed to lawyers and judges for comment. After their responses and suggestions for change, a revised draft was submitted to the Lord Chancellor at the beginning of May 1935. He proposed that the married women's bill be combined with a bill drafted by the committee to change the law of tortfeasors. The parliamentary counsel disagreed with this idea, arguing that the Tortfeasors Bill involved limited law change whereas the married women's bill went "deep into the roots of the common law." But the Lord Chancellor countered with the point that although some women in Parliament and various women's organizations wanted the reforms to go farther, in general they had accepted the married women's bill.

Sankey brought a bill for reform of the law relating to both married women's legal status and tortfeasors to the Cabinet. After the usual review by the Committee on Home Affairs, the Cabinet agreed to introduce the bill in the House of Lords. It included the following provisions: abolish the concept of married women's separate property and render her equal property rights; establish liability of married women for contracts and torts as if they were single; abolish restraint on anticipation of married women's property after 1 January 1936; abolish the husband's liability for wife's torts or antenuptual contracts and obligations.

One of Sankey's last acts as Lord Chancellor was to open the Second Reading debate on the Married Women's and Tortfeasors Bill on 5 June 1935. It received Royal Assent five weeks later, possibly a record for passage of a reform bill. The conflicts had been resolved and the legislative ground prepared before the bill came up for formal debate. Demands to abolish the concept of married women's separate property and give them equal rights came from the top levels of the legal community and from feminists. The lawyers considered removal of a husband's liability to be in the interest of men's rights. Feminists saw the change as a step toward financial and legal independence for women. Lord Chancellors in two successive governments were in favor of the change.

Parliamentary experts drafted the bill based on recommendations by legal experts. The legal community made further suggestions for polishing and refining the language. Finally, women in Parliament had their say. There, the only opposition was that the reform did not go far enough. The proposal had the support of lawyers, men, women, the government, and all of the parties. It would be difficult to find a substantive bill with more likelihood of parliamentary success.

Sankey's Second Reading speech, which had been reviewed by the parliamentary counsel, emphasized the careful work of the Law Revision Committee and the adequate input by leaders of the law profession. He reported that he set up the Revision Committee "for the purpose of considering how far, having regard to the statute law and to judicial decisions, such legal maxims as the Lord Chancellor might from time to time refer to them required revision in modern conditions."[47] He summarized the report of the committee quoting: "the day has now come when a married woman should answer for her own liabilities whether in contract or in tort, as if she were not married."

The Earl of Listowell agreed that the Law Committee was the proper way to achieve law reform, not as a political issue but as a matter for the professional expertise of the legal profession under the Lord Chancellor's leadership. The only suggestion for change came from two Lords who wanted married men to be relieved of the burden of their wives' income tax. The Lord Chancellor pointed out that matters of taxation were properly brought up with the Treasury. The only change in the bill was its title, from Law Reform (Miscellaneous Provisions) to Law Reform (Married Women and Tortfeasors) Act. It passed quickly through the House of Lords. The Second Reading was on July 8 in the House of Commons. Only one question was raised regarding restraint on anticipation. This was merely to give the MP a chance to explain that the original purpose of the provision was to allow the father of a married woman to prevent her husband from confiscating her property and to protect her from the workhouse, not to defraud her creditors. The bill passed through the Third Reading without amendment and received Royal Assent.

Married women's legal disabilities with respect to separate property were thus removed by the Law Reform (Married Women's and Tortfeasors) Act of 1935. The process of reform was different from divorce reform in several respects. First, the 1935 act was a government measure. It benefited from all the resources of the majority: parliamentary counsel, whips, and adequate time for debate. Second, the measure was part of a law revision package prepared by the Lord Chancellor with the expert assistance of the Law Revision Committee. This committee consulted lawyers and lined up their support. It was an early step in the establishment of permanent machinery for law reform. Third, the measure was not viewed by Parliament as a political, a religious, or even a feminist issue, but as a legal adjustment. Since the legal experts accepted the change, politicians had little justification for tampering with it.

A great deal of the credit for the proposal's relatively painless passage into law is a result of the manner in which it came to public attention. Deficiencies in the Married Women's Property Act were discovered in court decisions. If many husbands, wives, or creditors were suffering under the act, they failed to bring their problems to the public arena through interest-group activity. Rather, the House of Lords learned of the problem through one of its own decisions, forty-three years after the Married Women's Property Act was passed. Since the problem came through a legal channel, it did not arouse public controversy; it did not become partisan. Feminists included proposals for reform of coverture in their legislative action program in the 1920s. However, they were able to present their demands only after the government had introduced proposals for reform of property law.

CONFLICT RESOLUTION AND FEMINIST INFLUENCE

The divorce and married women's statutes enacted in the 1920s and 1930s completed the patchwork of alterations in divorce and matrimonial property law begun in the mid-nineteenth century. Demands for equality and removal of coverture brought by the first English feminists were only partially answered by nineteenth-century reforms. These laws tempered inconsistencies between official norms and actual behavior of men and women in marriage and divorce for a while, but soon the gap between the law and behavior widened again. Two groups, the poor and the women, had difficulty in getting divorces. The single ground, adultery, forced many couples to resort to collusion and perjury to make the facts of their marital breakdown fit the requirements of the law. Similarly, contradictions were found in the marital property laws. The 1882 act left husbands liable for their wives' debts and torts, despite the fact that married women had a claim to their own property and earnings. This situation became especially ludicrous after women gained the vote: how could a husband remain liable for the actions of his wife who was in every other way his equal in law?

DIVORCE

Demands for divorce reform became a public concern through the efforts of judicial and legal elites, especially Lord Gorell, former president of the Divorce Court and member of the House of Lords. In 1909 the Liberal government appointed a Royal Commission to consider reform proposals. The commission, composed of legal, religious, and feminist leaders issued a majority report and a minority report. Agreement was unanimous that the grounds for divorce should be equal for husband and wife. Eleven of the fourteen commissioners favored expansion of grounds to include cruelty, desertion, insanity, drunkenness, and penal servitude.

Feminists were divided over the expansion of grounds and made little effort to influence the commission's decision in that area. They took a limited part in the consideration of equal grounds. Millicent Fawcett testified at the commission, and Lady Balfour was a member. The deliberations, however, were dominated by legal reformers who supported equal grounds because of justice in the marriage law rather than because of women's rights. It is highly likely that the commission would have recommended equal grounds regardless of feminist testimony. The feminist argument in favor of an equal moral standard put forth by Mrs. Fawcett and others is mentioned in the commission report but not emphasized:

> Our conclusion is that no satisfactory solution to the problem which is raised as to the personal feelings between husband and wife, can be found except by placing them on an equal footing. . . .[48]

The commission met during the heat of the militants' battle with the government over the suffrage. Matters of divorce reform were not in the forefront of that movement. Law reformers probably assumed that their campaign could not benefit by being too closely associated with the issue of votes for women.

The Royal Commission developed proposals that eventually became law. Although it resolved some conflicts in the drafting of the reports, its work did not lead to a formal enactment of reforms. The fact that two reports were prepared indicated fundamental conflicts that would persist for many years. These conflicts made it difficult for any proposal regarding divorce to reach the public agenda. Finally, the proposal for equality was separated from that of expanding grounds, and the two issues followed separate although similar paths through the legislature.

Feminists played a central part in obtaining equal grounds for women during legislative consideration of the issue in 1923. The principal feminist group, the NUSEC, and its lobbyist took charge of all steps of the policy process: drafting the bill; contacting MPs for the private member ballot; extracting statements of support from the Prime Minister; avoiding any damaging amendments to the bill. Opponents said it would increase divorce and that men and women were not equal and required different moral standards. Others argued that the bill didn't go far enough in granting relief to unhappy couples. Conflicts were resolved in the legislature in favor of equality. Through deliberations of the Houses of Commons and Lords, the bill passed with little change.

This was the NUSEC's first and last successful postwar legislative campaign. Many of its goals were eventually achieved, but never again could the union take personal credit for an act of Parliament. As it reported in June 1923:

> Although modesty should forbid we cannot help congratulating ourselves upon the triumphant success of the Matrimonial Causes Bill! It is the first time a bill we have directly promoted has passed through all its stages in the House of Commons; its prospects in the House of Lords look really rosy and although we must not be premature in our rejoicings, there appears every hope of successful issue.[49]

The NUSEC was effective in its influence for a number of reasons. It enjoyed the postwar post women's suffrage momentum when measures on equality for women tended to get support. Many legislators were not sure of the influence of their newly enfranchised constituents and heeded, as the suffragists had hoped, communication from women's groups nationally and in their districts. The NUSEC became the leading feminist group after its successful role in putting suffrage over the top in the last years of the war. It was still a unified group and could claim a large membership. Issues of new feminism and social reform versus equality were only just being considered. Rathbone's second inaugural address questioning equality was given in March after Major Entwistle had introduced the bill.

Entwistle summed up the reasons for his success:

> The bill found its salvation in the fact that it was restricted to the one clause dealing with equality between the sexes in grounds for divorce, in the tremendous unanimity of opinion behind it in the country and its appearance at just the right psychological moment.[50]

It was because of the feminists in the NUSEC that the bill was put forth at the time so favorable to its passage.

The legislature also made the crucial decisions leading to the expansion of divorce grounds in 1937. However, the intensity of conflict over the liberalization of the law made conflict resolution more complex and required a more active role for the government than in the earlier reform. After the issues of equality and expansion were separated in the early 1920s, little attention was given to the expansion issue until the Knight proposals of the early thirties. The bill that ultimately became law was written and introduced by an Independent MP. His proposal was based on previous campaigns for divorce reform by groups such as the DLRU and the NCEC, but these groups were not directly involved during this legislative stage.

Catholic and Conservative MPs hoped not to prevent liberalization, but to limit it and to delay its passage if possible. However, opposition existed among Conservative law officers concerning certain clauses extending jurisdiction of the courts. Reformers had to settle these conflicts with the government before they had hope of overcoming parliamentary opposition. In return for nonobstruction by opponents and government benevolence, several changes were made in the bill: reducing the number of grounds; changing the separation provision; eliminating the extension of court jurisdiction. These conflicts were effectively resolved in the committee of the House of Commons. Conflicts within the government were resolved in the Cabinet; the government gave assistance to the reformers in the Commons. Still another compromise was required in the House of Lords where Liberals and churchmen argued over the number of years a couple should be married before petitioning for divorce. Important issues were settled in the House of Commons committee, the Cabinet, and the House of Lords. As with equal grounds, the legislature resolved conflicts over expansion of grounds, but with special assistance from the government.

Feminists did not seem to perceive the divorce bill of 1937 as an issue of central concern to them, although they voiced their opinions as they did on all policy affecting the family. Feminist individuals and groups had little influence in determining the outcome of this legislation. Without their support, the act would very likely have gone into effect anyway with one important exception: the contribution of Sir John Simon, the Home Secretary. As a member of the government, he was no longer active in feminist organizations, but he had been a member of the NUSEC and had sponsored the equal grounds bill in 1923. His support for the divorce bill and his influence in the Cabinet were very significant in gaining the government's assistance. As Deputy Leader of the house, he was able to help guide the bill through the floor debate. Herbert commented on his role after the Second Reading debate:

> Sir John Simon, the Home Secretary, sat down beside me and congratulated us on our discretion; and he carried to his colleagues, I believe, the report that, if we had our chance, we might be trusted not to abuse it. Sir John seldom seems to receive due credit for anything he does; so let me say here that he, too, again within the limits of his authority, did all he could for us throughout the year.[51]

Other than Sir John, feminists were on the periphery. Eleanor Rathbone cosponsored the bill in 1936 and lent her support; she was not particularly active, however, since she was occupied with her own family-assistance bill. Maud Tate assisted Herbert by speaking in debate but was not present during the crucial conflict resolution stages. The NCEC and the NCW were in support of reform and studied the various stages, but they did not wage a campaign. They were useful to Herbert to counteract the attempt to defeat the bill by the Mother's Union who claimed to represent "the women of England."

MARRIED WOMEN'S PROPERTY

The administration dominated the decision-making process over married women's property in 1935. The need for law reform came to public attention through a decision by the Law Lords. The Lord Chancellor Lord Cave introduced a bill to abolish a husband's liability for torts. Proposals came from interest groups: feminists wanted to abolish coverture entirely; creditors demanded protection and asked that separate property and proprietary liability be eliminated. The major conflict was over how far the reform of the law of coverture should go in requiring equal responsibility for men and women.

The conflicts were resolved by the Law Revision Committee (LRC), a standing committee of legal experts advisory to Lord

Chancellor Sankey. He asked his committee to consider torts and contract liability of married women. It expanded its study to include all aspects of the doctrine of separate property including restraint on anticipation. The LRC report advocating abolition of separate property, proprietary liability, and restraint on anticipation became the basis for a government bill. Potential conflicts were resolved between the Lord Chancellor and the women MPs. The Chancellor received deputations, letters, and petitions from interested groups; most were in support of the reforms and some advocated expanding them. None of these communications resulted in a change in the bill. The Cabinet agreed to the proposal on the grounds that it was noncontroversial, and neither House had any opposition.

Although they were active on the property bill, feminist groups had limited input on the reforms of 1935. The NCEC, the NCW, the Six Point Group, and the Equal Rights Committee sent letters to the Law Revision Committee. However, they were not present during the crucial steps of conflict resolution in the committee. A few individual women MPs were consulted by the Lord Chancellor. Conceivably, if they had been adamantly opposed to his bill, he might have reconsidered. As it turned out, their objections were that it was too limited. It is likely the bill would have been enacted without their support. The major problem in getting the bill through was gaining the approval of the government. Lord Sankey and the Law Revision Committee were largely responsible for gaining that support.

The central role of the LRC in the law reform process and conflict resolution should be noted. Some previous reforms in family law had been the result of conflict resolution in Royal Commissions that met publicly, received witnesses and other evidence, and issued detailed, highly publicized reports. Law reforms in less controversial areas were usually the concern of interest groups, such as the Law Amendment Society and the NAPSS or of individual peers. As a result, bills were often poorly written or provoked such controversy that the legislature was unable to resolve it, and the government refused to sponsor reform measures.

The LRC was a new approach to law reform: a standing committee of experts who considered those areas of law that the Lord Chancellor referred to them. The lords viewed the LRC as a way of removing politics from the law reform process by getting the important interest groups to agree to the proposals in bill form before any introduction in Parliament. Such a procedure didn't remove politics from the decision-making process; it moved the conflict from the legislature to the administrative offices where it could be resolved away from public view. In this way, the Lord Chancellor and the legal elite could maintain greater control over content and have more confidence in their ability to get reforms through Parliament.

CONCLUSION

Feminists were largely responsible for the 1923 act that achieved equality for women in divorce, arguing that it would establish an equal moral standard for men and women. Other reforms for divorce and equality in the 1930s attracted less attention and little influence from feminists. From the early 1900s on, the policy process was heavily dominated by the government and party leaders in the House of Commons. The trend of interest-group politics was away from pressure on the political system and toward consultation at the initiative of government elites with group leaders. The smooth path to law revision that could follow from governmental assistance in a noncontroversial policy area like property law was strewn with obstructions when the law involved liberalization of divorce.

Exception to a pattern of dependence on governmental assistance was the influence of feminists brought about by the massive campaign for the vote. But as the energy from the suffrage campaign waned, so did the initiative of the feminists, until in the thirties their legislative program, like that of other interest groups, consisted largely of reactions to proposals by government officials.

NOTES

1. Matrimonial Causes Act of 1923, 13 & 14 *Geo. 5,* XIX.

2. Matrimonial Causes Act of 1937, 1 *Edw. 8* & 1 *Geo. 6,* LVII.

3. Law Reform (Married Women and Tortfeasors) Act of 1935, 25 & 26 *Geo. 5,* 30.

4. Glen Petrie, *A Singular Iniquity: The Campaigns of Josephine Butler* (New York: Viking Press, 1971).

5. Oliver R. McGregor, *Divorce in England: A Centenary Study* (London: Heineman, 1957), chap. 1.

6. The Matrimonial Causes Act of 1878 gave magistrates the power to grant a wife a separation and maintenance order if her husband was convicted of wife beating. Subsequent statutes expanded the grounds for separation and maintenance orders to include cruelty, desertion, and neglect to maintain. The Courts of Summary Jurisdiction, easily accessible to the poor, had been presided over by lay magistrates and had dealt primarily with petty crimes. They became involved in matrimonial matters in 1857 when separated women could get an order for control of property.

7. Royal Commission on Marriage and Divorce, 1912-1913, *Report* (Cmnd. 6478), 371.

8. Graham Wooton, *Pressure Groups in Britain, 1720-1970* (London: Allen Lane, 1975).

9. Emmeline Pankhurst, *My Own Story* (London: E. Nash, 1914).

10. Ethel Snowden, *The Woman Socialist* (London: George Allen, 1907).

11. Victor Gollancz, ed., *The Making of Women: Oxford Essays in Feminism* (London: Allen & Unwin, 1917).

12. National Union of Societies for Equal Citizenship, "Why Join," Pamphlet for recruiting members, Fawcett Library, London.

13. Parliamentary Debates, Official Report, V *Hansard* (House of Lords) 39, c. 342+.

14. "The Matrimonial Causes Bill," *Women's Leader and Common Cause* 13 (11 March 1921).

15. Reported in National Council of Women, *Women in Council* (November 1922), NCW Archives, London.

16. "NUSEC Report," *Women's Leader and Common Cause* 14 (22 December 1922).

17. V *Hansard* (House of Commons) 160, c. 2355.

18. Ibid., c. 2371.

19. *Women's Leader and Common Cause,* 15 (9 March 1923), 411.

20. National Union of Societies for Equal Citizenship, *Annual Report* (1931), Fawcett Library, London.

21. V *Hansard* (House of Commons) 235, c. 2263-70.

22. Ibid., c. 2268.

23. A. P. Herbert, *The Ayes Have It: The Story of the Marriage Bill* (London: Doubleday, 1937), 60.

24. *Times,* 21 March 1936.

25. Peter G. Richards, "Private Members' Legislation," in *The House of Commons in the Twentieth Century,* ed. S. A. Walkland (Oxford: Clarendon Press, 1979), 292-328.

26. Merriman J. to Claud Schuster, Permanent Secretary to the Lord Chancellor, 16 November 1936, from Lord Chancellor's Office, Marriage Bill, 2 1195.

27. Schuster to Merriman, ibid.

28. V *Hansard* (House of Commons) 317, c. 2079.

29. Ibid., c. 2106.
30. Herbert, *The Ayes Have It,* 111.
31. Merriman to Schuster, Lord Chancellor's Office, Marriage Bill 2 1195.
32. Sir John Simon to Cabinet, 18 March 1937, ibid.
33. V *Hansard* (House of Commons) 322, c. 1338.
34. Ibid., 324, c. 574.
35. V *Hansard* (House of Lords) 105, c. 730.
36. *Times,* 24 July 1937.
37. Quoted from *Law Quarterly Review* 7 (1891) 313, by C. Morrison, "Contracts," in *A Century of Family Law 1857-1957,* ed. R. H. Graveson and F. R. Crane (London: Sweet & Maxwell, 1957), 124.
38. Schuster to the Home Office, 11 April 1923, Lord Chancellor's Office, Married Women's (Torts) Bill, 2 777.
39. V *Hansard* (House of Lords) 61, c. 61.
40. Ibid., c. 62.
41. National Conference of Labour Women, *Report* (1932), 5, Labour Party, London.
42. Lord Chancellor's Office, Law Revision Committee, 2 1969.
43. Law Revision Committee, *Fourth Interim Report* (1934).
44. *Times,* 21 December 1934.
45. *Times,* 24 December 1934.
46. Schuster to the Lord Chancellor, 23 January 1935, Lord Chancellor's Office, Law Revision Committee, 2 1969.
47. V *Hansard* (House of Lords) 97, c. 297.
48. Royal Commission on Marriage and Divorce, *Report,* 1912-1913, 89.
49. *Women's Leader and Common Cause* 15 (15 June 1923), 58.
50. Ibid., 15 (3 August 1923), 210.
51. Herbert, *The Ayes Have It,* 98.

Divorce and Matrimonial Property, 1969-1970 5

THE ACTS

The latest reforms of divorce and matrimonial property law introduced new concepts into English family law. The first is the principle of divorce on irretrievable breakdown of marriage. This policy treats marriage as a partnership of roles and responsibilities shared by husband and wife. Irretrievable breakdown makes no assumptions about the conduct of either spouse, viewing each marriage on an individual basis. Partnership coincides with the second new principle of shared assets or family property. Since marriage is a partnership, ownership of property acquired during marriage must be attributed to the spouses jointly.

Between 1857 and 1969 divorce law was based on matrimonial offense, a doctrine consistent with official norms of separate sex roles and responsibilities in marriage. Civil divorce had arisen at a time when men and women were expected to adhere to different standards of sexual morality. Divorce was the punishment for the violation of these standards. Later, although men and women assumed equal moral status in the law, the policy of separate roles and responsibilities in marriage remained. Desertion and cruelty became additional matrimonial offenses punished by divorce. Legally, only one spouse could be responsible for divorce through his or her separate misconduct. Legislators expected that wives and husbands would make different use of these grounds according to their separate functions.

The Divorce Reform Act of 1969 departs from matrimonial offense and introduces irretrievable breakdown as the state's condition for granting a divorce.[1] "After the commencement of this Act the sole ground upon which a petition for divorce may be presented to the court by either party to a marriage shall be that the marriage has been broken down irretrievably'' (Section 1). The doctrine of matrimonial offense remains in the statute as proof of breakdown. The proofs are that one spouse has committed adultery, and the other finds it intolerable to continue cohabitation; that one spouse has behaved in such a way that the other cannot reasonably be expected to continue cohabitation; that one spouse has deserted for two years. Proof of breakdown may also be indicated by separation for two years with consent of the respondent or five years regardless of consent. This policy provides a number of alternatives for terminating a marriage legally: with consent, without consent, with offense or without offense.

The statute charges the courts and law officers to encourage reconciliation. A solicitor must urge clients to seek marriage counseling. The court may postpone a divorce hearing to give the couple a chance to make up. Attempts at reconciliation do not void proof of breakdown if they are unsuccessful. A second responsibility of the court is to protect a respondent from financial hardship as a result of the divorce. The court has authority to deny a petition if it ''will result in grave financial hardship to a spouse or that it would in all circumstances be wrong to dissolve the marriage.'' A respondent may also petition the court to review a financial settlement and postpone or deny the divorce if it is obtained through separation without mutual consent. This provision is to protect the spouse from loss of a benefit, such as a pension, that would have accrued if the marriage had not been dissolved. Courts have little discretion, however, in accepting or denying proofs of marital breakdown offered by couples.

The principle of divorce due to breakdown of the marriage is consistent with the concept of marriage as a relationship of shared roles and responsibilities where each spouse is expected to contribute to the marriage and share responsibility for its success or failure. In its pure form, breakdown means the state does not require guilt or innocence of the spouses but considers whether the marriage, as a shared relationship, remains viable. The law does not assume that women will all choose to be full-time mothers and husbands full-time breadwinners. It treats each marriage differently depending on the pattern of roles the couple has chosen.

The Divorce Reform Act of 1969 does not wholeheartedly embrace the concept of irretrievable breakdown. Although matrimonial offense remains in the law as proof of breakdown, its importance in defining public policy toward marriage has been reduced. Breakdown has replaced offense as the major principle of civil divorce. Consequently, the official policy toward marriage in England fosters the new concept of shared marital roles and responsibilities. Much of the rest of the act sustains traditional notions of women's dependency in marriage. The provisions for maintenance are based on the expectation that the husband will be the provider, and the wife will need to be supported.

The enactment of this new policy of marital breakdown brought about a reexamination of the effect of matrimonial property laws on husband and wife in divorce. The separate-but-equal policy of matrimonial property established in 1935 was the result of reform of the common law coverture, bringing married women out from the legal and economic cover of their husbands. As far as the law was concerned each spouse was entitled to own and use his or her property and earnings independently. This policy is inconsistent with modern views of marriage as a partnership. If marriage means shared roles and responsibilities, it follows that it also means shared family assets. The doctrine of separate-but-equal matrimonial property also revealed real injustices to married women fulfilling their duties as wives and mothers: they were unable to accumulate property, and their work had no economic value.

The Matrimonial Proceedings and Property Act of 1970 (MPPA) introduces the concept of family property into English statute law.[2] It is not a bold reform, but a tentative step in a new policy direction. The act provides guidelines to the courts in making property and financial settlements in divorce for spouses and children. As such, it indicates the possible property rights spouses have during marriage. It authorizes courts to require periodic payments, lump-sum payments, or the transfer of property between spouses in a divorce. In making such a settlement, the court will take the following circumstances into account (Section 5):

(a) the income, earning capacity, property, and other financial resources which each of the parties is likely to have in the foreseeable future

(b) the financial needs, obligations, and responsibilities which each of the parties to the marriage has or is likely to have in the foreseeable future

(c) the standard of living enjoyed by the family before the breakdown of marriage

(d) the age of each party to the marriage and the duration of the marriage

(e) any physical or mental disability of either of the parties to the marriage

(f) the contributions made by each of the parties to the welfare of the family, including any contribution made by looking after the home or caring for the family

(g) in the case of proceedings for divorce or nullity of marriage, the value to either of the parties to the marriage of any benefit (for example, a pension) which, by reason of the dissolution or annulment of the marriage, that party will lose the chance of acquiring

The court is admonished to leave parties in a financial position as close to that before the divorce as possible, but may take the conduct of the parties into account in making a financial settlement. A similar set of guidelines is provided to the court when making arrangements for the support of any children. Under the MPPA either spouse may receive maintenance and a share of matrimonial property (most typically a home or business) based on contributions to the care of the home and family or helping out in a business (Section 5 [f]). Although men and women are equally liable according to their circumstances, they are not subject to the same enforcement. According to Section 6, the court may order a husband to pay maintenance to the wife if he has willfully neglected it. A wife can be ordered to pay only if the husband "by reason of his earning capacity, through age, illness, or disability of mind or body . . . it is reasonable in all circumstances to expect the respondent to provide or contribute" (Section 6 [b] i). In other words, the husbands are expected to be adequately employed; the wives may be maintained. The husband, according to the act, would need to be maintained by his wife only under unusual circumstances.

The MPPA enables an unemployed spouse to gain an interest in property acquired during a marriage without actually contributing money toward its purchase. Such interest is obtained by work in the home or assisting in a family business. This provision is based on the principle that a married couple acquires a home, furniture, or a business through their joint effort, despite the fact that one spouse may be formally paid more for that effort than the other. The law considers such property as far as divorce is concerned to be assets of the marriage, rather than of individuals, and each spouse has an interest in it.

New concepts of marriage partnership and family property are now part of Englsh family law. Yet the economic dependence and inequality of married women also remain a basis of policy. The

MPPA empowers the court to divide family property between the husband and wife according to the special circumstances of each divorce case. It does not, however, guarantee the unemployed wife or secondary earner equal rights with the employed husband or primary earner. A few clauses of both the Divorce and Matrimonial Proceedings and Property Acts were included to empower the court to protect the income of middle-aged dependent wives who are divorced against their will, are unlikely to remarry, and have little opportunity to be employed. Such protections, rather than guarantee economic rights, reinforce the dependency of married women.

THE DEMANDS

The impact of one law reform leads to demands for additional reforms. That was certainly the case with the 1937 Matrimonial Causes Act, which expanded the grounds for divorce but retained the fault concept. The act had a shorter period of acceptance than most reforms, since its enactment had been postponed so long after the initial tensions between the law and actual marriage problems appeared. Immediately following the act, the number of divorces increased, mostly as a result of the additional grounds, especially desertion (see figure 1).[3] During and immediately following World War II, the number of divorces rose as much as seven times prewar annual figures; 1947 was the high point with 52,249 compared with 7,621 in 1938. As the postwar social turbulance began to settle, the Legal Aid Act of 1949 contributed to another boost in the divorce rate. During the 1950s the rate began to fall. An expansion of the Legal Aid Act in 1960 led to another jump in divorce; this time the rate did not fall but continued climbing during the 1960s.

Grounds used for divorce changed during the 1950s and 1960s (see table 2). By 1966 over half of the divorces were for adultery. (During the war nearly three-quarters of the petitions were on that ground.) Desertion was the second most used offense. For a short time in the early 1950s, more divorces were granted for desertion than adultery: this was a consequence of new legal-aid programs that enabled couples who had long been separated to end their marriages. By the 1960s, however, the use of cruelty as a ground had increased, and the use of desertion had experienced a large drop.

Changes in the grounds for divorce coincided with changes in the share of divorces granted to wives in comparison with husbands. Most war-time divorces were granted to men, as many as 65 per-

Figure 1
Divorce Rates, per 1,000, Married Population, 1954-1968

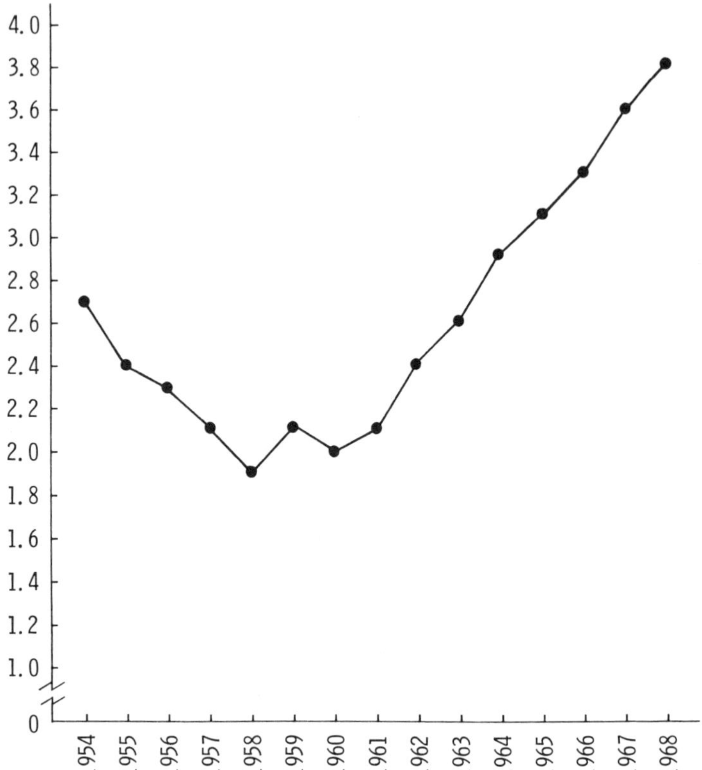

Source: Registrar General's Statistical Review, 1968.

cent in 1946. Otherwise, women received more than half the divorces. The Legal Aid Act of 1960 benefited many more women than men and led to an increase in their share of petitions: from 55 percent in 1954 to 59 percent in 1966. Most of the women petitioning for divorce received legal aid compared with about half the men. Men and women petitioned equally on adultery and desertion; 95 percent of the petitions based on cruelty were made by women. The increase in the frequency of cruelty as a basis for divorce in the 1960s was largely due to the increase in numbers of women petitioning for divorce. That, in turn, was affected by legal aid. These figures support the expectation of law reformers that the new grounds added in 1937 would benefit women desiring divorce. Due to economic dependency, however, women were able to take advantage of the law only with financial assistance.

Increases in divorce began to put pressure on courts with limited facilities to deal with large numbers of cases. It became more and more difficult for judges to determine guilt and innocence in every case. This was especially a problem when lawyers and clients presented evidence that satisfied the form of the divorce law rather than reflected the realities of the marriage. Courts began to develop their own formulas for granting divorce that resembled tests of breakdown more than determinations of guilt.

After World War II, lawyers and lay people continued to discuss the need for reform of divorce laws. Although the Matrimonial Causes Act of 1937 had expanded the grounds for divorce, reformers wanted a revision of the overall policy of matrimonial offense. The first proposal came from the Divorce Law Reform Union. It suggested that a new ground for divorce be added to the existing law: to grant divorces after a couple had been continuously separated for seven years. Proponents argued that the law based solely on the notion of fault was unrealistic and contributed to the suffering of many couples who had broken marriages but not

Table 2
Divorce Statistics, 1954 and 1966

	1954	*1966*
Number of divorces	27,353	38,352
Rate per 1,000 marrried	2.5	3.2
Percentage petitioners female	55%	59%
Percentage on grounds of:		
Adultery	43%	53%
Cruelty	13%	19%
Desertion	42%	26%
Number of women with legal aid	15,805[a] (women and men combined)	22,429 (72%)
Number of men with legal aid		8,749 (18%)

Sources: Registrar General's Statistical Review, 1968; Royal Commission on Marriage and Divorce, *Report* (1956); Civil Judicial Statistics, 1960-1968.

a. Numbers not available by sex.

the formal grounds for divorce. This proposal would legally end such marriages and would allow these couples, long apart, to form new legal families.

A proposal by the law profession for more basic reform was to make irretrievable breakdown of marriage the sole grounds for divorce. Proponents of this reform viewed fault divorce as so fundamentally out of touch with realities of marriage that it led to disregard for the law and individual unhappiness. They argued that the law should recognize that marriage is a complex relationship to which both spouses contribute equally and that divorce is the result of a failed human relationship, not the guilt of one spouse. Couples whose marriages have broken down and who have no hope for reconciliation should be able to divorce. Courts should assist in ending marriages legally that are proved to be dead. "It is therefore desirable so to alter the grounds of divorce that the law will afford legal recognition to the end of any marriage which has clearly broken down, and will do so at a cost which does not prevent ordinary people from exercising their legal rights."[4]

Increases in divorce, the changes in the status of women, and the advent of the welfare state prompted research and discussion by sociologists about the state of the family and women's place in it.[5] Social health depends on family health. Could the family perform its proper function of raising the next generation in the midst of easy divorce, equality for women, and a paternalistic state? Yes, because modern marriage was based on equality and sharing. It was agreed that the wife would be primarily responsible for small children and housework, but this work was as important as the husband bringing home his wages. The welfare state planners did not have the means to provide community services for every family. Women would have choices, however. Homemaking was easier because of better housing. Increased affluence meant that most families could afford laborsaving appliances. More and more women would be able to combine homemaking and childrearing with part-time work. The percentage of married women in gainful employment soared from 18 percent in 1947 to 40 percent in the late 1960s. Yet politicians praised women primarily for their work in the home, emphasizing the importance of the housewife in the new age of affluence and the welfare state.

The realities of divorce, however, revealed the financial hardships suffered by homemakers and mothers. Each divorce required a decision of some sort with respect to maintenance for dependent wives and children. Two facts became evident as divorces increased among the lower income families: a husband's salary was not enough to maintain his divorced wife and her children as well as a new wife and family if he remarried; a wife who earned no money had no property rights in a divorce. The equal rights that married women had achieved over their own property and earnings had little value for those married women who raised children and kept a home and were dependent on their husbands. In other words, family law based on separate-but-equal sex roles in marriage led to economic and financial dependency for most married women who pursued the duties expected of them as wives and mothers.

During the fifties Lord Denning introduced a new concept of family assets into his decisions on property settlements in divorce cases. This offered a means whereby a dependent wife through her work in the home might secure an interest in property paid for by her husband. In *Rimmer v. Rimmer,* 1953, he concluded that the "assets between husband and wife ought not to be governed by the same strict considerations both at law and in equity, as are commonly applied to the ascertainment of the respective rights of strangers when each of them contributes to the purchase power of property."[6] In *Fribance v. Fribance,* 1957, Denning pointed out that family assets bought for joint use by a husband and wife cannot be considered in terms of who paid for them.

> It does not depend on how they happened to allocate their earnings and their expenditure. The whole of their resources were expended for their joint benefit—either food and clothes and living expenses for which there was nothing to see or on the house and furniture which are family assets—and the produce should belong to them jointly. It belongs to them in equal shares.[7]

This principle could not be applied to most divorces, however, unless it became part of a statute on matrimonial property.

When proposals for divorce by consent or irretrievable breakdown surfaced, women's rights groups expressed concern for their effects on the economically dependent wife and mother. Under the 1937 law, as long as a wife committed no offense, she could not be divorced against her will. Her husband was legally required to provide for her support. Under no fault divorce she could be divorced against her will and left without adequate income either for herself or for her children. Reformers criticized property law that viewed the role of the wife and mother as separate and dependent. Praise from politicians for the work of the homemaker was not enough. They wanted the government to recognize that child-rearing had both social and economic value and that a wife's home-making duties made it possible for her husband to accumulate property. Laws should be changed to give economic worth to the wife's contribution.

Three proposals were made for changes in matrimonial financial and property law. One set of demands sought to remedy the immediate effect of no fault divorce on a dependent spouse: divorce would be granted only if a wife had the guarantee of a certain portion of her ex-husband's salary and pension. Another proposal would require the husband to pay the wife a certain part of his income or some other allowance during marriage, thus recognizing her right to earned income for her duties as wife and mother. A third proposal advocated some form of community of property in marriage, a major change from the concept of separate property. Community of gains, for example, was suggested to give spouses equal rights to family assets upon divorce; or the law might require joint ownership of the matrimonial home, furnishings, and savings during marriage and an equal division upon divorce.

These various demands for law reform involved different perspectives on family sex-role patterns. Divorce after separation, added to existing grounds, was consistent with the view that marriage required separate roles and responsibilities by sex, rather than a sharing of responsibility. The measure was advocated for the relief of men, primarily, who had left their wives and established new, but illicit, families. It was expected that the wife would be the one divorced against her will, not the husband. On the other hand, the major tenet of the proposal of divorce on irretrievable breakdown of marriage is that marriage is a relationship involving a sharing of roles and responsibilities. The adoption of breakdown in the divorce laws would mean a basic change in the official view of marriage. Proposals to change property laws are consistent with the legal notion of shared responsibilities and shared rewards in marriage as well. However, only community of property would provide for equal economic status for husband and wife with respect to the assets of the marriage.

The two issues, divorce reform and matrimonial property rights, were interrelated: the discussion of one inevitably led to the other. After World War II both were popular subjects for public debate. However, they suffered from the intense controversy aroused by the liberalization of divorce. Politicians' fear of the controversy had delayed the previous divorce reform for twenty years. In 1945 advocates of new divorce grounds wanted to include a change in family law as part of social policy in the new Labour government. It was not difficult to get initial action from the government. However, reformers had to wait another twenty years for the settlement of a conflict between church and state before family law reform found a safe place on the public agenda.

In March 1951 Eirene White introduced a private member bill to permit divorce after seven years' separation without proving any additional grounds. A divorce would be granted if no "reasonable prospect of reconciliation" existed and if the husband proved he had maintained his family during the separation. The latter provision was a safeguard for the wife, so that she could not be divorced against her will if her husband deserted her. In the Explanatory Memorandum to the bill, White presented separation as a breakdown measure: "The bill invokes a new principle in that it looks to breakdown of the marriage as a grounds for divorce, instead of to the proof of a marital offense having been committed by one partner against the other."

In the Second Reading debate, March 9, White pointed out that the purpose of the bill was to provide a remedy for couples who for various reasons lived permanently apart.[8] Many of them started new families but because they were unable to meet the criteria for divorce could not legally remarry. Their children were illegitimate, and the mothers had no financial security. She estimated that there were 100,000 or more such people. White brought out the problems created by the financial dependency of married women. She pointed out the inadequate provisions in the law for maintenance of wives and ex-wives. Many refused to sue their husbands for divorce even though they had grounds, not for religious reasons, but because they did not want to relinquish rights to old age pensions. She considered her bill a first step: "we ought to settle in our own minds the principle on which marriage and divorce should be settled, and then we should try to face any economic consequences in a larger and more intelligent way."[9]

During the debate MPs opposed to divorce reform presented their arguments. The debate was a preview for the controversy that was to follow. White's opening argument visited an old theme of reformers: liberalization of divorce law would reduce suffering. Opponents countered that some people will always suffer no matter what the law is. They are "hard cases" and "hard cases make bad law." Rather, the opponents argued, the goals of law reform should be to strengthen marriage by making divorce difficult. As Lyall Wilkes said in debate: "The extent to which easier facilities for divorce are provided, the extent to which we increase the number of grounds upon which divorce may be granted, will facilitate the breakup of marriages."[10] When divorce is made easier, in other words, people will not work as hard at saving their marriages.

Another criticism was that an innocent spouse could be divorced against his or her will. This might be emotionally trying for the husband, but it would be devastating to the innocent wife, who is more likely to believe that divorce is contrary to her religious views. By this reform, said the opponents, the nonreligious would force divorce on those with conscientious scruples against it. The proponents of reform countered with the charge that many times the law can be used to prevent divorce for merely vindictive reasons. A selfish and vengeful spouse, although technically innocent, could hold the other captive or alone for life. As far as religious views were concerned, White asked: "Why is it that those who put forward this point of view have no objection to one [religious spouse] forcing his or her religious views on the other? That seems to me a fundamental offense against the freedom of the human spirit."[11]

A final argument of the reformers was that since the existing law based on matrimonial offense was unrealistic, the lawyers and courts twisted it. The result was disrespect for a law that could be so easily violated. The opponents countered, somewhat weakly, that there were dangers to the basic legal code from removing fault and allowing a person to benefit from his own wrong by making marriage intolerable and then suing for the divorce. Said Wilkes: "If we eliminate innocence and guilt concepts from the law here—where will it end? With the elimination of all guilt?"[12]

White's bill passed a Second Reading in the House of Commons, 131-60, despite government opposition. The issue received widespread attention in the press. During the Second Reading debate the matter of a Royal Commission investigation was raised. White pointed out that petitions had been received from various groups asking that such a commission be established. One petition was from Edith (later Baroness) Summerskill, active at the time in the Married Women's Association (MWA): "We pray that legislation may be passed which will make the working housewife a partner by giving her a right to an equal share with her husband of the home and its income."[13]

When pressure for basic reform in the divorce law builds in Parliament and intervenes upon the government's consciousness, a Royal Commission to study the matter has often been a attractive alternative, as it was in the 1950s (unless one has just recently met). However, its work often does not result directly in statutes. Most of the proposals for policy changes come, not from Royal Commissions, but from standing advisory committees in government departments. Commissions placate proponents, postpone reform as opponents hope, and relieve the government of a disagreeable controversy. By the time the report is received, it is likely a new government will have to contend with it. Therefore, a Royal Commission is a useful alternative to a government that views divorce reform as an unwelcome source of nonpartisan, religious, moral, and legal controversy.

This occasion, although a Labour party majority was in power for the first time, was no exception. On 14 March 1951, in response to a question from Major Vernon, Eirene White, Cyril W. Black, and Lt. Colonel Lipton, Prime Minister Clement Atlee announced that he would recommend that His Majesty appoint a Royal Commission to review the law relating to divorce. White asked that the charge include a review of the law of marriage and separation as well, including matters of finance, pensions, insurance, and guidance and counseling. In return for the government's action, White withdrew her bill; otherwise it would have faced insurmountable opposition.

THE CONFLICT

ROYAL COMMISSION ON MARRIAGE AND DIVORCE

The Royal Commission on Marriage and Divorce, chaired by Lord Morton of Henryton, was appointed in September 1951. On 5 October 1951 the Labour government resigned. The election twenty days later returned a Conservative majority that would remain intact for the next thirteen years. The charge to the commission reflected the interests of both divorce reform and legal and financial status of married women as well as some other long-standing issues:

1. Review the law of divorce and matrimonial causes in England and Scotland.
2. Examine powers of magistrates courts affecting husband and wife.
3. Consider the property rights of husband and wife both during and at the termination of marriage.
4. Suggest any changes in the law of marriage and the degree of affinity.

Points 1 and 3 are relevant to the process of law reform in this study.

The Morton Commission met for longer than anyone had anticipated. It issued a wide call to groups and individuals to present evidence. Sixty-seven organizations and forty-eight individuals were represented in testimony. However, less than half of the 102 meetings were spent hearing testimony, most of them during the first year. The report was so long in coming (four years) because of deep division on the major issues. The final report in the winter of 1955-1956 was immense, extending over 400 pages, and yet resolved none of the major issues of divorce and property.

The commission's general views toward marriage are instructive in its apparent failure to understand the changes in marriage and family life in the last century. It was often callous and strict, with an unrealistic approach to the law. It agreed that marriage should be monogamous and for life and that its mission was to strengthen marriage, not destroy it. It's not unusual to approach the subject of divorce reform by advocating marriage and family stability. Herbert had even called his divorce bill the "Marriage Bill." But this commission went further than others in seeking to eliminate the causes of marriage failure, rather than only assisting its legal demise. After noting the problems of housing, and other social and economic pressures, it settled on the psychological reason for divorce: changes in values that had led to a lack of responsibility toward the obligations and duties of marriage. The remedy for the problem of marriage breakup would be to foster a proper sense of responsibility toward marriage obligations through education and counseling. It pointed out that unless lifelong monogamy were saved, the community would be seriously injured. Some wanted the government to protect the community by enforcing the ideal despite the consequences:

> There are some of us who think that if this tendency [to divorce] continues unchecked, it may be necessary to consider whether the community as a whole would not be happier and more stable if it abolished divorce altogether and accepted the inevitable individual hardships that this would entail.[14]

The chief demand for liberalization of the divorce law was that matrimonial offense be eliminated and replaced by the principle of marital breakdown. The concrete proposal for breakdown was White's bill for divorce after a seven-year separation. The commission faced two major issues: (1) whether to abolish matrimonial offense and replace it with some version of breakdown or (2) whether to expand the law to permit some breakdown provision in addition to fault.

The church, the Mothers' Union, and other conservatives strongly opposed any change in the law, and they appeared united. They were unhappy with any law that made divorce easier and moved away from the teachings of Christianity. Some argued that the stability of marriage and the family was so basic to the continuation of Western civilization that a proposal to allow an increase in divorce, despite the immediate relief to a few people it might bring, would have drastic social effects. Advocates of breakdown argued that divorce after seven years' separation for couples who agreed there was no hope of reconciliation would relieve suffering of unhappy people whose marriages had already ended. To this argument opponents replied: there will always be some suffering; we can't change the law on the basis of that—"hard cases make bad law."

Although public opinion was divided on the issue of abolishing fault, the commission was not. All but one of the nineteen members voted to retain the present law of matrimonial offense. Of the eighteen who wanted to retain fault, nine voted for the addition of a breakdown provision and nine opposed breakdown. Lord Walker was the only member of the commission favoring elimination of matrimonial offense. He advocated three years' separation be the only ground for divorce. The 9-9-1 division left the Morton Commission with no clear recommendation other than to retain the law as it was. As such, the commission reflected "the state of unsettled English public opinion on divorce."[15]

The Morton Commission also made the first full-scale official investigation of the property rights of husband and wife. Most of the testimony agreed that despite the Married Women's Property Act, the present law was unfavorable to women, especially to unemployed wives. The problem involved the following:

1. Women had no means of ensuring adequate support from their husbands.
2. Husbands were not obliged to give their wives any money at all or tell them what their earnings were.
3. If a wife were frugal with an allowance, by law her husband was entitled to any savings.
4. The woman who had worked in the home or family business had no right to any furniture, home, or income.

The report noted that the wife's economic dependence was "one of the basic and most insidious factors contributing to the stresses and strains of married life." Of course, the wife's lack of property rights continued in the divorce.

A number of proposals for changes in the law were made by women's groups and legal experts. The women's groups' proposals concerned the way in which the wife might be guaranteed a portion of her husband's earnings. One group advocated a 50-50 split of family income between husband and wife after household expenses were taken out. Another offered separate testimony for a compulsory personal allowance to be paid to the wife, not necessarily based on an equal division of income but an amount agreed by both spouses.

Other suggestions from the legal community involved some form of community of property. These proposals were that property and income of both husband and wife acquired during a marriage be jointly owned and equally divided at a divorce. The MWA and Council of Married Women (CMW) declined to support community property, arguing it would be harmful to employed women who were just beginning to acquire independent incomes. Individual feminists supported the idea of community, however, as the only way an unemployed spouse could acquire property. MWA and

CMW proposals required the husband to give money to his wife, rendering her a "protected" dependent. They saw guaranteed rights to property the only way to prevent women from being abused at the will of their husbands.

Opposition to these proposals for changes in matrimonial property law was subtle: all recognized that the unemployed dependent wife and mother deserved just treatment, but many (especially lawyers) argued that the various proposals were unworkable and unrealistic. After a divorce, they pointed out, a husband might be financially able to provide for one wife and family but not two. If he remarried he would be responsible for his new wife. There would not be enough money in the average pay packet to assure the first wife's maintenance. Other proposals to guarantee a portion of the husband's income to the wife would involve the courts in the expenditure of private income, a proposal viewed as entirely inconsistent with English law and the rights of privacy. As far as community of property was concerned, it was thought to be too complicated, unfair to a hardworking and frugal spouse, alien to English law, and revolutionary.

The commission agreed with all of the evidence presented about injustices in the law and that marriage was an "equal partnership." "We fully endorse the view that marriage should be regarded as a partnership in which husband and wife work together as equals and that the wife's contribution to the joint undertaking, in running the home and looking after the children, is just as valuable as that of the husband in providing for the home and supporting the family."[16] Then the commission failed to agree on any specific proposals for change in the law, although it noted that some amendment was probably necessary. It agreed that proposals for giving a wife a legal right to some portion of her husband's income would be impracticable and found it inconceivable that a court might be involved in deciding the expenditure of personal income. A majority (twelve) of the members opposed community of property, which they considered a startling break with tradition. The defects in community of property regimes were that they take no account of the "natural and normal desire" to acquire property, are too complicated especially in determining who is to be responsible for decisions about the property and still maintain equality, and may be unfair when one partner is industrious and the other is not. Seven members supported the idea of community, either as a general principle of marriage law or applied to matrimonial home and furniture. The commission did make some recommendations it thought might alleviate some of the injustices of the present law without disturbing the basic principle of separate property: household savings should belong equally to husband and wife; wife should have the right to a pension even though divorced; the spouse left in the matrimonial home should have the right to prevent its sale.

Thus the Morton Commission agreed on the following points: marriage should be monogamous and for life and the law should strengthen marriage; the present law of matrimonial offense should be retained; marriage should be considered an equal partnership between husband and wife; law should protect the financially dependent wife by guaranteeing her right to occupy the home, to receive a part of the household savings, and to receive a pension despite divorce. But the commission was deeply divided over whether to add a marital breakdown provision and whether to recommend some form of community of property in marriage and divorce.

Most of the publicity about the report covered the failure of the Morton Commission to agree on a change in the divorce law. The 9-9-1 split meant that the group had not resolved public controversy on the issues and had merely reflected the deep division between reformers and religious conservatives. The report offered no policy alternatives on divorce that had any likelihood of passing Parliament. In 1957, therefore, the Conservative government announced that it would not introduce legislation to implement any of the proposals made by the commission. Since controversy had not been cleared up, the government decided to wait until public opinion could be expressed more definitely.

The subject of property rights of husband and wife received little notice outside feminist organizations. They were pleased that an official body had finally recognized the equal partnership in marriage concept. They were disappointed since they had hoped at least to bring public attention to their issues through the commission's meetings and report. Lady Helena Nutting planned to persuade Parliament to act on the strength of the commission's recommendation that "something" should be done to alleviate effects of financial dependency on marriage stability.

Lack of publicity for women's rights issues plagued activities of feminists during the 1950s and 1960s. A generation of women grew up believing that feminism was as dead as the suffragettes. Despite this lack of attention, feminist politics actually revived after World War II. Those who had been active in the thirties, such as Eva Hubback and Helena Normanton, continued their campaigns. Old issues, such as equal pay and employment opportunity, gained new ground in the trade unions and the Labour party. More women entered politics and several MPs, such as Eirene White and Joan Vickers, made women's rights their special legislative concern.

The relationship between Dr. Edith Summerskill and the advocates of married women's rights exemplifies feminist political activity of the period. The Married Women's Association was organized in 1938 by a group of married women in another feminist organization, the Six Point Group. As a single-issue pressure group, its organization consisted of an Executive Committee, a chairman, a newsletter mailing list, and a large group of honorary vice-presidents, mostly MPs. The MWA prepared bills for married women's economic rights. It testified before the Royal Commission. Summerskill, a member of the MWA, spoke for its goals in the House of Commons and later in the House of Lords. Until her death in 1979, she was known as the parliamentary spokeswoman for the dependent wife.

Even a small organization like the MWA suffered from internal conflicts. In 1952 the Executive Committee split over its testimony before the Royal Commission on Divorce. The members, led by Juanita Frances, wanted a 50-50 division of family income between husband and wife. Helena Normanton persuaded a majority of the Executive Committee to take a more moderate stand. This difference of opinion and personality led to the formation of a new group, the Council of Married Women, led by Normanton and Lady Helena Nutting. The two women soon quarreled, and Nutting remained to preside in solitude over the lobbying activities of the CMW for the next twenty years. Frances became the president of the MWA.

Most feminist interest groups were similar to the MWA in size and organization. Many of them worked for a number of women's rights issues. The Six Point Group had organized in 1921 to campaign for six equality goals. They included equal pay, equal opportunity, and equal partnership in marriage. The Women's Freedom League (WFL) traced its origins to the suffragette campaign. It broke away from the Pankhursts, yet retained their ideas of militancy. In the 1950s the WFL followed the campaigns for equal pay and education and against sexism in the media. Other descendents of the suffrage movement also hung on: The National Association of Women Citizens was the daughter of the National Society for Equal Citizenship and the great-granddaughter of the National Union of Societies for Women's Suffrage. The Fawcett Society had been called the Women's Service League in the 1920s and kept the records of the women's movement at the Fawcett Library. All of these organizations derived their energy from a few dedicated women who had in the 1920s and 1930s made women's rights their life's work.

In 1960 Dame Joan Vickers (now Lady Vickers) invited organizations interested in women's rights to send representatives to a Status of Women Committee. In addition to the small, specialized feminist organizations, larger groups also sent representatives. Some promoted professional, religious, or peace issues: Society for Ministry of Women in the Church, St. Joan's Alliance, the Society of Women Writers and Journalists, the Open Door Council, and the Women's International League of Peace and Freedom. A few were large service associations, such as the National Council of Women of Great Britain (NCW), the British Federation of Business and Professional Women, the Federation of Soroptomist Clubs, and the Women's Liberal Federation. They are composed of local branches under the umbrella of a central committee and executive office in London. Since their members are women, the leaders concern themselves with activities and issues pertinent to women, including equal rights. Usually, a national officer is responsible for monitoring political and legal matters, especially bills introduced into Parliament that may affect women. Each organization enacts resolutions indicating support or opposition to these matters at the annual general meeting. In the case of the NCW, the active working parties also prepare position papers on important issues to advise government agencies.

THE DEADLOCK

After the Morton Commission made its report in 1956, feminists and divorce reformers alike were frustrated by the absolute refusal of the government to take up their demands. The inability of the commission to come up with some sort of proposal for change reflected the deadlock between religious conservatives, represented by the Church of England, and the reformers, represented by divorce lawyers. The matrimonial property issue did not attract enough attention to be taken up separately from the other subjects in the report. Feminists could not get their issue on the public agenda unless Parliament was willing to make a decision about divorce, and that would not occur until the deadlock was broken. Activity did not cease, however, and proponents of both reforms continued to keep their issues before the public and wait for a break in the impasse. Such impasses are not unusual in British politics and political activists learn to respect the importance of proper timing in proposing change.

Divorce. There was widespread disappointment and criticism of the outcome of the Morton Commission's deliberations in the area of divorce reform. In 1957 Oliver McGregor analyzed the report in *Divorce in England.* He attempted to correct some of the misunderstandings about the rising divorce rate. He argued that an increase in divorce was the result of many factors, mainly economic and social variables, reinforced by the increase in available grounds. McGregor saw little cause for alarm from divorce statistics. He found no evidence that the population was "divorce-minded" as some members of the commission had charged. Marriage as an institution had not weakened; in fact, most divorced people remarried. Married couples accepted their responsibilities to their children: divorce rates were low among families with young children. The notion that divorce was used mainly by men to rid themselves of middle-aged wives was contradicted by the fact that wives were just as likely as husbands to sue for divorce.

McGregor suggested that the views of the church should not be a barrier to divorce reform. Most people rejected the notion that secular law be based on canon law. Even the Archbishop of Canterbury had recognized this in 1937, when in the debate on the Herbert Marriage Bill, he agreed that public policy in a democracy must allow religious sects to impose their rules on their own members, but not through the public policy itself.

McGregor concluded that the Morton Commission reflected a disagreement about the importance of people versus institutions. He clearly came down on the side of freedom of choice for individuals over the maintenance of institutional norms: "The essence of democratic living is the exercise of choice. Choice necessarily implies change and fear of change has never been a successful guardian of morality. Free men and women ought not to tolerate barriers erected as safeguards against their assumed irresponsibility. In any case, they won't.''[17]

Parliamentary attention to divorce did not cease because of the government's unwillingness to sponsor legislation affecting matrimonial law. Several backbenchers sought to introduce private member bills for reform. Leo Abse, Labour MP from Pontypool, Wales, received a low number in the ballot in 1963 and introduced the Matrimonial Causes and Reconciliation Bill. It had two major provisions: to allow divorce after seven years' separation (similar to the 1951 White bill) and to permit couples to try reconciliation after matrimonial offense had been committed without losing the grounds for divorce.

In the Second Reading debate, Abse explained the dual purpose of the bill: to encourage estranged couples to ''make a bid for happiness'' and permit parents cohabiting in permanent unions to end previous marriages and make their children legitimate.[18] He realized that the addition of the separation provision was controversial but argued that objections to it were hollow. The law, by adding insanity as a grounds in 1937, had already departed from matrimonial offense. He pointed to safeguards in the bill whereby an innocent spouse being divorced against her will could protest, and the petitioner had to show her previous misconduct.

The strongest opposition came from outside the Commons: from the church and from Sir Jocelyn Simon, president of the Probate, Divorce and Admiralty Court. Simon delivered a well-publicized address in opposition before the Magistrates Association. Although the separation clause survived the Second Reading and committee stages, Abse withdrew it during the report stage. He believed it was a mild reform and that the bill had adequate safeguards to protect dependent wives and children. Yet he realized significant opposition was coming from the church and the courts. He accused Simon of behaving as if he were still an MP. Since Abse had been informed that several MPs intended to talk out the entire bill, he withdrew the controversial separation clause to save the reconciliation provisions.

An attempt was made in the House of Lords to revive the breakdown principle in what was then referred to as Abse's ''Kiss and Make Up'' bill. That provided Lady Edith Summerskill, who had become a peer in 1961, with an opportunity to present the arguments of those concerned with the effect of the separation clause on dependent wives.[19] She referred to it as the ''compulsion'' clause.

Summerskill argued that marriage has different value to men and women. A woman views it as a way of establishing a home for her children. She will fight against the breakup of the home even if it means ill treatment from her husband. Children can survive with quarreling parents better than with the breakup of their home. A woman can lose everything in divorce: maintenance, home, insurance, and pension. A wife raises the children and cares for the home, freeing her husband to pursue his business. She is not entitled to one penny of the housekeeping allowance and any savings belong to the husband. "Most deserted wives therefore have not a penny in their own right."[20]

The separation clause was not put back, but a step was taken during the debate that turned out to be more significant in the process of reform in the long run. The Archbishop of Canterbury stated that although this proposed separation clause was unacceptable, he believed the divorce law needed reforming:

> Again, if it were possible to find a principle at law, of breakdown of marriage which was free from any trace of the idea of consent, which conserved the point that offences and not only wishes are the basis of the breakdown, and which was protected by a far more thorough insistence on reconciliation procedure first, then I wish to consider it. . . . I am asking some of my fellow church men to work on it sociologically and doctrinely.[21]

Matrimonial property. The Married Women's Association and the Council of Married Women turned toward parliamentary lobbying after they realized nothing would come from the Morton Commission report. The MWA prepared a new bill. "The status of married woman must be raised so that she has not only a share in the family income or its surplus if any, but an equal share in the question of how that money is to be spent to the family's best advantage. Her work in the home in bearing and rearing children must be seen to have an equal share with her husband's work outside it."[22]

The MWA's proposal, called the Married Women (Financial Status) Bill, contained the following provisions: the matrimonial home and its contents were to be the common property of the spouses; all income after marriage was to be common property unless both spouses formally agreed otherwise; money in excess of household expenses must be divided equally; income tax returns made by one spouse must be signed by the other; each spouse was to have joint financial responsibility for children; property purchased out of the common income was to be owned jointly. The Married Women (Financial Status) Bill was based on the idea of sharing income and property of the marriage; its proponents claimed it did not go as far as continental systems of community property. In community of property the husband manages the money, apart from what a wife earns on her own. The MWA called for equal division of income after household expenses, giving the unemployed spouse a legal right to the control of some of the family income.

Meanwhile, the rival Council of Married Women was preparing its own bill. Lady Helena Nutting criticized the MWA proposal as "ridiculous and impractical." She considered it to be too revolutionary and was convinced that men would never accept such a law; it was too drastic. "It is a very vast question and would, I am told, affect the whole wage structure of the country which is based upon a married man having a housekeeper free in most respects."[23]

The CMW put together the Married Persons (Allowances) Bill, which would provide that a portion of the income of the husband (or employed spouse) be paid directly to the wife (or unemployed spouse) for her own use. The amount to be paid could be worked out between the spouses or in the event of conflict by the courts. The MWA criticized the CMW bill as being fundamentally at odds with the goals of equal status in marriage; instead of equal status, it charged, it would put the wife on a par with the children, receiving an allowance from the husband, but still dependent on him. If adopted, even in principle, it would put the fight for equality back fifty years, said Executive Committee member Lady Ormrod.

The two bills appeared in 1958 and circulated for the next few years. The organizations' activities focused on stimulating public interest through distribution to clubs and large organizations for support and allies; circulation of MPs for possible interest as a private member bill; submission to prominent individuals who might have government contacts; review by lawyers for suggestions in drafting; letters to ministers asking to review the issue; public meetings for publicity. The leadership of the two groups took all of these steps during 1958-1964 with little immediate result. Even organizations like the NCW were lukewarm to the proposals; MPs were not particularly interested; the government saw no need to consider the problem any further in light of the recent Morton

Commission study. Neither bill received so much as a First Reading in Parliament. They remained proposals, thus far not officially recognized.

Other feminist groups expressed support for reform of the law affecting the financial status of married women. The Six Point Group advocated economic, legal, occupational, moral, social, and political equality for women. It included the status of married women under its first point, economic equality: "We want to change the law so that marriage shall be an equal partnership—each partner making those contributions which he or she is best fitted to make and the results of their combined labours being shared equally as a right between them. The group believes that the good wife's work in the home is of equal value with the good husband's work outside it."[24] Still associated with the Six Point Group in 1961 were suffragists Lord Pethick-Lawrence and Lady Mary Stocks, as well as Lady Summerskill and Dame Joan Vickers, MP.

Vickers' Committee on the Status of Women included a plank on married women in its policy statement of 1960: "Both spouses should be entitled to share in the family home, goods and income. In the event of a breakdown of a marriage, there should be an equitable distribution of such assets as have been acquired and accumulated as the result of the work of the two spouses."[25] The National Council for Women supported the CMW concept of allowances. It resolved at its 1956 annual meeting that the common law obligation to allocate and transfer to her a portion of his income free from his control. In turn, if the husband were disabled, the wife should pay him an allowance out of her separate resources, if possible. Later in the 1960s the NCW changed its policy to advocate community of property.

Although a good deal of activity had taken place over divorce and property law reform during the fifties, the Conservative party's rule ended in 1964 without any change in the statutes. Plenty of support for a change existed, especially in the legal community, but fear of staunch religious objections and the tendency during the decade away from major reform policies deprived the issues of necessary political initiative. Evidence of changes in marital behavior and attitudes toward the family in the early sixties accumulated. Divorce rates showed an upward turn, and birth rates showed a decrease. It was widely recognized that people wanted a marriage where they could share happiness and were impatient with traditional notions of authority and responsibility. In a study of the British family in 1962, Ronald Fletcher found it had the following characteristics: small in size, consciously planned; "entered into and completely maintained on a voluntary basis by partners of equal status, and therefore entailing a marital relationship based on mutuality of consideration; democratically managed, in that husband and wife (and frequently children) discuss family affairs together when decisions have to be taken."[26] The reality of a democratic family of equals based on shared responsibilities and buoyed up by improved status of women was inconsistent with the law of divorce and matrimonial property. Social conditions were becoming favorable to the resolution of the conflicts over family law reform.

What was needed was the political leadership to bring issues of divorce reform and matrimonial property back to the public agenda and to start up the processes of decision making. The Divorce Law Reform Union (DLRU), which had been active in the campaign for changes in the divorce law for decades, tried to fill the needed role. The union consisted of a small group of MPs and officers and about 300 members who contributed to its meager budget. It held public meetings, visited MPs, and published pamphlets. In a time of large, professional, broadly based interest groups, the DLRU had few resources to get the attention of government leaders. In the mid-1960s a new group of leaders took office in the union, led by R. V. Banks. Banks in turn recruited Alistair Service as chief lobbyist. Service had recently been successful in a similar job for the Abortion Law Reform Association. Despite these changes, the DLRU, like the single-issue feminist groups, was unable to bring together the opposing sides on the divorce question. What they could and did do was lobby once a private bill was prepared and introduced.

Although single-issue reform groups persisted, the initiative for law reform no longer came from individuals and groups such as those of the nineteenth century. It came from standing advisory committees in the administration. Responsibility for various legal areas was interspersed among several government departments: the Board of Trade, business law; Ministry of Labour, factory law; Ministry of Health, housing and sanitation law; the Home Office, criminal law. No coordination existed, nor was any agency interested in family law. The staff of the Lord Chancellor had increased, but he had only partial authority and no control over the legal network.

The Law Revision Committee of 1934 appointed by Sankey was followed by the Law Reform Committee under Lord Chancellor Simonds in 1952 "to consider, having regard to judicial decisions what changes are desirable in such legal doctrines as the Lord Chancellor may from time to time refer to the Committee."[27] One of the members of the Law Reform Committee for ten years was Gerald Gardiner, a Labour barrister. When asked by the Lord Chancellor which areas of the law needed revision, Gardiner replied that the whole of the law needed reform.[28] He found the law reform machinery "hopeless": no full-time staff was available and it took two to three years to produce any proposal that would then likely be ignored unless the Lord Chancellor agreed to push it. Interest in law reform came from a wide variety of sources, but especially among the Labour lawyers. The Haldane Society advocated a Ministry of Justice to coordinate and codify all of English law.[29]

Before the 1964 election, Gardiner and Andrew Martin edited *Law Reform Now,* a blueprint for Labour's policy. "The problem of bringing the law up to date is largely one of machinery; . . . it must be kept in continuous operation and minded by full time personnel."[30] They proposed that there be a permanent group of Law Commissioners charged with the review and updating of all areas of law in cooperation with the Lord Chancellor but independent of any government department.

Events moved quickly after the Labour party victory. Gardiner became Lord Chancellor. He drafted a White Paper and then introduced the Law Commission Bill, which received the Royal Assent on 15 June 1965, eight months after the election. Law Commissioners were appointed the next day. The commission submitted the First Program to the Lord Chancellor on July 19 and to Parliament in October. "It is rumored that early implementation of 'Law Reform Now' proposals was made a condition of Gerald Gardiner's acceptance of the Lord Chancellorship in the Wilson Government."[31]

The statutory duties of the commission are (a) to review the law to achieve systematic development and reform; codify; remove obsolete sections, anomalies, contradictions, and thus simplify and modernize the law; and (b) to consider proposals for reform, to study and formulate proposals; and to draft appropriate bills. One task is the reform of "lawyers law," where goals are agreed upon but procedures need to be revised. The second is social reform where law would be changed to achieve a new political or social objective. Any proposal might involve both types of law and the Law Commission was established to consider both. The role of the commission is advisory to Parliament, although no machinery is in the act whereby proposals are to be introduced. The commission must depend on the Lord Chancellor, the government, or a private member to pick up its proposals. Between 1966 and 1976 the commission made sixty reports calling for new legislation; all but seven have resulted in statutes.[32]

The first commission was composed of Sir Leslie Scarman, chairman, a judge of the High Court; Professor L.C.B. Gower, solicitor and academic lawyer; Neil Lawson, leading counsel at a commercial bank; Norman Marsh, director of the British Institute of International and Comparative Law; and Professor Andrew Martin, academic lawyer and coeditor with Lord Gardiner of *Law Reform Now.* Cartwright Sharp was appointed secretary and administrator. A staff of lawyers and parliamentary draftsmen were assigned to special sections according to their expertise. Each commissioner assumed responsibility for one of these areas. Gower was in charge of the family law section, and Scarman, as well as Gardiner himself, had special interest in divorce reform.

The first commissioners developed the procedures. After the commission decides to review a subject, the appropriate law team studies the problem and prepares a working paper. Each paper includes a review of statutes and case law on the subject, a discussion of problems with current law, and specific suggestions for change. The full commission reviews each working paper. It then distributes a revised paper to a wide variety of individuals and groups for comment. The list of distribution is drawn up by the commissioner in charge. This stage is called "consultation" and was Scarman's contribution: requiring such input was neither in the act nor in *Law Reform Now.* The commission regards this stage as the most important step in the law reform process.

The effect of consultation is to determine the levels of support for proposals among lawyers and interest groups. As Scarman pointed out, without consultation, opposition and misunderstanding may result that will make it difficult to get reforms through

Parliament.[33] By circulating proposals to legal experts and lay interests alike, the two aspects of law reform, technical and social, can be fully considered. A lesser effect of the consultation stage is the occasional revision of the proposal itself. Sometimes, the paper will include an unusual suggestion just to gauge the reaction. Observations about the effects of reforms and interpretations in courts may suggest revisions that had not occurred to commissioners. After consultation, the staff prepares the final report. At this point parliamentary counsel on the commission's staff drafts a bill. When the report is approved by the commission as a whole, the draft bill is appended. Thus either the Lord Chancellor or a member of Parliament can submit a correctly drafted bill to the Parliament without delay.

The Law Commission is an important addition to the machinery of law reform in England and Wales. (Scotland has its own commission.) It is a permanent institution that has the time and resources to carry through codification as well as propose basic reforms. The two tasks, reform and codification, must occur together. The commission has the expertise to codify law and make it more certain and accessible to practitioners and citizens alike. At the same time, through consultation, it can propose necessary reforms that are consistent with social values and political realities. The Law Commission was able to provide the leadership to solve problems of divorce and property law reform.

RESOLUTION OF THE CONFLICT

THE ARCHBISHOP AND THE LAW COMMISSION

The impasse over divorce reform was broken by a change in the position of the church. The input from the church in previous divorce debates had been either negative or reactionary. In the 1850s it opposed legal divorce, but accepted the single ground of adultery as consistent with the Bible. Later, the church opposed any liberalization of the 1857 law and frustrated recommendations of the Gorell Commission. The Herbert act of 1937 caught the church off guard, but it focused its opposition in time to testify at the Morton Commission against the separation proposals, which it regarded as divorce by consent. When the archbishop appointed an advisory group in 1964 to review the law of divorce, proponents of reform began to see some hope for change, especially since the charge to the group specifically separated church rules from public policy and asked only that the recommendations not make it impossible for church beliefs in lifetime marital stability to be realized.

The Labour governments headed by Harold Wilson, formed in 1964 and 1966, also made it possible for a reform proposal, once agreed upon by the church and the lawyers, to be enacted. Part of that job was accomplished by the creation of the Law Commission in 1965. However, the Labour Cabinet was no more anxious to take official responsibility for the controversies surrounding divorce than any previous government. What made the new Parliament more receptive to change was the composition of the Labour majority in the Commons. The most important aid to social reform was the ideology of MPs in the Labour party, how they viewed controversial issues, and their willingness to pressure their leaders. Forty percent of the labour MPs elected in 1966 were young, middle class, well educated, and classified as social as well as economic liberals. Nineteen of them were women, many active in women's rights. They shared a view of socialism put forth by Anthony Crosland in *The Future of Socialism* in 1956, which emphasized continuous, peaceful, and moderate change. They were more likely to support and understand national legal reforms than were their working-class colleagues. The workers and economic reformers often viewed issues of public morality as "some unfathomable mystery, like the sacraments of the Church or the evolution of the Leader of the Conservative Party."[34] These younger MPs thought issues such as abortion, homosexuality, and divorce were as politically important to them as nationalization of steel was to the older Labour MPs.

Important changes had taken place in the House of Lords as well. Although the Parliament Acts of 1911 and 1949 had severely limited the constitutional powers of the upper house, the Life Peerages Act of 1958 brought in new membership, including women. Among these new life peers were politicians, lawyers, and other public figures who combined status with expertise. The House of Lords began to seek a new more creative role for itself. It took over responsibility for policies that did not pertain to party programs and were of little interest to the government. In the Lords, these issues could be considered in a leisurely way, not possible in "another place." Members discussed issues of abortion, capital punishment, divorce, homosexuality, and matrimonial property. In earlier days the Lords had done the same (recall Gorell and Buckmaster's attempts to reform divorce law in the 1910-1925 period). But what was different in the 1960s was the presence of more professional and public figures who took an active interest in the business of the House and the presence of women, twenty-five appointed between 1958 and 1970. On the whole, the House of Lords became more active in reform efforts during the late 1950s and early 1960s than it had been before.

The House of Lords was discussing one of these reforms, Abse's "Kiss and Make Up Bill," in 1963 when the archbishop announced his intention to ask his fellow churchmen to develop a new principle of divorce that would be acceptable both to the state and the church. He asked R. G. Mortimer, the Bishop of Exeter, to chair the group composed mostly of lay people: a barrister, a solicitor, judges, sociologists, a writer, a legal scholar, a psychiatrist, and two canons of the church. They received testimony from a number of experts including Lady Ormrod, a member of the MWA and the Marriage Guidance Council; Justice Ormrod and Sir Jocelyn Simon of the Divorce Court; and Sir Leslie Scarman, head of the Law Commission. Despite its emphasis on the secular and its advisory role, the group became associated with the Church of England, and its report was considered to be representative of official church thinking.

Two extremely important recommendations were in the group's report, *Putting Asunder: Divorce Law for Contemporary Society,* which was published in July 1966. The first was that secular law should not be the same as church law, since it must apply to many people who are not connected with the church. The state divorce law had developed in an atmosphere where the church made any rational consideration of the divorce law impossible: "there can be little doubt that, if the existing law embodies uneasy compromises they are partly due to the state's desire not to cause unavoidable conflict with the Church."[35] The separation of secular and church law would provide the first opportunity for Parliament to consider a humane divorce law without the constant spector of church opposition. The group realized that only a church body of some sort could begin this process. For this reason, regardless of the substance of the recommendations, the process toward real divorce reform had begun with the Archbishop's Group, perhaps for the first time in English law.

The second major recommendation of the group dealt with the

divorce law itself. It recommended sweeping away current laws based on matrimonial fault. Everyone testifying before the group agreed that present law was unsatisfactory, and the reasons given provide a good summary of the criticisms offered by reformers over the years: (1) an innocent spouse proving offense by the other spouse had little to do with marriage failure; (2) current law prevented legitimizing a second union after separation; (3) accusatorial procedures were unrealistic and led to bitterness; (4) through collusion many couples received divorce by consent, thus removing any effective participation by the court; (5) the law unfairly branded one spouse as guilty, whereas both were probably responsible for marriage failure; (6) grounds were inconsistent, since there was already one non-fault ground, insanity.

All agreed that divorce should be granted only after the marriage has completely broken down. The group recommended that the secular law on divorce be based on the principle of marital breakdown as proved by court investigation or inquest. Rather than asking who committed a grievous act against another, the question concerning breakdown would be: "Does the evidence before the court reveal such failure in the matrimonial relationship, or such circumstances adverse to that relationship, that no reasonable probability remains of the spouses again living together as husband and wife for mutual comfort and support?"[36] The court would be charged with investigating, through a procedure similar to an inquest, the circumstances of the marriage to see if there were any chance of its being saved. If there were a chance, the court would help a couple to solve their problems; if not, the court would legally dissolve the marriage, giving legal expression to what had already happened in fact.

Breakdown is based on the principle that marriage is a lifelong covenant but allows for circumstances that may lead to marriage failure. In fact, the group viewed the breakdown with inquest principle as much more compatible with Christian values than doctrines of matrimonial offense that involved the idea of winning or losing—guilt or innocence—in what is in fact a social failure. Under matrimonial offense, the state authoritatively gave permission for one spouse to put away the other for an offense, "separating what God has joined." Whereas, in breakdown, the court would say: "We find on inquiry that this marriage relationship has so irretrievably disintegrated that it is no longer qualified to receive legal recognition: therefore recognition is withdrawn."[37]

The group recommended that reform include specific charges to the court to make provision for reconciliation, to establish procedures for presenting evidence of breakdown, such as are provided with respect to grounds, and to expand the court staff, especially with social workers. Breakdown with inquest would differ from both divorce by consent and offense by the creative and expanded role of the court in helping marriages in distress, either to save them or to end them. The group was adamant that if the law were changed, breakdown with inquest must be the sole grounds for divorce and not be added to current matrimonial offenses. To retain offense would perpetuate all the drawbacks of the present law and not involve the state effectively and meaningfully in investigation and reconciliation. Most couples would probably continue to use the fault grounds, thus destroying the purpose of the reform.

Putting Asunder considered objections to the breakdown principle that had been raised by the Morton Commission, especially those dealing with the "innocent wife" divorced against her will. It broke the problem into two parts—finance and status. The financial disadvantages to wives of divorce were not due to divorce law, but to the existing system of financial settlements: "a wife's claim to a proportionate share in insurance benefits and her husband's pension should be recognized and protected; questions of property, maintenance, and enforcement of maintenance should be examined with a view toward improvement . . . our belief is that the establishment of community of property in some form would do much to prevent injustice."[38] The group cautioned that divorce on the basis of breakdown should be made conditional on the financial protection of the respondent and any children.

The Morton Commission had accepted the fact that these financial problems were augmented for most workers whose pay was only enough to support one wife and would not stretch to maintain both a first and second family; a man was obligated to his current wife and a law that required him to pay maintenance he could not afford was useless. The group suggested some restraint: "If society is to have successive polygamy, then the rule must apply that a man may not acquire more wives than he can afford to support. Successive polyandry, though not uncommon, does not as things are, create financial problems so frequently."[39] The second problem, that a married woman would suffer loss of status through no fault of her own, is just not solvable said the group: "when a marriage comes to grief wounding cannot be avoided. Thus it would be an empty title in a marriage that no longer exists in fact."[40]

Putting Asunder, therefore, recommended that the proper divorce law for contemporary society would be based on the principle of marital breakdown. Whether a marriage were broken would be determined by the courts after a thorough investigation. Such a law would be compatible with church teachings if it removed all trace of offense and provided for legal procedures to save troubled marriages and end broken ones. The Archbishop's Group suggested also that the financial and property laws be revised to protect dependent wives, preferably through some form of community of property.

The report was received as a fundamental change in the church's position toward divorce law, even though it was not from an official body. It was praised for its persuasiveness and for generating discussion and study in public opinion and public life. It gave some hope to reformers that the law could at last be changed. Leo Abse announced his intention to introduce a private member bill under the ten-minute rule to add a breakdown provision to the existing law. McGregor commented that the report helped "release the log jam which had obstructed the shaping of a new divorce law . . . the group has done an invaluable service by creating a new atmosphere for the consideration of the proposals for reform already promised by the Law Commission."[41] The most important and immediate effect of the publication of *Putting Asunder* was to encourage the Law Commission, charged with responsibility for law reform, into action.

In its first proposal to the Lord Chancellor and Parliament in 1965, the Law Commission included a carefully worded recommendation that preliminary examination be made of a number of topics in family law including divorce. Lord Gardiner, Scarman, and Gower considered divorce law reform to be a top priority of their work but had been reluctant to proceed remembering the stalemate following the Morton Commission. Gower had testified before the Morton Commission about the abuses of procedures in divorce courts and still recalled the shock with which his revelations were received. "At the time, I was still a practicing solicitor and I thought everybody knew about the practices in the divorce court. They acted as though I was really terrible."[42]

Then in July 1966 *Putting Asunder* was published. Cartwright Sharp, secretary to the commission, suggested that they ask the Lord Chancellor to ask them to comment on the Archbishop's Group's report. This was the break needed to get the commission started working on reform of the divorce law. They sponsored a seminar at Oxford to discuss the reforms and invited judges and law officers. Other than that, they did not consult outside groups in preparing their report. They felt the issue had already been adequately discussed and the major lines of debate fully formed.

The *Field of Choice* was published in November 1966.[43] The title is appropriate, because the report reviewed various suggestions for reform. Instead of advocating a particular choice, as Cartwright Sharp commented, it showed the Lord Chancellor "what is not on" and which of the reforms would be reasonable and workable. The goal was to "mark out the boundaries of the field of choice," leaving it up to Parliament to settle the social issues involved. Before reviewing the field, the commission recommended proper goals for marriage and divorce law:

"(i) to buttress, rather than undermine, the stability of marriage;

(ii) when, regrettably, a marriage has irretrievably broken down, to enable the empty shell to be destroyed with the maximum fairness, and the minimum bitterness, distress and humiliation."[44]

The report summarized both arguments in favor and opposed to current law. However, it was clear that the commission considered the present law to be incompatible with its goals. Although the law made divorce difficult, it was unrealistic and in disrepute. It caused unnecessary bitterness and through collusion and perjury gave undue advantage to the least scrupulous.

The commission argued that any change in the divorce law would be limited by certain assumptions:

Public opinion would not support any restriction in the divorce law.

The breakdown of marriage usually preceded matrimonial offense on which divorce would be based.

Reconciliation at the time of divorce, as recommended by the group, would be too late to do any good.

Little support would exist for an increase in funds to be spent on divorce proceedings.

Divorce should not be automatic.

Courts must make sure that an economically dependent spouse is fully provided for.

The commission agreed that breakdown should be the underlying principle of the divorce law, rather than offense, but they opposed the group's recommendation that the court investigate every marriage and get involved with reconciliation before granting divorce. With the volume of divorce, such services and inquests would be much too costly. They suggested, rather, that divorce be based on breakdown with a simpler test:

1. Has the marriage broken down?
2. If the marriage has broken down is there reasonable prospect for reconciliation?
3. Is there any reason of public policy (such as, justice to wives and children) why the marriage should not be dissolved? If not, what are the arrangements made for the financial care of the parties and the children?

Under this test, breakdown might be based on the testimony of the parties concerned or a period of separation. "The parties are likely to be better judges of the viability of their own marriage than a court can hope to be, even with the most elaborate and searching inquest."[45]

The commission considered divorce by consent and separation. The former would require elaborate safeguards to make sure that the spouse was not coerced into giving consent. Other grounds for divorce would be retained for cases where there was no consent. Separation might be workable if there were two periods—one for divorce with consent and one, longer, where there would be divorce regardless of consent.

A number of safeguards were suggested to be part of any reform: a three-year waiting period as in the current law; power of the court to adjourn proceedings if reconciliation seems possible; discretion to refuse divorce if the attempts were made to deceive the court; adequate provision made for dependent spouse and children. The commission considered the latter point in terms of the problems brought up in *Putting Asunder* of an innocent wife divorced against her will. They noted that the economic interest of the wife was in her pension and the shelter of the matrimonial home. In divorce her security would inevitably diminish, they reported, as few wage earners could afford to support more than one home. More radical reforms were needed if wives were not to suffer materially, and the commission alerted the public that it was working on the problem: "We agree with the Archbishop's Group that if the law changes so an innocent wife can be divorced against her will, there should be a bar where the court could refuse if not satisfied the property settlements were equitable."[46] Referring to the loss of status the innocent wife would suffer, the commission agreed with the group that divorce is really a symptom of marital breakup. It made little sense for a wife to be able to retain a status in name only. "From the point of view of the wife herself, it is not clear that the status of rejected wife is at present day superior in society's esteem to that of a divorcee."[47] A wife may feel insecure in her marriage as she grows older, but keeping the law as it is is no bar to the philandering husband. If he wants to find a younger woman, he will, and the law can do nothing about it.

According to the Law Commission, the field of choice for divorce law reform did not realistically include either retention of the current law or adoption of a new law based on the Archbishop's Group's suggestions. It agreed that the breakdown principle was sound but considered the expense in investigating and counseling every couple filing for divorce to be excessive and prohibitive. The commission suggested instead that breakdown be combined with fault and separation provisions. It considered the need for financial safeguards for the dependent spouse and children and especially for a wife divorced against her will under a separation provision.

The Lord Chancellor initiated a debate on *Putting Asunder* and the *Field of Choice* in the House of Lords, 23 November 1966. The debate indicated that the gap between the Law Commission and the Archbishop's Group would have to be bridged before a formal proposal for reform could be introduced. During debate, the ground rules for such an agreement were put forward. First, the principle of breakdown had overwhelming support. Lord Denning reported that in practice the principle was already used in the divorce court. "In law we have to find cruelty, adultery, or desertion, and we have to use our discretion, but the day to day practice of our courts is to act on the principle of the breakdown of the marriage."[48] For example, he said, fifteen years before, judges had redefined cruelty to include the intent to injure. Since 1964 proof of intent was no longer required, only that an intolerable situation had been created.

Second, there was little interest in requiring investigation in the face of the Law Commission's conclusion that it would be too expensive. Lady Summerskill argued that an inquest was unrealistic: people don't want to bring all their troubles out in the open—that's why there are so many undefended divorce cases. Denning said inquests would be unnecessary in most cases. He observed that judges usually have little difficulty in determining breakdown, since most couples have already separated permanently. Most of those who spoke saw no reason why breakdown could not be combined with offense and separation provisions instead of investigation. However, some were concerned about the effects of "compulsory divorce."

The Lord Chancellor notified the peers that the government would remain neutral on the divorce issue but indicated his own sympathy with the proposals for reform. The Archbishop of Canterbury agreed that reform was advisable and that the church no longer demanded that divorce laws be similar to church doctrine. However, the church would not favor a law where civil marriages could be broken at the will of the spouses rather than the court speaking for the community. The Bishop of Exeter, chair of the Archbishop's Group, closed debate by informing the Lords that he would have "a friendly discussion with Mr. Justice Scarman and one other member of the Law Commission about this gap between divorce with inquest and divorce without inquest."[49] He believed that gap was bridgeable and that the two groups could come to an agreement on a practicable way of having a divorce law based on the breakdown principle.

It took seven months for an agreement acceptable to both the group and the Law Commission to be reached. The "Consensus" published 2 June 1967 proposed that divorce law be based solely on the breakdown principle that had been accepted by the church assembly in February. "'But in place of the proposed inquest the court is directed to infer breakdown, in the absence of evidence to the contrary, on proof of the existence of certain matrimonial situations.'"[50] Situations signifying breakdown would be intolerable adultery by the respondent, intolerable conduct by the respondent, desertion for two years, separation for two years and agreement by the respondent, and separation for five years. Safeguards would require a three-year waiting period after marriage to petition, notification by the court of reconciliation opportunities, the right of the court to dismiss proceedings in the event of reconciliation, and satisfactory financial arrangements for the respondent and children.

The compromise between the church and the Law Commission prevented the adoption of a policy wholeheartedly embracing the concept of marriage as a relationship of shared responsibilities between the sexes. It retained the idea of matrimonial offense as a means of defining breakdown, because the church would not accept a policy based totally on consent, denying the court discretion in determining whether to grant a divorce. The separation provisions provide couples with such an alternative but require a longer waiting period than other proofs based on fault.

In April the Law Commission published Working Paper No. 9 on the financial aspects of family law in divorce and circulated it among various interest groups and individuals.[51] This action had been long awaited by the feminists seeking to achieve equal financial status for married women. The Working Paper, however, was limited to the subject of maintenance and did not discuss property rights. In determining the adequacy of a maintenance agreement as a result of divorce, the Law Commission recommended that the court look at the following: conduct of the spouses in relation to each other; duty of spouses to care for and bring up any children in the family; domestic arrangements of the spouses; earning capacity of each spouse and the extent, if any, to which that capacity has been impaired through age, illness, or disability of mind or body and has for the time being diminished by reason of the fact that the spouse is receiving instruction at an educational establishment or is undergoing training for a trade, profession, or vocation; the earnings and other resources, if any, of each spouse; financial obligations of each spouse regardless of matrimonial offense. The report included what was by now ritual admonition that the law should protect the wife from the loss of her pension.

WILSON DIVORCE BILL 1967

Now that agreement on a viable reform of the divorce law had been reached, the problem arose of how to introduce it into Parliament. The Law Commission could not introduce legislation, sensitive as it was to the prerogatives of Parliament. Even after all of the compromise between the commission and the church, the government still refused to sponsor any bill on divorce. Lord Gardiner, who had advocated reform, explained that no government had ever sponsored a bill expanding the grounds of divorce. Gower, a member of the Law Commission, commented that although there were Catholics in the Cabinet, the real reason for not sponsoring the reform was the belief that no votes would be gained, and many would be lost from such purely social issues. A sponsor of the reform in the Commons explained that divorce, like homosexuality, abortion, and hanging was an issue that government would not touch.

Leo Abse, MP, realized that divorce reform must originate as a private member bill. After the ballot in 1967, newspapers reported that William Wilson, Labour MP, had received fourth place and was the chosen one, even before Wilson himself had been told. He was a likely sponsor. A solicitor with some experience with divorce law, he was interested in social reform and was a member of the Labour party that had a substantial majority in the House.

Notwithstanding their official reaction, the government lent support to the sponsors of the bill in a number of ways. First, a bill based on the "Consensus" report was drafted by a parliamentary counsel at the Law Commission. The commission staff was not under the control of the government, but the Lord Chancellor accepted the active role of the staff in assisting preparation of the bill. Then commission members, especially family law expert Gower, assisted sponsors with drafting problems and wrote commentaries on various sections of the bill. Finally, the government provided parliamentary time to finish deliberations on the bill.

The bill was printed in November 1967. It provided that breakdown be the sole ground for divorce and that the proof of breakdown be intolerable adultery, intolerable conduct, desertion or separation for two years with consent, separation for five years without consent—in other words, precisely what the Law Commission and the Archbishop's Group had recommended. Between 1 November 1967 and February 1968 when the Second Reading was held, widespread discussions of the bill took place among interest groups and newspapers. In general, the sponsors received support for the principle of breakdown. A poll published in the *Sunday Times* in June 1967 had indicated that 72 percent of the public agreed with breakdown as the only basis for divorce. Reports in January 1968 confirmed this support. A National Opinion Poll and Gallup Poll showed majority support for provisions in the bill, even the provision for divorce after five years' separation when only one party consents.[52]

The Divorce Law Reform Union (DLRU) offered its services in lobbying for the bill. In October Alistair Service joined the union and changed its primary focus from public-opinion education to pressure on Parliament. Service, fresh from a successful stint with the Abortion Law Reform Association, knew what was required to obtain success with a private member bill. Although the DLRU had been active in the area for nearly sixty years, it changed its goal and its tactics. Until 1966 the organization spoke for the White bill for separation. Now it lobbied for the breakdown principle.

During the months between the First and Second Readings, the outline of controversy on the bill became clear. In favor of the bill were Labour reformers, lawyers, and most women MPs. Opposed were a small coalition of conservatives, Catholics, and Anglicans. A third group supported the bill "with reservations." Most in that group agreed with reform of the law to dissolve marriages upon breakdown rather than matrimonial offense. However, they were concerned about divorce by consent, an innocent wife being divorced against her will, and inadequate financial safeguards and property rights.

The provision of the bill allowing divorce after two years of separation was, in effect, divorce by consent, a principle that had been opposed by the church as well as the Morton Commission. The five-year clause made it possible for an innocent wife to be divorced against her will. In that case, no financial safeguards were in the bill, according to the critics, to protect a wife's pension, financial support, and the children of the first marriage.

Several women's groups were especially active on this point. The Mother's Union, which had opposed all previous attempts at reform, favored the provisions, but opposed divorce by consent and expressed concern about the financial status of women. The Mother's Union fought against the separation clauses, especially the five-year clause, because they meant no one was safe from divorce. The union also wanted satisfactory safeguards for the innocent wife.

The National Council of Women (NCW) of Great Britain considered the divorce bill at its annual general meeting just before the Second Reading. It too agreed with the provisions of breakdown but was opposed to the automatic divorce after five years of separation regardless of consent. The NCW resolved that divorce after separation must be dependent on adequate financial safeguards for wife and children, and courts should be empowered to prevent divorce without such provisions. The council argued that suffering of a deserted wife with children was much more than that of a deserted husband, because prolonged financial stringency was less likely in the latter case. The divorce bill was of special concern to women.

The most publicized argument against the bill with respect to its effect on women came from Lady Edith Summerskill in a speech before the Married Women's Association at Caxton Hall in January 1968. Lady Summerskill had been interested in economic protection for dependent housewives through her work in the MWA and through her sponsorship of the Matrimonial Homes Act in 1967.[53] She dubbed the Divorce Reform Bill a "Casanova's Charter." She described the five years' separation provision as an open invitation for a middle-aged man to cast aside his wife in favor of a younger woman. The devoted wife, aging, no longer attractive, and financially dependent, was vulnerable to divorce and had no guarantee of financial support in her old age.

During the Second Reading debate, Wilson defended the financial safeguards in his bill.[54] As the DLRU had pointed out on the eve of the debate, the bill provided more financial security than the present law. Specifically, Wilson referred to Clauses 5 through 7: the court could refuse a divorce if it imposed financial hardship, such as loss of a pension (Clause 5). The court must be satisfied that the provision made for the wife be "reasonable and fair or the best that could be made in the circumstances" (Clause 7); the respondent may object to divorce decree if misled about the financial arrangements after the divorce (Clause 6).

Sponsors believed little else could be put in the bill that would be realistic in a measure on divorce. A man with two families to support would be bound to have financial difficulties, and little could be done about that. Joan Lestor pointed out that the position of women had changed fundamentally over the previous forty years, and that most women were no longer financially dependent. Lena Jeger accepted the criticisms and remarked that other legislation on property and pensions was needed to solve them. Norman St. John-Stevas agreed, but suggested the problems of the financially dependent spouse be taken care of before a potentially unjust divorce reform was passed.

In general, the sponsors insisted that their bill provided the best financial safeguards possible and suggested that those concerned with the issues of property and finance look elsewhere for necessary reforms. Leo Abse considered the criticism symptomatic of a broad social problem that could not be resolved by the divorce bill. The debate brought out "the avalance of protest, anxiety, and interpretation, mainly from middle aged, middle class, deserted housewives, that I endured with each post [which] taught me that all the compromises, additions and alterations we could make in the bill could not give those sad women the emotional security they sought."[55] So the sponsors went ahead with their bill as it stood, confident that adequate support was there in the Commons, and concentrated on securing time for all parliamentary stages.

The Wilson bill passed a Second Reading, 9 February 1968, 159-63, and was committed to Committee C. The committee met weekly during March, April, and May. Considerable discussion and lobbying occurred at this stage, but the bill came through with little substantial change. The Lord Chancellor's Office and the Law Commission helped to draft amendments. But the bill had to be withdrawn, since it was too late in the session for the government to afford to give the necessary time. The fact that it had survived both the Second Reading and committee stages encouraged reformers and government supporters that it would eventually become law. The steps taken on the Wilson bill were not in vain. As B. H. Lee noted, "it transformed public opinion into legislative opinion and established a *fait accompli* by providing a ready made bill for the next round."[56]

JONES AND BISHOP BILLS, 1968-1969

The next round began with the opening of the parliamentary session in the autumn of 1968. Divorce reformers announced through the newspapers their intention to press on. Again, they had to find a sponsor from the private member ballot. They recruited Alec Jones who had drawn ninth place. The Second Reading debate was held before Christmas but did not go as smoothly as before. Jones reviewed the goals and provisions of the bill repeating many of Wilson's arguments from the year before. He summarized the financial safeguards that had been moved by the committee to Clauses 4, 5, 6. The opposition was under the vocal and enthusiastic leadership of Bruce Campbell: "Every time one makes a divorce easier, one makes marriage cheaper, and people tend more and more to enter into marriage as an experiment, feeling that if it doesn't work out there is always the divorce court—in rather the same way they enter into a business partnership."[57] He considered this a weakening of marriage and family stability: the bill gave license to husbands to desert their wives.

The proponents sought to establish their arguments about the need for divorce reform and show the support that the concept of marital breakdown received from the community, especially the church, lawyers, and women's groups. They argued that the picture painted by the opponents of legions of innocent, frightened, middle-aged, dependent wives was unrealistic and certainly exaggerated. Young people received the most divorces, and both men and women petitioned. Seventy-five percent of divorced women remarried. As Abse summed up the debate: "the bill affirms its intention not to have an easier divorce law, but to have a more rational one, one that is more humane, more compassionate, and in my view more in keeping with the civilized feelings of our people."[58]

The Second Reading debate lasted five and one-half hours over two days. The government allotted four hours the second day (a Tuesday) in keeping with its commitment to give divorce reform a fair hearing. The vote, 183-106, in favor showed a majority of seventy-seven, smaller than the year before. The bill was then sent to Committee B. Opponents took their arguments to the press and urged women to fight it. The *Economist* advised that if the bill's suppporters wanted to be sure it became law, they should offer to try to strengthen the clause, giving financial protection to the unwilling respondent.[59]

The criticism of the financial provisions of the Divorce Reform Bill intensified. The bill's supporters continued to defend the financial clauses as adequate. Out of the controversy came specific proposals for a complete reform of matrimonial property law. Olive Stone, senior lecturer in family law at the London School of Economics, was the chief advocate for "community of gains." An article by Stone and Antonia Heald outlining her proposal had been included in *Law Reform Now,* Gerald Gardiner and Andrew Martin's 1963 book proposing the Law Commission. In their essay, they criticized proposals for community property. Rather, Stone and Heald advocated equal partnership in marriage based on a "community of gains" or "community of surplus." The problem with community of property was with management. To have the manager be the husband would be inconsistent with equality of the sexes. Without clear lines of authority, however, spouses would be running to court all of the time to settle their differences.

Under community of gains, each spouse would retain his or her separate assets. Neither could dispose of the matrimonial home without the consent of the other. Upon termination of the marriage, any assets above what was held at the beginning of the marriage would have to be shared equally. Stone and Heald agreed that the court decisions had been proceeding in the direction of shared gains in marriage, but these gains could not be relied upon in every case, since such decisions conflicted with the established statutory principle of separate property.

As legal advisor to the National Council for Women, Stone criticized the Law Commission's Working Paper No. 9 for failing to deal with the issue of matrimonial property. Stone's chance to influence policy came through her work with Justice, the British Section of the International Commission of Jurists. Justice was an organization of 1,500 lawyers interested in law reform and representing all three political parties. In 1968 the issue of marital property came up before the Civil Law Committee of Justice, and a subcommittee on matrimonial property was formed to study it. The committee was composed of Olive Stone; Joe Harper, a barrister and member of Justice; and Joseph Jackson, QC, prominent divorce lawyer and author. They held discussions, and Stone drafted a bill based on her proposal for community of gains. The committee intended to append it to its report, but did not expect much support from Justice. According to one member of the committee, the leadership did not want to support any reforms that might be considered too radical, and community of gains would substantially alter the doctrine of separate property that had been evolving since the 1800s.

At the beginning of the 1968-1969 parliamentary session, Edward Bishop, Labour MP, received third place in the private member ballot. He had been concerned that the divorce bill lacked adequate financial provisions and that neither its sponsors nor the government seemed to be doing anything about it. He had been discussing a bill for joint ownership of the matrimonial home proposed by the Married Women's Association. He asked Justice for assistance in drafting a bill. Bishop worked closely with Olive Stone, and they drafted a bill that went beyond the ownership of the home and provided for equal division of family property in divorce.

The bill enabled the court, upon application of either spouse at divorce or separation, to divide equally all property of the marriage except separate property, that is, property owned by either spouse at the time of the marriage or obtained as a result of gift or bequest. If a couple disagreed about the value of any item of property, the court would be required to determine its value. The spouses could refuse to have property divided if each were advised by a different solicitor and signed the agreement out of the presence of the other spouse or his/her relatives.

The Matrimonial Property Bill, more commonly known as the Bishop bill, was given a First Reading and was printed on 27 November 1968, a week or so before the Second Reading debate on the Jones divorce bill. It was cosponsored by Peter Archer, Dan Awdry, Robert Edwards, Dame Joan Vickers, Dr. Shirley Summerskill, Eric Heffer, Joyce Butler, Gordon Oakes, Eric Lubbock, Jill Knight, and Douglas Houghton. Some of them had opposed the divorce bill because of the inadequate financial provisions.

Bishop's proposal received enthusiastic support among interest groups that had been concerned about the injustice of the new divorce bill to dependent wives. In 1967 the National Conference on Labour Women had adopted a resolution urging the government to introduce legislation for joint ownership of the matrimonial home. A new resolution adopted in 1968 was reported by the Chief Woman Officer:

> The National Joint Committee accepted the principle that breakdown of marrriage be the criteria for divorce but felt the provisions for financial arrangements embodied in the bill before Parliament were unsatisfactory and that the reform of the matrimonial property laws should proceed simultaneously with reform of divorce laws. Full support was given to the private member's bill on matrimonial property laws and the National Joint Committee asked the government to give the same facilities to this bill that are being given to the divorce law reform bill.[60]

The Six Point Group supported the Bishop bill. They reported: "At long last we have a bill based on equal partnership in marriage . . . the implications of the bill can easily be recognized as stabilizing the institution of marriage, to provide for the wife in every case and at the same time allowing the judicial flexibility necessary in an inherently complex relationship."[61] The Mother's Union viewed the Bishop bill as a step in the right direction, but only a limited one. It signed a joint resolution with the Council of Married Women to that effect. It continued to oppose the separation clauses in the divorce bill and maintained that more fundamental reforms in family property law would be required before the divorce bill would cease to be a hardship to women.

The Lord Chancellor, the Law Commission, and much of the legal community opposed the Bishop bill. They viewed property law, unlike divorce law, as a matter for legal experts, not private members. It was automatically assumed that a private member bill in this area would be poorly drafted. Bishop met with the Lord Chancellor and discussed his proposal. Gardiner strongly urged him to introduce another bill. Bishop argued that no safeguards were in the divorce bill, and he considered the issue to be of vital importance. Gardiner countered by reminding him that the Law Commission was working on a family property report, and the government would oppose all attempts at amending the law before it appeared, despite the fact that the report would not be available until the next session after the Jones bill was passed. Bishop decided to proceed with his property bill.

Between Christmas and 24 January 1969, the day for the Second Reading, Bishop mounted a big campaign on television and radio. He spoke to women's groups and asked them to lobby their MPs. The DLRU thought the Bishop bill might win more support for the Jones bill and helped to mobilize support. Many women's groups who had opposed divorce said they would be a lot happier with the principle of marital breakdown if something like the Bishop bill were passed.

On the eve of the Second Reading, an editorial in the *Times* agreed with the government's support for the Jones divorce bill and opposition to the Bishop property bill. The Bishop bill was not the way to solve the problem:

> It picks up the promising idea of community of matrimonial property but leaves the legislature with too little, and the courts with far too much, of the work of translating the idea into a system of law.[62]

The *Times* advised Parliament to wait for the Law Commission report and not to rush the issue.

A *Guardian* news story on the Tuesday before the Second Reading reported on a conflict within the Parliamentary Labour Party (PLP) over the Bishop bill. Lord Gardiner, adamant that the matter be left to the Law Commission, issued a three-line Ministerial Whip against the bill. This meant that Ministers had to be there and vote against the bill. Bishop did not hear of the government's action until he read about it in the paper; he was furious. As a Labour backbencher, he felt he had been struck by his own party leaders on a matter that was within his rights as a private member. With a third place on the private member ballot, he did not need the government's assistance to get adequate time for a Second Reading. He did not expect such opposition to his measure. The government apparently considered the bill a serious threat. The Whip was recognition of the support for matrimonial property rights Bishop had been able to gain in only two months.

The matter was vigorously contested in the PLP meeting on Thursday night, the eve of the Second Reading debate. Bishop and Gordon Oakes led the protest against the leaders with the support from women MPs. Prime Minister Wilson, after the debate and consultation with the Lord Chancellor, removed the Whip and made the matter a conscience vote. The next morning the *Times* reported that Bishop was prepared to listen to offers from the Front Bench that might meet the need that prompted his bill, that is, "fair financial provision for wives who may be divorced against their will."

The Second Reading debate took place on Friday, 24 January 1969. Leo Abse, chief proponent of the divorce bill, later wrote that the whole Bishop business had taken him by complete surprise. He tended to think the issue a bit overblown and described the bill as "hideously drafted by some supporting shameless academics."[63] He was impressed that the opponents of his divorce bill were willing to reconsider if the Bishop bill or something like it were adopted. He thus planned to feign support for the bill during the debate and at the proper time (timing in these matters is most important) ask the government to introduce a bill based on the recommendations of the Law Commission. The government would agree, and the Bishop group could safely withdraw its bill, thinking it had won concessions from the government. "And meantime the way to the conclusion of the divorce bill would be clear. I laid on the scheme with the connivance of those in authority."[64]

Bishop opened the debate, and he and Jill Knight (Conservative) presented the major arguments in favor of the bill. The basic argument was two-fold. First, statutes based on separate property made it difficult or impossible for married women to obtain any property, since a majority were not employed and instead were homemakers and mothers. They could not depend on maintenance alone:

> Young children in a home prevent a married woman going out to earn and have all the protection of the 1882 Act. Such a woman has no legal rights to income and is dependent on her husband. On divorce, the wife is even more conscious of dependence with maintenance orders which can be enforced only if the ex-husband can pay. The problem is that so many husbands either have not the means to maintain a wife and family or more often, do not intend to do so and the wife is left high and dry.[65]

The second part of the argument was that the unpaid work of a wife and mother had economic value that should be recognized in the family property law. The wife's work taking care of the home and family allowed the husband to concentrate on his job or career. Yet in the law the contribution of the wife and mother was thought to be of negligible worth when the marriage broke down. As Knight pointed out: "it is not until a man is left with young children to look after that he begins to realize the great benefit of his wife to him in economic terms."[66] The proponents urged the bill in view of the imminent divorce reform and the fact that the government and the Law Commission were moving so slowly. They warned that it would be a grave injustice for the divorce reform to go into effect with no change in the property law.

Early in the debate, Abse made his move. It's a good idea, he said, but let's leave it to the experts in the Law Commission, and by next session we'll have a really good bill. He asked the Solicitor General: "Is it not correct that it is possible and practicable to have in the hands of the government, in sufficient time before the next session begins, the full proposals relating to financial relief together with a draft bill from the Law Commissioners? Secondly, is it not correct that it is presently anticipated that such proposals should include new powers to break up family property?"[67] He then noted that the wisest course for the Solicitor General to follow would be not to oppose or seek to destroy the bill, but to pledge to implement Law Commission recommendations the next session, and then the proponents would be satisfied that the problem would be solved.

The Solicitor General failed to give any guarantees with respect to future legislation. He opposed the Bishop bill as an impracticable and impossible burden on the judiciary. He noted the Law Commission was working on the problem and would have a report by July. He cautioned that passing a reform measure while the Law Commission was working on it might jeopardize relations between Parliament and the commission, a point that was not very favorable to supremacy-conscious MPs. He did not give guarantees that the government would solve the problem in the next session.

The debate continued, and Abse's plan failed. It became evident in the course of the debate that not only would no guarantees from the government be forthcoming, but that the report of the Law Commission, due the following July, would not include any provisions for property. They had divided the question of matrimonial finance into issues of maintenance and property. The first working paper had dealt with maintenance only and *that* report was due in July. No working paper on property had yet appeared. Even if the bill's sponsors waited for the Law Commission to act, it appeared that such action would not come until the 1970s, and in the meantime, all knew an election would be held that could change everything.

The rest of the debate brought out opposition arguments. Some opposed the principle of community of gains as "wholly inapt and unadapted to a sophisticated modern society."[68] They argued that the only way to protect women would be to maintain the separate property system and provide for adequate maintenance of the dependent wife in divorce. The drafting of the bill received much criticism. Supporters often agreed with the drafting critique but pushed for acceptance of the bill's principle of equal property division.

The closing argument by Gordon Oakes for the supporters confirmed the importance of the bill as a means of prodding the government to act on issues of property in marriage and divorce. "It is a revolutionary bill. It seeks to revolutionize the status of married women. That is the whole object of it. This is not some icing on the cake for married women. It goes to the root of marriage for the benefit of the wife."[69] He concluded that although the bill had weaknesses, the Commons should approve its principle.

The Bishop bill passed a Second Reading, 86-32. There was jubilation among the floor supporters and the women in the gallery.

Bishop realized, however, that his bill would face obstacles in committee due to the government's opposition. The purpose for sponsoring and supporting the bill in the first place had been to force the government to take action. Now that they had a Second Reading victory to bargain with, Bishop and Oakes decided to make an arrangement with the Lord Chancellor. They chose Awdry, a Conservative, and Lubbock, a Liberal, to represent the bill's sponsors. Bishop wanted an all-party group, so he would not be accused of selling out to his government to get them out of a tough spot. The Attorney General and Solicitor General were there from the government and Scarman and Gower from the Law Commission. Scarman and Gower reviewed their work to date on financial provision in marriage and divorce; it appeared that they still had not thought much about property but promised a report by July. The compromise reached between the Bishop coalition and the government made no guarantees with respect to property, but referred to financial provisions generally.

The Lord Chancellor drafted the following statement to Bishop:

> Sir Leslie Scarman agreed that the Law Commission would be able to report before the end of July on their proposals for matrimonial financial relief. The Divorce Reform Bill contains a provision that it will not come into effect until an order is made by the Lord Chancellor. Without of course committing the Government on its programme for legislation, which I know you would not expect me to do at this stage, I agreed that if you withdraw the Matrimonial Property Bill, I would undertake not to make such an order until Legislation, based on the Law Commission's proposals, had been introduced the next session.

The compromise was that the Law Commission agreed to hurry up its report, the Lord Chancellor (if the government agreed) would sponsor a bill in the next session providing financial security in divorce, and the Lord Chancellor would not let the divorce bill go into effect until such legislation was passed. In return, the sponsors agreed to withdraw the Matrimonial Property Bill. The Attorney General read the agreement during the debate on the Divorce Reform Bill to convince those who had backed Bishop that something would come out of it all and also to gain their support for the divorce reform itself. On 25 February 1969 the Bishop bill on matrimonial property was withdrawn.

Meanwhile the Jones Divorce Reform Bill was in committee. Protest continued about the separation clauses and the financial provisions. The bill passed through intense committee debate with few changes. The grueling sessions of the Report stage continued through the middle of May. The bill's sponsors had to make sure at least 100 supporters were present at certain times to avoid having the bill talked out. With 100 affirmative votes, debate could be ended. After debate on three consecutive Fridays, the government delivered on its promise by allocating time: four weeks hence—an all-night session on June 12. The lobbyists spent the next four weeks making sure enough MPs would attend and remain all night if need be. They received just over 100 pledges of support.

During the all-night session, opponents introduced numerous amendments, most to limit the scope of the bill. None passed, but they used up the time. The most crucial vote came at 8 A.M. when, after ten hours, 177 supporters remained to close debate successfully and defeat an amendment to make religion a bar to divorce. The bill was safe. The Third Reading was completed at 11:40 A.M. The debate had lasted more than thirteen hours; the vote was 109-55. The only significant change in the bill in all that time was to make it mandatory for lawyers to encourage reconciliation.

The House of Lords considered the bill during the summer of 1969. Again, the problem was to make sure enough supporters were present at every stage to defeat the opposition. The DLRU led this work, helped by Mrs. Undine Barker, secretary to the Liberal peers. Lord Stow Hill sponsored the bill, and his main concern was to answer the criticism from Lady Summerskill that the bill was a "Casanova's Charter." She was most concerned that divorce was being made easier without adequate provision for the first wife and children. Lord Gardiner did not repeat his promise to seek to introduce a bill in the next session but touted the adequacy of Clause 6 of the divorce bill: no one could wave a magic wand and make a limited wage packet provide for two families as easily as it did for one; this was the best that could be expected in the circumstances.

The debate lasted about seven hours, and the bill passed Second Reading, 122 Contents-34 Not Contents. The House of Lords met in committee of the whole in July. The proponents of the bill lost one division and accepted an amendment requiring the active consent of the respondent after two years' separation rather than the more passive original language that the respondent "does not object." It was the only defeat for the bill's sponsors on an amendment in either House. The Report stage was completed on July 24, but the long summer recess intervened before the Third Reading on October 13. The Lords' amendments were accepted in the House of Commons on October 17 with Royal Assent on the 20th.

Matrimonial Proceedings and Property Bill

In July 1969 the Law Commission's *Report on Financial Provision in Matrimonial Proceedings* was published. In the preface the commission noted:

It should be emphasized that this report does not attempt a root and branch reform of family property, a far more intractable problem on which we hope in the next few months to publish a preliminary study in a further Working Paper. Nevertheless, if our proposals are implemented they will go some way towards enabling the court on the breakdown of marriage to deal with family assets on an equitable basis, and will therefore achieve some of the objectives sought in the Matrimonial Property Bill. . . .[70]

The commission recommended the following criteria when ordering financial provision in divorce cases:

(i) respective means, needs, earning capacity and financial responsibilities of each spouse;

(ii) the standard of living of the parties;

(iii) the parties respective contribution, direct or indirect, to the welfare of the family, including any contribution looking after the home and children;

(iv) in proceedings for divorce or nullity the value of any benefit such as a pension which by reason of the dissolution or annulment either party will lose the chance of acquiring; and the courts should exercise the powers, so far as is possible, and so far as it is just to do so having regard for the conduct and needs of the parties, to put the spouse in the position he or she ought to have been in had the marriage not broken down.[71]

The commission recommended that the court be given power to transfer property, that damages for adultery be abolished, along with wife's agency of necessity, and that the wife be made liable to pay maintenance on the same basis as the husband.

The report was based on Working Paper No. 9 but was different in a number of important respects. The Working Paper had involved guidelines for maintenance and child support only; the report considered marital property as well and suggested that the court be empowered to transfer property from one spouse to another. The guidelines in the Working Paper involved need and ability to pay only; the report added that the court should take into consideration the contribution of the spouses to the welfare of the family, including work in the care of home and children. This report recommended for the first time that in a divorce, contributions made by an unemployed spouse, usually the wife, to the home and the family entitled that spouse to a claim on the property as well as maintenance. The report, by discussing property rights, went further than the commissioners had promised the Bishop supporters. As a result of the events of 1968-1969, especially the debate on the divorce bill and the support for the Bishop bill, the Law Commission produced a report that substantially augmented the Working Paper.

The Law Commissioners denied that the Bishop bill had any effect on their work. Cartwright Sharp remarked in an interview that its only effect was to slow their progress. Gower admitted that the Bishop agreement probably encouraged the government to consider the report more quickly than it might have otherwise. Proponents of the Bishop bill remained convinced, however, that the Law Commission included the property provisions and recognition of the economic worth of home and child care because of the pressure brought by the Bishop coalition.

Evidence supports both claims. On the one hand, the Law Commission very likely took the debate on the Bishop bill into account when preparing its report. Originally, it did not plan to include any proposals with respect to property in its report on financial provision but save its recommendations for a complete report on family property due in the early 1970s. The commission had been eager to propose reforms that would be accepted widely and not provoke strong opposition in the public or Paraliament. Interest in community of gains shown by the publicity surrounding the Second Reading debate was a measure of the opposition it could expect from a report that failed to take any steps on the property issue. On the other hand, the Law Commission usually is conscious of developments in case law. Since the idea of family assets had been developing in the courts, something about it may have been included regardless of the Bishop bill debates. Denning's decision in *Gissing v. Gissing* (1969, 2 WLR 525) was consistent with his earlier point of view in the *Fribance* and *Rimmer* cases. Gissing involved a divorce where the husband had earned more money than the wife and the matrimonial home was in his name. As part of the settlement, the wife remained in the home while the husband paid for it and she accepted no maintenance. After the husband had remarried, he tried to turn his wife out. While married, she could have prevented the sale. But in divorce, she could not. The court ruled that the house was a family asset in this case, despite the fact that it was in the husband's name:

It comes to this: where a couple by their joint efforts, get a house and furniture, intending it to be a continuing provision for them for their joint lives, it is prima facie inference from their conduct that the house and furniture is a "family asset" in which each is entitled to an equal share. It matters not in whose name it stands: or who pays for what: or who goes out to work and who stays home. If they both contribute to it by their joint efforts, the prima facie inference is that it belongs to both equally: at any rate when each makes a financial contribution which is substantial.

The Law Commission report provided for division of property but stopped short of recommending the share that each spouse should have, leaving that to be determined by the courts in each case. The recommendations were disappointing to Olive Stone, but she was not surprised. In a letter to Lady Helena Nutting of 19 August 1969, she pointed out that the Law Commission was opposed to her proposals for community of gains and had brought up the criticism of "poor drafting" as a red herring hiding its opposition to the principle of her bill.

My own impression is that we shall delude ourselves if we think that the Matrimonial Property bill had done its job. It has raised a real and substantial point and the judges have shown since that they largely agree with its aims. But property is the holy of holies. If women want it they will have to go in and get it. Nobody will offer it to them on a plate, but all sorts of smokescreens about bad drafting and the like will be raised to head them off. I hope they will keep on target.[72]

The report included a draft bill that the Lord Chancellor introduced on 29 October 1969, at the beginning of the next parliamentary session, right after the Royal Assent on the divorce bill. Since the Matrimonial Proceedings and Property Bill was a government measure, it had all the advantages of time and the Whip. In the House of Lords the major opposition came from a frustrated Lady Summerskill: "I really feel that a confidence trick has been played on the women of this country. . . . I believe they felt that this was the year they would be protected and of course it is now too late."[73] She argued that the government had promised to protect deserted wives, but nothing in the Matrimonial Proceedings and Property Bill would do that. "In a situation where a well-behaved wife can be divorced against her will, it is to me grossly inequitable that this puny bill should be offered as a safeguard to herself and her family."[74] As a gesture she proposed an amendment to divide the property in equal shares, but withdrew it due to government opposition.

In the House of Commons, frustration was also evident, especially among the women MPs. They stayed out of the debate. Bishop and Oakes considered the government bill to be a first step. Although an equitable division of family property upon divorce was not included, said Oakes, the Law Commission was reportedly working on an extensive report on family property. "This present bill is a good half loaf; the other half is in the oven."[75] Nevertheless, Bishop's supporters attempted to broaden the bill to include the concept of community during the various stages, with little hope of success due to government control of the proceedings.

The most controversial aspect of the bill turned out to be a procedural provision that urged the courts to consult the Law Commission report in the interpretation and application of the act. This was strongly opposed in the House of Commons as a breach of parliamentary supremacy and occupied much of the debate. The provision became useful to Gardiner in the end. The bill did not get to the Commons for the Report stage until May 26, and by then dissolution was imminent. Gardiner had to pressure the house to get it through. He offered to withdraw the controversial section regarding interpretation in return for a Third Reading before the end of the session. The Report, Third Reading, and Royal Assent were accomplished 26-29 May 1970. On May 29 Parliament was dissolved. A Conservative majority was returned in June, and the government changed. Gardiner barely made good his promise to have a financial bill through before the Divorce Reform Act was due to take effect. Both became the law in January 1971.

What was the importance of the Bishop bill to the policy outcomes on divorce and matrimonial property? Most observers agree that the opposition to the divorce measure might have been much more successful without the government's pledge to introduce a bill with more extensive financial provisions. It is certain that many of the women's groups who had opposed the divorce bill were satisfied with the government's assurances. Although they continued to voice concern about "the innocent wife," they were not as adamant against the reform as previously; this was especially true of the Mothers' Union.

No doubt the government hurried the Law Commission's Report on Financial Provision in response to demands from the Bishop coalition. Its report included property provisions and recognition of the economic worth of the unemployed spouse's contribution to home and children in order to answer demands made by the Bishop coalition, which sought community gains in matrimonial property. Recognition of trends in case law and consultation with interest groups on the Working Paper may also have contributed to the change in the commission's recommendations.

The government seemed very reluctant to deal officially with the financial issue until the Law Commission had made its report. The support shown the Second Reading of the Bishop bill forced the Lord Chancellor to consider the issue. The government was prodded into making the divorce act contingent upon the acceptance of a property act. That this Matrimonial Proceedings and Property Act did not include the concept of community of property indicates the limits of the influence of the Bishop group. But as Bishop and Oakes noted in debate, the concept of equal sharing of family assets is not dead, either in the courts, the Law Commission, or the Commons.

CONFLICT RESOLUTION AND FEMINIST INFLUENCE

Although demands for changes in the law of divorces were often accompanied by criticism of the law as it affected financially dependent married women, the process of decision making was different on the two issues. Demands for divorce law reform centered on some form of marital breakdown. The most limited proposal was to add a provision to the existing fault grounds allowing divorce after a seven-year separation. More basic suggestions were to substitute marital breakdown completely for the doctrine of matrimonial offense as the basis of the law. Opponents of the changes in the divorce laws also ranged from moderate to extreme. The church defined separation as divorce by consent and considered it to be incompatible with public policy, which should encourage the stability of marriage and the family. Some conservatives opposed any change in the law that would make divorce easier, fearing that it would undermine the family as the foundation of society.

The first attempt at resolving conflicts over divorce reform, the Morton Commission in the early fifties, failed. The commission report reflected rather than reduced the divisions in public opinion over divorce; the vote was 9-9-1: nine wanted to keep the law unchanged, nine wanted to add a breakdown provision; and one wanted breakdown to be the sole basis for divorce. The only recommendation agreed upon was to retain matrimonial offense. The effect of the Morton Commission was no change in the law. The demands for reform and the problems that provoked them remained. Another effect of the commission was to postpone the likelihood of any action on the issue for several years. Although the House of Commons had indicated as far back as 1951 that it was ready to consider proposals for divorce reform, the commission deadlock and the Conservative majority in Parliament dimmed hope for a solution.

The second attempt at resolving the conflict over divorce reform was successful. Three important events made a decision possible: change in the church's attitude toward reform; leadership from the permanent Law Commission on all issues of law reform; a Labour majority in the House of Commons committed to change. A group advisory to the Archbishop of Canterbury proposed a reform of the existing divorce law that would completely eliminate matrimonial offense and establish the principle of marital breakdown with court inquest as the sole basis for divorce. The Law Commission agreed that breakdown was the best principle but that inquest by the court in each case would be impossible. The Law Commission and the Archbishop's Group resolved their differences and reached a compromise that combined the three principles of breakdown, offense, and consent in the law. Two of these principles are new and are consistent with the view of marriage as a shared relationship with joint responsibility. The Labour majority did not participate directly in this agreement that broke the deadlock over divorce and made parliamentary enactment of the reform statute possible. But in several ways, having the Labour majority contributed to the outcome. The Law Commission was the creation of the Labour Lord Chancellor Gardiner. The commission staff drafted the divorce bill and assisted the private member sponsors during important legislative steps. The Lord Chancellor was amenable to the change, and the government allowed sufficient time in Parliament for a full consideration. The Labour MPs were reform-minded and had supported substantial changes in abortion, homosexuality, and capital punishment laws.

The conflict resolution process on divorce reform took place in the administration rather than the legislature. Leaders of the church and the Law Commission consolidated proposals for reform. Compromises were reached between the Bishop of Exeter, chair of the Archbishop's Group, and Scarman and Gower from the Law Commission. The Lord Chancellor and the government law officers hovered in the background all during parliamentary consideration. Although it was a private member bill, with extensive lobbying from the Divorce Law Reform Union, the crucial step in the decision-making process, which resolved conflict and allowed a decision, was the agreement between legal and church elites, with government assistance and approval.

Demands for equal financial status for married women accompanied proposals for divorce reform but originated in feminist groups, rather than among divorce lawyers. Proposals ranged from court-enforced guaranteed maintenance through wages for housewives, both of which would retain separate property, to a complete revision of family law to introduce the concept of community of property. There was little opposition to the underlying concept that marriage was an equal partnership. However, opponents found something impractical or radical in every proposal to give financial expression to the equality idea. Court-enforced, guaranteed maintenance was impractical, said opponents, because a man who divorced and remarried would be able to support only one wife and family. Wages for housewives would involve courts in the expenditure of family income, which was a violation of rights of family privacy. Community of property was too drastic a change, alien to English law, and unworkable. Proponents of matrimonial property and financial rights faced the toughest sort of opposition: opponents who agreed with the values but could not envision any way they could be put into effect. Their attitudes were similar to those encountered by Caroline Norton 100 years before as she listened to the House of Lords discuss the financial plight of married women: she likened their attitude to a "Party of miners who have given up the attempt to dig out persons buried in the superincumbent earth. They would be very glad to do something toward amending the laws for women but, really 'the subject is so surrounded with difficulty.' "[76]

The Morton Commission, the Archbishop's Group, and the Law Commission all considered the problem of the financial status of married women, especially as it affected the financially dependent wife in divorce. The Morton Commission agreed with the equal partnership concept and suggested that an overhaul of the entire matrimonial property law might be required if wives and children were not to suffer as a result of divorce. However, they offered no suggestion for policy.

The Law Commission and the Archbishop's Group concentrated on specific problems of the financially dependent spouse in divorce. Both said that divorce should be granted only if the dependent spouse were adequately provided for, but both recognized the difficulty of trying to require one wage earner to support two families. In preparing the divorce reform, the Law Commission staff left specific financial safeguards in the hands of the courts, empowering them to hold up a divorce until the pension and maintenance had been secured, as much as was "reasonable under the circumstances." The Commission's Working Paper suggested some detailed guidelines of reasonableness. They were all based on need rather than rights and reinforced married women's financial dependence both during and after marriage. None of these suggestions satisfied demands, mostly from feminists, for financial guarantees in divorce.

The Bishop coalition became crucial to the resolution of conflicts on matrimonial property rights in divorce. Bishop had sponsored a community of gains bill in the House of Commons that received a Second Reading. His success was due to a lively campaign waged in the press and Parliament by a coalition of feminist groups, the DLRU, and individual peers and MPs. The government that had delayed action on demands for property reform and that had opposed the Bishop bill met with representatives of the Law Commission and the Bishop coalition. The result was an agreement that the government would sponsor a bill based on the Law Commission's report on financial settlements in divorce before the Divorce Reform Act went into effect. The commission report included a provision for transfer of property, rights to property, and maintenance accrued through unpaid labor in the home. The resulting policy introduced into English statute law the concept of family property that must be divided between the spouses upon divorce. Husband and wife do not automatically have equal shares to property; division is a matter for the courts in each case.

The government and legal elites managed the resolution of conflict over matrimonial property reform with important input from backbenchers and interest groups represented by the Bishop coalition. Decision making, therefore, combined administrative and legislative bodies. The government and the Law Commission were responsible for drafting major provisions of the Matrimonial Proceedings and Property Act. Parliamentary support for more attention to rights of dependent spouses as evidenced by the Second Reading on the Bishop bill forced elites to include additional safeguards. MPs met with government and Law Commission leaders to resolve differences and make sure that the government would take these legislative demands into account. Without these guarantees, both the divorce reform and the property acts would have had much greater difficulty. The mechanism of the private member bill allowed interest groups to obtain effective access to the decision-making process through legislative representatives.

Feminists were much more interested in the effects of marital breakdown on the financial status of women than they were on the issue of breakdown itself. There were several channels of expression on the issue: private individuals, MPs, and peers who took advantage of the forum in Parliament to bring the matter to public attention. Lady Edith Summerskill was especially vocal in calling attention to the so-called Casanova's Charter. Olive Stone used her legal contacts to promote, through her writings and organizational activities, the doctrines of community of gains. Special-interest groups were often led by one or two active women: Juanita Frances and Lady Summerskill of the Married Women's Association and Lady Helena Nutting of the Council of Married Women. Larger women's organizations—the National Council of Women, the Federation of Business and Professional Women's Clubs, the Mother's Union, and the Six Point Group—publicized their resolutions about divorce and property issues, wrote members of Parliament, and consulted with the Law Commission on Working Paper No. 9.

How important were these feminists in influencing the policy giving legal recognition to the economic value of the labor of homemakers? To what extent did these groups and individuals have effective input during the stage of conflict resolution on either divorce or property policy? Feminists did not participate in conflict resolution on divorce reform. That was accomplished among church and legal elites. Feminists did, however, have direct input into the outcome of the property statutes through the Bishop coalition, which in turn was present during the conflict resolution stage. Bishop himself was an advocate of women's rights. Olive Stone, a feminist lawyer, took the lead in drafting the bill Bishop introduced on community of gains in divorce. Feminist groups helped pressure Parliament to pass it on the Second Reading. Those who had been wary of the divorce bill, because it endangered the status of married women, indicated they would support that bill if some sort of property reform were undertaken by the government. The activity of these individuals and groups gave Bishop and his parliamentary supporters the resources and leverage needed to pressure the government and the Law Commission to act. It was only through the private member bill mechanism that groups outside the elite, such as the feminists, were able to have an effect on the policy outcome.

CONCLUSION

The major reforms described in this chapter took place at a time when there was activism in both social reform and lawyer's law. Official legal and religious bodies, along with interest groups, recognized that marriage was an equal relationship, not a patriarchal one. It became widely recognized that people wanted happiness from marriage, and if they did not attain it, they would end their marriages whether the law helped them or not.

English public policy toward the family has been significantly altered through the introduction of the concepts of marital breakdown and family property into divorce and matrimonial property law. Since 1970, proposals for further changes in both divorce and the new doctrine of shared family assets have come from the feminists, the Law Commission, and the church.

NOTES

1. Divorce Reform Act of 1969, 17 *Eliz. 2,* LV.
2. Matrimonial Proceedings and Property Act, Public General Acts, 1970, 45.
3. Statistics on divorce are from the Royal Commission on Marriage and Divorce, 1956, *Report* (Cmnd. 9678); Registrar General's Statisical Review, 1968; Civil Judicial Statistics, 1960-1968.
4. Glanville Williams, ed., *The Reform of the Law* (London: Gollancz, 1951), 142.
5. Ronald Fletcher, *Britain in the Sixties: The Family and Marriage* (Bath: Penguin, 1962); Michael Young and Peter Willmott, *Family and Kinship in East London* (London: Routledge & Kegan Paul, 1957); Elizabeth Bott, *Family and Social Network* (London: Tavistock, 1957).
6. Rimmer v. Rimmer, 1953, QB 63 (C.A.), 76.
7. Fribance v. Fribance, 1957, AER 357 (C.A.), 99.
8. Parliamentary Debates, Official Report, V *Hansard* (House of Commons) 485, c. 926.
9. Ibid., c. 931.
10. Ibid., c. 965.
11. Ibid., c. 935.
12. Ibid., c. 965.
13. Council of Married Women, *Committee files* (1952-1959), Fawcett Library, London.
14. Royal Commission on Marriage and Divorce, 1956, *Report* (Cmnd. 9678), 19.
15. B. H. Lee, *Divorce Reform in England* (London: Peter Owen, 1974), 31.
16. Royal Commission on Marriage and Divorce, 1956, *Report,* 175.
17. Oliver R. McGregor, *Divorce in England: A Centenary Study* (London: Heineman, 1957), x.
18. V *Hansard* (House of Commons) 671, c. 806.
19. V *Hansard* (House of Lords) 250, c. 389.
20. Ibid., c. 400.
21. Ibid., c. 1528.
22. Married Women's Association, Papers, 1952-1970, Fawcett Library, London.
23. Council of Married Women, *Committee files* (1952-1959), Fawcett Library, London.

24. Six Point Group, "Pamphlet" (1961), British Library, London.

25. Status of Women Committee, *Manifesto* (1960), Fawcett Library, London.

26. Fletcher, *The Family and Marriage,* 128.

27. Quoted by John H. Farrar, *Law Reform and the Law Commission* (London: Sweet & Maxwell, 1974), chap. 1.

28. Reported by Cartwright Sharp in personal interview (3 February 1976), Law Commission, London.

29. Williams, *The Reform of the Law.*

30. Gerald Gardiner and Andrew Martin, eds., *Law Reform Now* (London: Gollancz, 1963), 1.

31. Farrar, *Law Reform and the Law Commission,* 22.

32. Law Com. No. 107/1981, *Fifteenth Annual Report, 1979-1980.*

33. Sir Leslie Scarman, *Law Reform, the New Pattern* (London: Routledge & Kegan Paul, 1968).

34. David McKie and Chris Cook, *The Decade of Disillusion: British Politics in the Sixties* (London: Macmillan, 1972), 199.

35. Archbishop's Group, *Putting Asunder: A Divorce Law for Contemporary Society* (London, 1966), 14-15.

36. Ibid., 38-39.

37. Ibid., 65.

38. Ibid., 47-48.

39. Ibid., 73.

40. Ibid., 49.

41. *Sunday Times,* 31 July 1966, 9.

42. Personal Interview with Gower (27 January 1976), William Goodenough House, London.

43. Law Com. No. 6/1966, *Reform of the Grounds of Divorce: The Field of Choice* (Cmnd. 3123).

44. Ibid., 10.

45. Ibid., 26.

46. Ibid., 22.

47. Ibid., 22.

48. V *Hansard* (House of Lords) 266, c. 310.

49. Ibid., c. 347.

50. Actual title of the agreement was "Reform of Grounds of Divorce. Result of Discussion between the Archbishop's Group on Divorce and Law Commission." Appendix III to Law Com. No. 15/1968, *Third Annual Report, 1967-1968* (H.C. 312), 30-32.

51. Law Commission Working Paper No. 9/1967 (25 April 1967) *Family Law, Matrimonial and Related Proceedings: Financial Relief.*

52. Reported in Lee, *Divorce Reform in England,* 97-107.

53. The Matrimonial Homes Act protects the right of a spouse occupying the matrimonial home not to be evicted by the other spouse who owns

the home except through court order. A dependent spouse may file claim at land registry office ensuring her an interest in the matrimonial home; it cannot be sold without her consent.

54. V *Hansard* (House of Commons) 758, c. 810.

55. Leo Abse, *Private Member* (London: Macdonald, 1973), 178.

56. Lee, *Divorce Reform in England,* 107.

57. V *Hansard* (House of Commons) 774, c. 2044.

58. Ibid., 775, c. 1130.

59. *Economist,* 14 December 1968, 44.

60. National Conference of Labour Women, *Annual Report* (1968), 9, Labour Party, London.

61. Six Point Group, *Newsletter* (January 1969), British Library, London.

62. *Times,* 23 January 1969.

63. Abse, *Private Member,* 190.

64. Ibid., 199.

65. V *Hansard* (House of Commons) 774, c. 805.

66. Ibid., c. 827.

67. Ibid., c. 824.

68. [Percy Grieve, MP] Ibid., c. 867.

69. Ibid., c. 888.

70. Law Com. No. 25/1969, *Family Law: Report on Financial Provision in Matrimonial Proceedings* (H.C. 448).

71. Ibid., 40.

72. Council of Married Women, *Papers* (1965-1970), Fawcett Library, London.

73. V *Hansard* (House of Lords) 305, c. 501.

74. Ibid., c. 504.

75. V *Hansard* (House of Commons) 794, c. 1575.

76. Jane Gray Perkins, *The Life of Mrs. Norton* (London: Murray, Albemarle, 1910), 244.

The Policy Process and Feminist Influence 6

THE POLICIES

This study has compared the provisions of several statutes that changed public policy toward sex roles in the family. English policy has evolved from fostering separate roles and unequal status for women toward viewing marriage as a shared relationship of partners with equal status. These revisions in the laws of divorce and matrimonial property law also demonstrate trends in modernization of the law. Each statute continued progress toward uniformity of application of legal rules, greater specialization in new principles and procedures to meet social needs, and equality of treatment according to sex, class, and income. Civil divorce and divorce courts established in 1857 were the first step in specialization. They were followed by the development of a new area of law regulating married women's property. Recent reforms again introduce new concepts—marital breakdown and family property. Each of these legal concepts has been brought into the law to accommodate demands on the legal system due to changes in the family structure, status of women, and work patterns.

Before 1857 parliamentary divorce and equity marriage settlements applied only to the rich. Nineteenth-century statutes sought to extend these legal provisions uniformly throughout the population. Demands for extension of divorce jurisdiction to county courts was also motivated by the need for uniformity. Concern that all people be able to secure benefits and rights under the law led to liberalization of the divorce law in the 1930s. It was not until legal aid reforms and extension of divorce jurisdiction to county courts in the 1950s and 1960s that all people had access to divorce regardless of income, and the law was administered uniformly.

Every liberalization of the divorce law permitted new groups to enjoy benefits of law previously reserved only for the wealthy. The more grounds for divorce and the more courts granting them, the narrower the gap between rich and poor. In addition, of course, these laws have greatly reduced the legal inequality of the sexes in marriage removing the common law principle of coverture almost entirely. At present, with the new concepts of equal partnership and family assets, policymakers are trying to come to terms with the economic dependency of women in marriage.

These law reforms also reflect the interplay between statutes and judge-made case law. Judges, through decisions in individual cases, begin to develop new ways of treating marriage and divorce. Typically, statutes are enacted when courts are unable to incorporate these new ideas fully into law through case decisions alone. Therefore, the statutes are not innovative in themselves but refine and extend practices already developed in the courts. The 1857 Divorce and Matrimonial Causes Act, which established civil divorce, was based on long-standing practices of the ecclesiastical courts and Parliament. The church had granted divorce *a mensa et thoro* (separation) when offenses of adultery, cruelty, or unnatural crimes had been committed. Parliament passed acts of divorce *a vinculo* on grounds of the wife's adultery and, in four cases, the husband's adultery plus incest or desertion. The 1857 act retained the principles of offense for both separation and divorce.

Long before the next reform in 1937, the simple ground of adultery, which had been extended to both men and women in 1923, became too restrictive to apply to the complexities of marriage. The law was stretched and manipulated both in and out of court. The 1937 act, which expanded the grounds of divorce to include desertion, cruelty, and insanity, was adopted to regularize and legitimize the marriage and divorce behavior already practiced.

The 1857 and 1937 acts were both based on the ecclesiastical principle of matrimonial offense that, as a violation of sacred, later civil, vows, was punished by separation or divorce from one's family. In 1969 a statute introduced a new principle of divorce into the law: irretrievable breakdown. This principle, too, had been practiced in the courts before its formal enactment. Divorce judges had found it necessary to look beyond unconvincing evidence of adultery, cruelty, or desertion to see if the marriage relation itself had broken down. The concept of matrimonial offense, despite the increased number of grounds, was not applicable to many contemporary marriages, and judges had begun to adjust the law to fit the cases before them.

Some statutory changes in matrimonial property law also have made existing practice in the courts uniform throughout the country. The 1882 act provided equity practices of protecting married women's property for all women in the guise of "separate property." As in equity law, a woman was not personally liable for debts and contracts but only to the extent of her separate property. In 1970 the new concept of family assets was introduced into statute law. Although the practice was not widespread, some courts were already making lump-sum maintenance settlements and awarding interest in the matrimonial home on other than purely financial contributions and need, that is, on the evidence of unpaid contributions to the home.[1]

The exception to this interaction between litigation and statutes is found in those matrimonial property statutes that introduced ideas of sexual equality previously avoided by the courts. When called upon to interpret the 1882 Married Women's Property Act, for example, the courts adhered to judge-made doctrines of coverture and equity marriage settlements. Neither was based on equal rights. It took four statutes and seventy-eight years for Parliament to guarantee that married women had equal rights outside the home with respect to their earnings and property. In 1857 a woman legally separated from her husband was given full *feme sole* property rights. The Married Women's Property Acts of 1870 and 1882 established married women's rights to own their earnings and property. The Law Reform Act of 1935 made married women liable for contracts, debts, and torts on the same terms as other citizens. Matrimonial property statutes are more likely to be innovative, because lawyers and judges are reluctant to press for equality in the courts. They are more responsive to the demands of husbands for easier divorce than to the demands of wives for equal treatment in property. The pattern continues to the present. Court decisions based on 1970's Matrimonial Proceedings and Property Act (MPPA) have been based on principles of unequal division of family assets. If and when spouses achieve equal shares, it will be through statutory reform, not court practice.

FAMILY LAW: A WOMAN'S ISSUE AND MORE

Divorce and marital property law affects the status of women. In each phase of reform, family law has been an issue of intense interest to women, especially feminists. However, this review of the policymaking processes has also showed that issues have been defined both inside and outside Parliament in other terms as well. Several themes other than women's rights in the family have recurred in debate each time divorce and marital property rights reached the public agenda and Parliament set about making a decision.

A theme that repeatedly became the major justification for divorce reform was that the law should be realistic to alleviate suffering of couples unable to divorce under old laws. In 1857 divorce was not available to middle and poor classes. Inadequacies in the law led to bigamy and illegitimate unions. A famous case in 1846 was evidence of what happened when a man whose legal wife had run off with his money and another man tried to remarry. Lacking £1000, he was tried for bigamy.

Again, debate in the 1930s focused on the plight of many thousands of couples who could not use adultery and would not commit perjury but who had ended their marriages and formed new families. The children of these families suffered the stigma of illegitimacy, again due to inadequacies in the law. The fact that nearly 100,000 couples lived in consensual unions with illegitimate children was brought up in debate on White's bill, the Royal Commission of 1952, Abse's Kiss and Make Up Bill and finally during debate on the Divorce Reform Act in 1968 and 1969. Supporters of divorce law reform argued every time that the law was not going to increase the breakup of families but would accommodate needs of the many couples who had already left unhappy marriages. Several generations of proponents have justified divorce reform not as a threat but as a salvation for the family. They have maintained again and again that by reducing the number of illicit unions and illegitimate children, respect for both legal marriage and the legal system would increase.

Another theme that extends through all of the debates on law reform is the need to extend the law to allow the poor the same advantages as the rich. Often the rich can make an inadequate law work for them by being able to employ good lawyers. Such was the case with parliamentary divorce before 1857, marriage settlements before 1882, perjury and collusive adultery before 1937, and divorce and maintenance of more than one family before 1969. Divorce law in 1857, the Married Women's Property Act, the divorce reforms of 1937 and 1969, were all to allow the poor as well as the rich to have property protected and obtain divorces.

Even when a reform proposal was defined as a woman's issue,

disagreement arose about the proper role of the wife and how the law should treat her. Voices are always heard in debates adamantly upholding a double moral standard in marriage. In the 1850s the view was widely accepted in the Lords and Commons that adultery by a wife had a different meaning from adultery by a husband. It was such a common belief that some speakers apologized for having to point out the grave implications to the family and society of a wife's adultery. All understood why it would be impossible for a husband to forgive such an offense in his wife. But a husband's adultery was only "a little profligate," and it would be unthinkable for a wife to let such occasional transgressions break up her home. The law was really protecting the wife by not allowing her husband to "force" her to a divorce merely by committing simple adultery. This double standard that disappeared from the statute has not disappeared from some people's thinking. Some MPs and peers continue to expect the husbands of England to be polygamous by nature and to be more likely to leave one woman and set up housekeeping with another. The charge that the 1969 Divorce Act was a "Casanova's Charter" reflected such thinking by implying that easy divorce would be an advantage to men and cause suffering for women. The 1981 Campaign for Justice in Divorce speaks for the second wife against the financial claims of the first wife.

In considering family law as it affects women, the legislators have frequently tended to emphasize protection rather than equality, especially in the nineteenth century. They described cases where poor women suffered at the hands of their husbands and argued that the law should prevent this injustice. Limits on liability and contract responsibility would protect married women, they reasoned. Many considered equality for women to be dangerous to the family and society. In alleviating the suffering of the poor married woman, most legislators believed they would neutralize demands for the suffrage. In fact, it was pointed out by proponents that unless the legislature responded to the needs of women, they would have a strong case for the vote to protect their own needs.

During parliamentary debate after the 1918 Suffrage Act, comment was made repeatedly that women were finally equal and that their disabilities were removed, although it was not true. The 1923 equal-grounds measure passed easily in the wake of the momentum of the suffrage movement. Some even said that women had benefited enough by all of the reform. The 1935 act was widely supported, because it removed liability from husbands, not because it finally gave married women equal status. It was referred to as the "husband's charter," and as one MP said, it was only just, after the women had gotten so much; it was time for the married men to have a break.

The notion of protection reappears in the debate on the Divorce Act in the 1960s. Those concerned about the financial status of married women can be classified in two groups: the ones who sought rights for women to property on an equal basis with husbands and the ones who wanted the law to protect the income of financially dependent wives by guaranteed maintenance or allowances. The idea of equal division of family assets was thought to be too radical. Many legislators preferred to leave issues of equality out of their consideration.

THE ISSUE OF WOMEN: FEMINIST INFLUENCE

Although family law may not always be seen by politicians as a matter of women's rights, British feminists have been interested in the outcome of every proposal for reform. As a matter of course, Parliament has sought the opinion of lawyers and the church; they readily influence policy in matters of marriage and divorce. Women, on the other hand, have had to push their way into the process from the outside, often with few political resources. A survey of all reforms demonstrates the range and variation of their influence from 1850 to 1970.

DECISION MAKING

Although seven statutes were under study, they involve ten specific policy outputs affecting changes in the policy toward sex roles in the family and the status of women. When listed according to these specific policy outcomes, the ten decisions are as follows:

1. 1857 (1) *civil divorce* in court
2. 1857 (2) *unequal grounds:* adultery for husband's petition; adultery plus grounds for wife's petition
3. 1857 (3) *feme sole property rights* for separated wife
4. 1882 (1) *married women's ownership* of earnings/property
5. 1882 (2) *limited liability* on separate property

6. 1923	*equal* divorce *grounds*
7. 1935	*equal liability*
8. 1937	*expanded* divorce *grounds*
9. 1969	*breakdown* principle in divorce
10. 1970	economic value in divorce to unpaid work in home: *family assets*

Table 3 presents the results of classifying the ten policy outputs according to the pattern of decision making. Particular structures of conflict resolution are listed for each policy. Four policies were decided in the administration, five in the legislature, and one combined administrative and legislative structures during crucial conflict resolution stages. Three of the legislative policies were decided in the House of Commons committees and two in the House of Lords. Administrative policymaking in law reform is dominated by law officers and structures advisory to them: the Royal Commission, the Law Revision Committee, and the Law Commission. One policy was settled through bargaining between the legislative and executive structures.

Table 3
Family Law Reform According to Type of Decision-Making Process

TYPE OF DECISION MAKING	*REFORM*	*STRUCTURE FOR CONFLICT RESOLUTION*
Administrative	1857 (1) civil divorce (D)	Royal Commission
	1882 (2) limited liability (P)	Cabinet, law officers
	1935 equal liability (P)	Law Revision Committee
	1969 breakdown (D)	Law Commission/Archbisiop's Group
Administrative/ Legislative	1970 family assets (P)	Law officers/Bishop coalition
Legislative	1857 (2) unequal grounds (D)	House of Lords Committee
	1857 (3) *feme sole* (sep. w) (P)	House of Lords Committee
	1882 (1) equal ownership (P)	House of Commons Committee
	1923 equal grounds (D)	House of Commons
	1937 expanded grounds (D)	House of Commons Committee

Note: D = divorce reform; P = property reform.

Although no clear trend can be seen away from legislative and toward administrative structures for conflict resolution, the process of decision making in family law reform has become more specialized and regular. An array of informal associations of reformers has been replaced by a permanent government commission with responsibility for the continual monitoring of the law. In the early nineteenth century, individual utilitarian lawyers such as the great Lord Chancellors Brougham and Lyndhurst promoted law reform. Brougham organized reformist Radicals into the Law Amendment Society (LAS), which studied areas of reform and presented suggestions to the government. The LAS joined with the National Association for the Promotion of Social Science (NAPSS), a larger organization including MPs, peers, and political activists. Still private, the larger organization sponsored annual Social Science Congresses to publicize needed reforms, their committees drafted legislation, and the NAPSS members who were in Parliament introduced bills. Law reform groups became more specialized and expert at pressuring Parliament. However, despite their close connections with politicians and government law officers, their reform activities remained private and intermittent.

In the twentieth century, the government began to take more responsibility for initiating reform. Committees to review law and recommend change were established in various departments. In the 1930s the Labour Lord Chancellor Sankey appointed the Law Revision Committee, which prepared the way for the married women's property law of 1935. A revision commission was reestablished in the 1950s under the Conservative Lord Chancellor. Dissatisfaction with the piecemeal approach of these ad hoc committees and the lack of support facilities led to the enactment of the Law Commission Act in 1965. The Law Commission is a permanent government institution for reform and codification of the law. It has a specialized staff and parliamentary counsel to assist in recommending changes in the law, publishing reports, and preparing Parliament-ready bills.

The development of the permanent commission for reform of the law has coincided with the demise of the Royal Commission as an effective structure for resolving conflicts. On only one policy—1857 (1), see table 3—did a Royal Commission contribute directly to resolving the conflict on an issue of family law. Although proposals of the Royal Commission of 1912 eventually became statutes, that commission's work must be considered preliminary, part of the process of formulation of proposals and demands rather than conflict resolution. Finally, the 1956 Royal Commission was little more than a forum for the various proposals for reform and did not even formulate demands. In fact, that commission's failure postponed action on divorce and property issues for another decade. Royal Commissions in the twentieth century seem to have a public relations role. Their reports may provide a basis for public discussion of controversial problems. The effective resolution of conflict leading to policy outputs is more likely to take place behind the scenes in government offices and committee rooms. As long as the Law Commission remains effective at solving conflicts about legal changes, it is unlikely that Royal Commissions will be established to study family law issues, unless they are part of some larger social question.

This specialization in policymaking has not led to a similar decline in the participation of the House of Lords in divorce and property law reform processes. In the 1850s the Lords were the dominant and liberalizing force in law reform. In the 1870s and 1880s they were obstructionist and vigorously opposed reforms passed by the Commons. In the 1920s the upper house was more interested in divorce than the Commons was and initiated several proposals that were too liberal for the lower house. Again in the 1960s the revitalized House of Lords took an active role in assisting the resolution of conflict over divorce reform.

The House of Lords and its leader, the Lord Chancellor, have retained responsibility for initiating law reform, despite statutory limits on their powers. The Law Commission and the government rely on the Lord Chancellor to sponsor their law reform proposals first in the House of Lords. The only law bills that originate in the lower house come from private members. Without support of the Lord Chancellor, however, controversial proposals have little chance of success. The House of Lords can no longer obstruct reform that the government wants. But on those issues where the government is neutral, the Lords have leeway to change proposals that come from the Commons. The House of Lords is thus likely to have an independent influence more frequently on issues of law reform than in many other policy areas. Retaining such influence is a result of its role as a high court rather than a legislative body.

Despite this concentration of power in legal and administrative bodies, it is still possible to expand the conflict on a reform issue to the legislature by means of a private bill. Sometimes a private bill is used by interest groups such as the Divorce Law Reform Union (DLRU) and the Married Women's Association (MWA) to persuade the government to take up an issue. Others allow the legislature to resolve conflicts. Three acts, 1923, 1937, and 1969, originated as private bills. The Married Women's Property Committee bill for earnings and property enacted in 1870 was incorporated by the government into its own bill in 1882. Resolution of the conflict on three of four policies took place in the legislature. Another, the 1970 act, was introduced after a private member bill forced the government to include a coalition of backbenchers in the policy-making process.

Private bills, especially if they are controversial like the divorce issue, can become law only if the government helps. In a way, this has been true since 1882, when private member bills sponsored by the Married Women's Property Committee were unable to complete all legislative steps until they were taken over by the Gladstone government. The Herbert bill in 1937 and the Divorce Reform Bills of 1968-1969 needed government assistance. The only bill that passed without active participation from the government was for equal grounds in 1923. This simple measure produced little opposition, and the Prime Minister approved of it. However, sponsors were warned not to allow any amendments expanding the grounds, or the opposition would obstruct the bill.

Time available for consideration of private bills has been reduced from the nineteenth century due to increasing centralization and control of parliamentary business by the Cabinet and party leaders. Nevertheless, in the time that remains, interest groups working with MPs can have some effect on policy outcomes as was shown by the Bishop bill in 1969.

Changes in formal legal-administrative and legislative processes have affected decision making in law reform; changes in the political party system have not. Between 1850 and 1970 political party organizations have become complex and centralized, and their leaders fill all of the top government positions. However, no clear trend in the party system over the four periods of family law reform can be related to the policymaking process. In the 1850s the parties were in disarray. In the 1870s and 1880s and the 1950s and 1960s, two well-organized parties alternated with convincing majorities in the Commons. In the 1920s and 1930s there was one strong party, two weak ones, and several coalition governments. The two periods when parties were not well organized were times of change in the party system itself. In the 1850s the Whigs and Radicals were regrouping and became the basis for the Liberal party of the 1860s, 1870s, and 1880s. In the 1920s the Liberal party was in decline, and Labour was becoming one of the two major parties.

What matters most to family law reformers is not the nature of the party system, but which party is in the majority. Advocates of change have found that a Liberal or Labour majority makes it more likely that their demands will find a place on the public agenda. However, divorce and property reforms have been enacted under all three parties: Liberal, Conservative, and Labour. Family law reform is not considered to be an important partisan issue. Textbook definitions of British government in terms of Cabinet and party dominance are not adequate to understand decision making about statutory reform of family law. Features of the British constitution often thought bereft of political importance, such as the House of Lords and private member bills, are more important to law reform than are political parties.

FEMINIST INFLUENCE

Influence by feminists has been defined in this book as the presence of feminist individuals, groups, or their representatives during the critical stage of conflict resolution on policies affecting the status of women. Table 4 shows this influence on the ten divorce and property policies. Feminists were found to have a direct impact on the outcome in five cases.

Feminists influenced the achievement of equal grounds in divorce (1923), equal ownership of property and earnings (1882-[1]), and *feme sole* property rights for separated women (1857-[3]—see table 4). They participated in the steps taken in the 1970 act toward the principle of family assets, giving legal recognition to unpaid labor in the divorce settlement, although they did not succeed in gaining equal rights to property. The feminists reduced inequalities in divorce proposals of 1857 (2)—see table 4—but were not successful in eliminating them. They did not affect the three divorce laws, 1857 (1), 1937, and 1969—see table 4—or policies dealing with married women's liability in 1882 or 1935.

Table 4
Feminist Influence on Divorce and Property Reform

POLICY	*STRUCTURE FOR CONFLICT RESOLUTION*	*FEMINIST REPRESENTATION*
1857 (1) civil divorce (D)	Royal Commission (ADM)	No
1857 (2) unequal grounds (D)	House of Lords Committee (LEG)	Yes
1857 (3) feme sole (P)	House of Lords Committee (LEG)	Yes
1882 (1) equal ownership (P)	House of Commons Committee (LEG)	Yes
1882 (2) limited liability (P)	Cabinet and law officers (ADM)	No
1923 equal grounds (D)	House of Commons (LEG)	Yes
1935 equal liability (P)	Law Revision Committee (ADM)	No
1937 expanded grounds (D)	House of Commons Committee (LEG)	No
1969 breakdown (D)	Law Commission/Archbishop (ADM)	No
1970 family assets (P)	Law officers/Bishop coalition (ADM/LEG)	Yes

Note: D = divorce reform; P = property reform; ADM = administrative; LEG = legislative.

Whether the policy is related to divorce or matrimonial property (D or P) has little effect on feminist influence. What seems to be more important, however, is the issue of the status of women in marriage. All five policies where feminists were influential concerned equality for married women (see table 5). Three—equal grounds, *feme sole* rights, and ownership of property and earnings—achieved equality. In two—divorce grounds in 1857 and family assets in 1970—policy outcomes did not guarantee equality but reduced differences between the legal rights of husband and wife. These reforms in the direction of equality were due to the influence of feminists, although complete equality was not achieved. In two other policies relating to equality, feminists were not influential. In 1882 they failed to secure their goal of equality in the use of property when the government law officers rewrote their bill.

In 1935 when their goal of equal liability was achieved, the Lord Chancellor monopolized the decision-making process.

Table 5
Feminist Influence and Type of Policy Issue

FEMINIST INFLUENCE	*TYPE OF POLICY*	
	Roles	*Status*
Yes		1857 (2) (D) 1857 (3) (P) 1882 (1) (P) 1923 (D) 1970 (P)
No	1857 (1) (D) 1937 (D) 1969 (D)	1882 (2) (P) 1935 (P)

Note: D = divorce reform; P = property reform.

The feminists were also influential in affecting those policies that were made in legislative structures rather than administrative. Table 6 classifies the policies according to the pattern of conflict resolution and feminist influence. The feminists had influence

Table 6
Feminist Influence and Pattern of Decision Making

FEMINIST INFLUENCE	*DECISION-MAKING PATTERN*		
	Administrative		*Legislative*
Yes		1970	1857 (2) 1857 (3) 1882 (1) 1923
No	1857 (1) 1882 (2) 1935 1969		1937

when conflicts were resolved in parliamentary committees, by individual MPs and through votes on the floor of the legislature. They achieved access to administrative structures in 1970 through legislative channels. Women's rights groups did not affect the outcome of one policy that was settled in the legislature, the divorce reform of 1937.

Feminists tended to be influential, therefore, on policies relating to equality that were decided in the legislature. What accounts for this interrelationship among the type of policy, pattern of decision making, and the level of feminist influence? Either of the following conclusions is possible:

1. When feminists define family law reform as affecting the goals of equal status for women, rather than sex roles in marriage, they use pressure-group tactics to transfer the conflict from the legal administration to legislative bodies where they can have influence. When they do not define an issue as a matter of equal rights, they show less interest in lobbying, and the issue remains in the hands of administrative committees and lawyers where outside pressure groups have little chance of participation.

2. Issues of equal status are resolved in legislative bodies, and issues of sex roles in marriage and divorce are settled in the administration. Feminists are interested in both kinds of policy outcomes and try to get their demands heard. As an outside pressure group with limited political resources, they are able to have an effect through the legislature, which is more accessible and receptive to them than administrative committees of lawyers. Therefore, feminists have influence only over policies affecting equality.

If the first conclusion is true, the amount of influence depends on the amount of pressure exerted by feminist interest groups. In comparing the processes on various reform policies, political activity would be greatest on policies affecting women's status. If the second conclusion is true, however, level of political activity would not vary according to type of policy. Then feminist influence would be limited to those policies that happen to be settled in legislative bodies.

Table 7 classifies policies according to type of issue decided and indicates the various sorts of political activities of feminist groups. *lobbying:* petitioning Parliament, visiting MPs, writing letters, testifying at committees; *public relations:* publishing pamphlets, taking a stand on policy proposals, holding public meetings, speaking, passing formal resolutions; *elite representation:* placing a mem-

Table 7
Feminist Activity According to Type of Policy Issue

TYPE OF POLICY ISSUE		*STRUCTURE*		*ACCESS*			
		Individual	*Group*	*Lobbying*	*Public Relations*	*Elite Representation*	*Personal Connection*
Status/Feminist Influence	1857 (2) LEG				X	X	X
	1857 (3) LEG	X			X	X	X
	1882 (1) LEG	X	X	X	X	X	X
	1923 LEG		X	X	X	X	X
	1970 ADM/LEG	X	X	X	X		X
Status/ No Influence	1882 (2) ADM		X	X	X	X	X
	1935 ADM		X	X		X	X
Roles/No Feminist Influence	1857 (1) ADM						
	1937 LEG		X		X	X	
	1969 ADM		X		X		

Note: LEG = legislative; ADM = administrative.

ber of the organization in an official position such as MP or member of the government; and *personal connection:* seeking to influence through personal relationships between members of the interest group and influential public figures. Marks in these categories give an idea of the extent of interest and activity feminists have exerted to influence policy.

In 1857 a single individual was able to influence a single peer to change the policy outcome to improve the status of women in divorce. In terms of pressure-group politics of the time, these feminists were interested and active. They did not get involved on the issue of sex roles in divorce. With the exception of the 1935 property act, organized feminists also exerted more activity on policies affecting the equal status of women than on those pertaining to sex roles in marriage. On three of the four policies where feminists waged a campaign, they were successful: the 1882 Married Women's Property Act giving equal ownership of earnings and property; the 1923 Matrimonial Causes Act establishing equal grounds; and the 1970 act gaining some financial guarantees for dependent wives in divorce. The feminists had only one major defeat in the entire array of policies: failing to get equal property rights under the 1882 MWPA. The Married Women's Property Committee exerted a full, detailed campaign for equal rights for married women, and they were denied in the end by law officers of the government. With three acts the feminists exerted less effort and had less influence (1935, 1937, 1969). They restricted their activities in these cases to passing resolutions and speaking personally or writing letters to government officials.

On the basis of these ten cases of policymaking, the variables of policy output, pattern of decision making, and feminist political activity may be interrelated as follows: feminist groups and individuals have been interested in family law reform as it affects women. They have been more likely to be active on issues of equality than on the more subtle effects of grounds for divorce on sex roles. They may be successful in placing an issue on the public agenda as they did in 1882 and 1923. Or when Parliament begins to make a decision, they may be able to persuade the legislature to redefine the family law proposals in feminist terms as they did in 1857 and 1970.

Feminists seek to influence the outcome through various combinations of lobbying, public relations, elite representation, and personal connections. The more active the pressure, the more effective they are likely to be. Legislative structures are most vulnerable to feminist campaigns. When feminists are successful, they get the conflict moved from the administration to the legislature for final resolution. Not all legislative decision making invites feminist input (e.g., 1937), but in every case where feminists have been effective, it has been through legislative structures. When they have had little impact, it has usually meant they were less active, and conflicts remained to be resolved behind closed doors in administrative bodies. Therefore, evidence supports the first conclusion offered above: When feminists define family law reform as affecting the goals of equality for women, rather than sex roles in marriage, they use pressure-group tactics to transfer the conflict from the legal administration to the legislature where they can have influence.

The level of feminist influence, then, is related to feminist interest in the issues of divorce and matrimonial property law reform and the intensity of feminist political activity. These factors are in turn affected by the general nature of feminist politics. Table 8 lists the types of feminist political activity according to periods of policymaking.

Table 8
Types of Structures and Access According to Time Periods

PERIOD	*POLICY*	*STRUCTURE*		*ACCESS*			
		Individual	*Group*	*Lobbying*	*Public Relations*	*Elite Repre.*	*Personal Connection*
I	1857 (1)						
I	1857 (2)	X			X	X	X
I	1857 (3)	X			X	X	X
II	1882 (1)		X	X	X	X	X
II	1882 (2)		X	X	X	X	X
III	1923		X	X	X		X
III	1935		X	X			X
III	1937	X	X		X	X	
IV	1969		X		X		
IV	1970	X	X	X	X	X	X

These four periods can be related to what else was occurring during the various stages of the feminist movement in Britain.

Period I preceded organized activism; political activity was limited to writing books and pamphlets on various aspects of the woman question. Period II coincided with the first wave of feminism, where demands for education, jobs, health, and votes accompanied demands for married women's property rights. Period III followed the successful suffrage movement, when the ideology of feminism was being altered by new feminists who sought to enact special legislation to aid and protect women rather than seek complete equality. New feminism was closely connected to socialism, and equalitarian feminist political activity declined during the interwar period. Period IV coincided with a revitalization of feminism and a new interest in the status of women brought about by the Women's Liberation Movement of the 1960s.

Table 8 demonstrates that feminist political activity in areas of divorce and married women's property fluctuated with the other aspects of the movement. The first period preceded development of organized interest-group activity. Of the periods when feminists were well organized, most interest was shown in the campaign for the Married Women's Property Act of 1882. The least activity occurred during the 1920s and 1930s, at first because of the momentum from the suffrage and later because feminists were not as interested in family law as family allowances. Because feminists were not active did not mean that equalitarian policies vanished (e.g., 1935). When groups are active, they will have impact, however. When the government ignores equalitarian issues and the status of women, a feminist campaign can be successful in changing policy outcomes, for example, to give married women an interest in family assets, in the direction of improved status for women.

THE POLICY PROCESS CONTINUES

The Divorce Reform Act and the Matrimonial Proceedings and Property Act went into effect in January 1971. Proposals for changes in family law have not ended with the passage and implementation of these reforms. If anything, they have increased. Some of the demands arise from implementation of the new statutes. Others would eliminate all traces of the common law and equity assumptions of fault and dependency from family law. Feminist political activity, deriving energy from the international women's rights movement of the seventies, has diversified both in its demands and organization. The process of family law reform in England continues to unfold, promising to keep legal procedures in line with social change.

Figure 2
Divorce Rates, per 1,000 Married Population, 1964-1978.

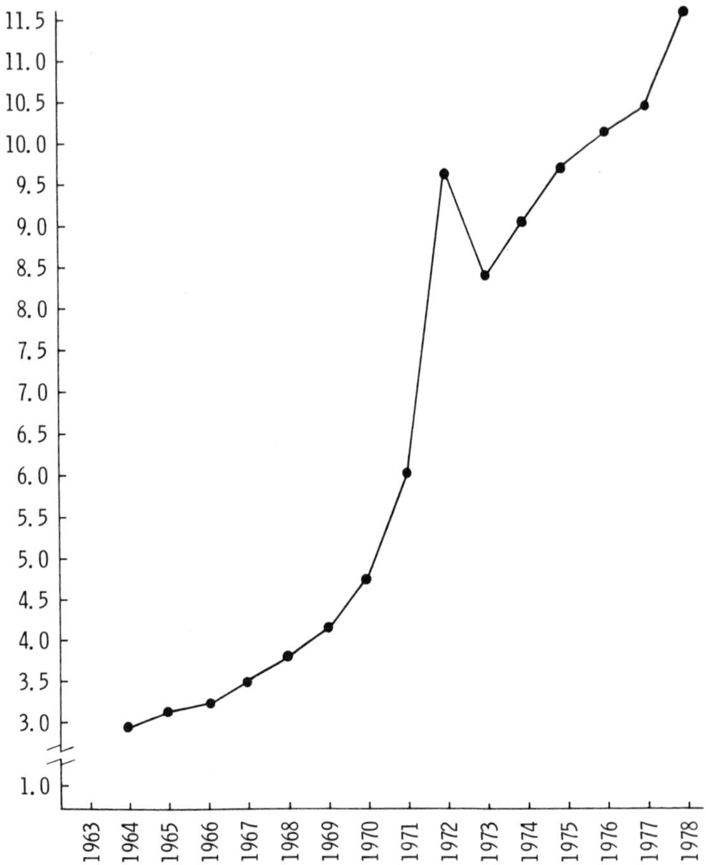

Source: Registrar General's Statistical Review, 1978.

Divorce rates have skyrocketed since the implementation of the Divorce Reform Act in 1971. Rates that had been increasing before 1969 at a rate of two-tenths of a point a year tripled between 1969 and 1978 at a rate of eight-tenths of a point (figure 2). The changes in divorce behavior can be seen when statistics for 1966, 1973, and 1978 are compared (see table 9).

Table 9
Divorce Statistics, 1966, 1973, 1978

	1966	1973	1978
Number of divorces	38,352	103,741 [a]	143,667
Divorce rate	2.5	8.4	11.6
Percentage of women	59%	64%	69%
Percentages of Divorces on grounds of:			
Adultery	47% (18,025)	30% (31,525)	28% (40,416)
Cruelty	22% (8,437)	21% (22,255)	31% (43,627)
Desertion	21% (8,053)	7% (7,565)	3% (4,854)
Separation (2 yr.)	——	22% (22,889)	27% (37,703)
Separation (5 yr.)	——	16% (16,935)	10% (14,387)

Source: Registrar General's Statistical Review, 1966, 1973, 1978.
a. On petitions since 1971.

In the twelve years there were four times the number of divorces, nearly six times the divorce rate per 1,000 marriages, and a steady increase in the percentage of women petitioning. For years women presented slightly more than one-half of the petitions: their share of suits has increased to more than two-thirds in two decades.

The new grounds of separation have steadily accounted for about 38 percent of the divorce petitions. Although the number of adultery petitions has increased, their percentage of the total has declined. The ground of cruelty has become more and more popular. The number of petitions on desertion remained the same until 1973 and has since declined. These petitions make up a mere 3 percent of the decrees.

Table 10 shows grounds used by men and women. The women take advantage of all grounds at a greater rate than men do. Men seem to prefer adultery as a ground more than women do; 40 percent of husbands in 1978 suing for divorce used that ground compared with 24 percent of the women. The cruelty petitions on which 31 percent of the divorces are granted are filed overwhelmingly by women. They also tend to sue for desertion more frequently than men. The use of cruelty and desertion by women suggests that a substantial number of marriages are based on separate sex roles. However, it is difficult to tell, because many couples use cruelty as a quick means to a mutually agreed upon divorce.

Table 10
1978 Grounds for Divorce and Sex of Petitioner

	GROUNDS BY SEX			*SEX BY GROUNDS*	
	Husband	*Wife*	*Total*	*Husband*	*Wife*
Adultery	43%	47%	100%	40%	24%
Cruelty	9	91	100	9	41
Desertion	27	73	100	3	4
Separation (2)	38	62	100	32	24
Separation (5)	48	52	100	16	8
				100%	100%

Source: Registrar General's Statistical Review, 1978.

Has the act become a Casanova's Charter? From examining variation in grounds by age and sex (table 11), some trends are noticeable. Adultery becomes less popular for both sexes as the age of the petitioner increases and the gap in rates between husband and wife narrows. Separation for five years constitutes a greater percentage of grounds as the petitioners get older. However, from the forties on, the men are more likely to sue for divorce after a five-year separation than women are. Forty-five percent of the husbands fifty-five to fifty-nine years old suing for divorce used this ground, contrasted with 28.6 percent of the wives. Ten percent of the men thirty-five to thirty-nine years old used this ground.

The largest single group suing for divorce were women twenty-five to twenty-nine years old (22,953). They used grounds of adultery, cruelty, and separation for two years. Men in the same age group sued for 8,500 divorces; they preferred adultery and two-year separation to cruelty. In 1978, 5,494 men aged forty or more, constituting 12 percent of all men, sued for divorce using the five-year separation ground. 4,803 wives over age forty sued for divorce after five years constituting 5 percent of the women. Women over age forty are more likely to be sued for divorce against their will than men are.

The increase in the divorce rates is no doubt in part due to the liberalizing effects of the Divorce Reform Act of 1969, especially the added separation grounds. But a number of changes in the administration of divorces were also made in the sixties and seventies. A long-standing demand to allow more access to divorce procedures was realized in 1967 with the passage of the Matrimonial Causes Act, which extended jurisdiction in divorce from the High Court to county courts. If a divorce petition in county court is defended, it is transferred to the High Court. In 1970 the High Court itself was reorganized, and a Family Division was established to deal with all family issues: separation, dissolution, property, adoption, custody, and so on.

The Matrimonial Causes Act of 1973 codified all existing statutes on matrimonial proceedings, maintenance, and legitimacy, including the entire Divorce Reform Act and most of the Matrimonial Proceedings and Property Act. The procedures for seeking divorce were also revised in 1973 in the Matrimonial Causes Rules. According to these rules, the 125 registrars of the county courts make initial disposition in divorce petitions. Most of these registrars have

Table 11
Grounds by Sex and Age, 1978 (in percentages)

AGE	*SEX*	*GROUNDS*[a]					
		Adultery	*Cruelty*	*Desertion*	*Separation (2 yr.)*	*Separation (5 yr.)*	*Total*
20-24	Husband	43.0	8.3	4.1	43.6	0.2	100
	Wife	18.7	45.6	4.3	29.7	0.5	100
25-29	Husband	45.8	7.5	3.0	40.1	2.7	100
	Wife	25.3	39.3	3.3	28.1	2.8	100
30-34	Husband	49.6	7.9	2.3	34.1	5.4	100
	Wife	28.1	40.1	2.9	22.8	4.8	100
35-39	Husband	49.1	9.3	1.7	28.8	10.1	100
	Wife	24.9	43.2	3.2	20.1	7.2	100
40-44	Husband	41.3	11.2	2.9	29.7	14.0	100
	Wife	23.0	41.6	3.5	20.1	10.4	100
45-49	Husband	32.5	10.9	3.3	30.2	22.3	100
	Wife	19.9	39.9	3.9	21.2	13.7	100
50-54	Husband	21.8	9.9	3.5	28.9	34.9	100
	Wife	18.3	37.1	4.1	19.7	19.3	100
55-59	Husband	14.7	10.2	3.6	25.1	45.2	100
	Wife	14.6	32.9	5.5	17.0	28.6	100
60 & over	Husband	6.6	8.3	4.6	17.9	61.7	100
	Wife	8.4	28.4	5.8	14.1	41.9	100

Source: Registrar General's Statistical Review, 1978.
a. "Other" grounds category constitutes less than 0.75 percent of the total.

legal training as solicitors. They handle the routine divorces, thus saving time and investment in additional courts.

In 1977 the "special procedure" was extended to divorce. For all cases of undefended divorce, neither party has to appear before the registrar or attend court. The registrar merely examines the papers substantiating the claims of breakdown, be it by fault or separation, and financial information. If he agrees with the papers, he issues a certificate for the county judge's formal pronouncement. For these "divorces by post," no legal aid is available; however, divorce by agreement is readily accessible to most citizens. If decisions are to be made by the registrar or judge about property, maintenance, or children, the couple may have to appear, and legal aid is available. The Family Court of the High Court of Justice in London decides defended cases. The vast majority of divorces are handled entirely by registrars in the county courts.

The registrars also make decisions about maintenance and property settlements; thus they implement the provisions of the MPPA regarding family assets. If some conflict over the settlement arises, the county judge reviews the case, and it might be appealed to the Family Division of the High Court. As with divorce, nearly all financial decisions in this case are made by registrars. No records are kept of their decisions, so it is difficult to know how well economically dependent wives are being protected under the new legislation.

The High Court ruling by Lord Denning in *Wachtel v. Wachtel* (1973, 2 WLR 366 [C.A.]) has come to be regarded in the legal community as the guiding interpretation on property division under the MPPA.[2] Denning defined the concept of family assets as those assets acquired in marriage for the joint use of the spouses. He divided them in two parts: (1) capital goods, such as home, furniture, savings; and (2) the earning power of the spouses. In divorce, capital assets must be divided and earning power apportioned. The *Wachtel* case involved a home valued at £20,000 bought with the husband's money and in his name. The lower court, based on MPPA, awarded a lump sum of half of the value of the house to be paid to the wife based on her work in the home, £1,500 per annum maintenance for the wife, and £1,500 for the support of their daughter. The High Court reduced the settlement to £6,000, £1,500, and £300 respectively.

Denning used the opportunity of the appeal to set down some guidelines for interpretation of the act while settling the *Wachtel* disagreement. In this case, the husband had claimed that the wife's share should be reduced because of her conduct. First, Denning noted that the conduct of the parties in marriage should not affect the financial provisions under the principle of marital breakdown. Only if behavior of one party is so "obvious and gross" that it would be unjust to ignore it should conduct be taken into account in a property settlement.

Denning then traced the development of the concept of family assets. Section 17 of the Married Women's Property Act of 1882 could be used by a wife to sue for interest in a house or other property proving an actual financial contribution to its purchase or improvement. The new concept of family assets gave a woman an interest in property based on nonmonetary contributions:

> By a long line of cases starting with Rogers' Question [1948] 1 AER 328 and ending with Hazell v. Hazell [1972] 1 WLR 301, it has been held by this court that, if a wife contributes directly or indirectly in money or money's worth, to the initial deposit or the mortgage installments, she gets an interest proportionate to her contribution. In some cases it is a half share, in others less.

But courts had never succeeded in actually awarding a share in the home without some financial contribution by the wife. The injustice of this situation was pointed out, Denning noted, by various groups and individuals: the Royal Commission on Marriage and Divorce in 1956; president of the Divorce Court, Sir Jocelyn Simon, who said in 1965, "The cock can feather the nest because he does not have to spend most of his time sitting on it"; House of Lords in *Pettit v. Pettit;* and the Law Commission's report of 1969, which recommended legal recognition of the economic value of the wife's unpaid labor in the home:

> This should meet the strongest complaint made by married women and recognized as legitimate by the Morton Commission in 1955, namely that the contribution which wives make toward the acquisition of the family assets by performing their domestic chores thereby releasing their husbands for gainful employment is at present wholly ignored in determining their rights.

Denning established that the concept of family assets and the right of wives to a share in the matrimonial home had been provided for in the 1970 act. He argued that there should, however, *not* be an equal division of assets as long as the husband's earnings were apportioned to the wife and children. If the wife only gets a portion of the capital assets, half would be fair. But most wives sue for maintenance as well: "In view of those calls on his future earnings we don't think she should have both—half the capital and half the earnings." It is best to start with one-third of joint earnings. Denning insisted that one-third was not a hard and fast rule but a starting place. All other things being equal, the wife should get one-third of the property and earnings. Other matters might then be taken into account: her age, earnings, disabilities, and so on. "But it is convenient to begin with a transfer to the wife in specie or as a lump sum payment, of one third of the capital assets and to order periodical payments to bring her income, if any, up to one third of their joint incomes." Thus the value placed on the wife's contribution to the marriage relationship by the High Court is one-third, not one-half.

A recent survey of registrars reveals that the majority agree that the one-third rule is a useful starting place in making decisions about property distribution.[3] However, one-third of the officers surveyed were more flexible, pointing out that when combined incomes are very high or very low, other fractions are more appropriate. On this as in most questions about property in divorce, substantial diversity of opinion occurs among registrars, revealing a lack of uniformity in administration of the MPPA. The act, for example, declares that the basic goal of the courts in making settlements is to place the parties in the position they would have been in had the marriage not broken down. Many registrars called this an "unattainable ideal" in all but the wealthiest cases. For most couples, one salary and one house could not be stretched to provide for two families.

Diversity is greatest in making maintenance awards. Denning had ruled that consideration of conduct had no place in a marital breakdown unless it was "obvious and gross." Nevertheless, one-third of the registrars considered less serious conduct in making financial orders. Most believed the wife should seek employment, as an alternative to support, especially if she were young. Others were prepared to lower the amount a wife would receive to make her eligible for supplementary benefits from the government. Most registrars have accepted the husband's own word about his assets and income.

A dependent wife apparently has few financial guarantees in divorce. Much depends on the personal values of the registrar in her county court. Some tend to treat spouses scrupulously as equal. Others hold more old-fashioned views of marriage. They believe that a wife should get some maintenance regardless of her age and earning capacity, since having been married once has damaged her chance of remarrying. Registrars are not necessarily bound by High Court precedent. They may ignore their superiors and do what they think is right. Colin Gibson, who conducted the survey of registrars, estimates that of the hundreds of thousands of divorces, only a few have been denied on financial grounds, confirming the fears of those who criticized this provision of the original bill as an inadequate financial safeguard for a dependent wife.[4]

REFORM ISSUES

Family court. The divorced mother often has had only one place to go for relief from poverty: the government. The relation between divorce, financial dependency of women, and welfare was fully explored by the Committee on One Parent Families, the Finer Committee. Its 1974 report reviewed, for the first time, the entire range of public policy affecting families, including law and social services. Its study of the law revealed two separate matrimonial jurisdictions, the divorce courts and the magistrates courts. Although a recent thorough review and change of policy had taken place with respect to grounds and financial provisions of divorce, the law of magistrates courts remained virtually unchanged from the basic policy of the nineteenth century. Divorce was based on principles of marital breakdown, and orders for separation and maintenance were given on a whole variety of fault grounds complete with bars of collusion, connivance, and condonation.

Inadequate enforcement of maintenance orders from either court forced a dependent mother to apply for income from the social security administration. No way existed under these separate systems of law and social policy for the government to have a consistent policy of aid to poor families. The Finer Committee recommended a unified system of family courts to replace the divorce and magistrates courts and allow the public authorities a coordinated approach to all family problems. Not only would such courts handle separations, divorce, and maintenance orders according to one policy of marital breakdown, but they would also include social services to help troubled families, prevent needless marital breakdown, and provide income for the needy.

The Law Commission was interested only in the Finer Committee's remarks about the two inconsistent systems of matrimonial law. Its 1976 report became the basis for the government-sponsored Domestic Proceedings and Magistrates Courts Act, 1978. The act substitutes "unreasonable conduct" for the long list of offenses previously used as a basis for magistrates orders. It also removes adultery by petitioner as a bar to a maintenance order and includes the guidelines from the 1970 MPPA as a basis for determining the amount of a financial provision. Excluded from this 1978 act is the policy that courts should try to place couples in the same financial position as if the marriage had not broken down.

Law reformers criticized the Labour government for sponsoring this act.[5] Many hoped that since the Labour party manifesto for the 1974 election campaign had supported the family court, the government would propose a bill based on the Finer Committee recommendations. Not only did this act not propose a family court, but by institutionalizing the magistrates courts, it was a step away from the unified system. No effort was made to bring together legal procedures with social policy to aid the single parent. In 1979 the Law Society, criticizing the Law Commission for its inattention, published its own report calling for a family court system.[6]

Ownership of the Matrimonial Home. The MPPA and *Wachtel* guidelines do not provide any property rights to a married woman while married beyond what she would have if single. If she is dependent while raising a family, she acquires no interest in family assets until there is a divorce. In the 1971 Working Paper on family property, the Law Commission recognized the limits of the 1970 legislation, pointing out that the divorced woman's property rights are better protected than those of widows or married women. The demands of feminists for equal property rights in marriage remained:

> In effect, what the women are saying, and saying with considerable male support, is: "we are no longer content with a system whereby a wife's rights in family assets depend on the whim of her husband or the descretion of the judge. We demand definite property rights,

not possible discretionary benefits.''[7] The Law Commission recommended that the law require coownership of the matrimonial home during marriage and use of its contents to resident(s) regardless of who paid for what: "it would acknowledge the partnership element in marriage by providing that the ownership of the principal family asset be shared by the spouses." It rejected adopting a complete community of property scheme.

In 1972 the Office of Population Censuses and Surveys published the results of a study of matrimonial property undertaken at the request of the Law Commission.[8] For the first time, evidence showed that a majority of English families were property owners. Their largest asset was the home; 55 percent owned their homes, and 45 percent were renters. The survey showed nearly unanimous approval of the principle of coownership of the home: 94 percent of the wives and 91 percent of the husbands. Most of the interest groups consulted by the Law Commission also agreed on the need for fixed principles of ownership of property, especially the home and its furnishings. Disagreement existed, however, about whether community of property should be the principle of family assets.

Since widespread support was evident for at least joint ownership of the home, since the home represented most of the matrimonial property, and since a lot of disagreement was evident about community of other forms of property, the Law Commission in its 1973 report recommended that the law be reformed to introduce the principle of coownership of the matrimonial home, "which, in the absence of agreement to the contrary, . . . would be shared equally between husband and wife."[9] In addition, it recommended that claims of a surviving spouse to the other's estate should be equal to the rights of a divorced spouse. It did not suggest any exact share that a surviving spouse should get, preferring to leave the division of assets to the courts.

In June 1978 the Law Commission completed its special report on the matrimonial home, embodying most of the proposals of the 1971 Working Paper.[10] It included a draft bill providing that by statute husband and wife be equal owners of the home, unless a private agreement existed between them to the contrary. Other sections of the report made recommendations about occupation rights and use of household goods.

Only two short debates in the 1979-1980 House of Lords, one on the report and one on a private bill, have been held.[11] They are interesting not only for their substance in defining the controversy, but because they gather together some of the old guard of family law. Lord Simon (the former Sir Jocelyn "the cock can afford to feather the nest because he doesn't have to spend most of his time sitting on it" Simon) emphasized the separate roles of husband and wife. He made a plea for economic justice for the women who still have a special social function in raising the children.

Lord McGregor (Oliver "the essence of democratic living is the exercise of choice" McGregor) focused on the need to eliminate marital inequality "intentionally institutionalized" by the Married Women's Property Act of 1882. Now married women work and most people think of marriage as an equal partnership. Lady Seear agreed that statutory coownership of the home would be "belated recognition of the true status of the wife in marriage"—as an equal partner, not a dependent. Lady Vickers (who as Dame Joan Vickers convened the Status of Women Committee in favor of equal partnership in marriage) gave support from the Married Women's Association to the substance of Seear's comment. Lady Lockwood (first chair of the Equal Opportunity Commission) disagreed with Simon, saying that the idea of separate functions of husband and wife does not apply. An increasing overlapping and sharing of all family activities is occurring, to which Lord Gardiner (*Law Reform Now*) agreed.

The only skeptic about the proposal was the Lord Chancellor, Lord Hailsham (whose father had opposed all extension of divorce grounds in the thirties). He suspected that the low turnout for the debate indicated either a lack of interest or hidden opposition likely to spring forth once the government made a committment. He noted a letter barrage from second wives against giving an equal share of the husband's assets to the first wife. He then announced that the Conservative government would not introduce a bill on this subject. Since then, another obstacle has arisen—a court decision in April 1980 calling for a complete review of the whole matter of land registration, affecting the legal aspects of the matrimonial home. Action on the proposal for giving married women statutory right to family assets, which seemed to enjoy such widespread support in the early seventies, has been indefinitely postponed.

Financial status of women in divorce. Controversy over ownership of family assets has been replaced by challenges to the policy about financial provision in divorce, set forth so recently in the

1969 and 1970 acts. In 1980 the Law Commission responded to the criticism these new laws provoked with a discussion paper on the financial consequences of divorce.[12] In it the commission outlined the arguments on all sides and summarized a number of proposals for change.

At issue is the contention that despite fundamental changes in the grounds for divorce, the concept of lifelong duty of one spouse, usually the husbnd, to support the wife remains basic policy. Some oppose the guidelines in the 1970 acts that courts "exercise those powers to place the parties, so far as it is practicable and, having regard to their conduct, just to do so, in the financial position in which they would have been if the marriage had not broken down and each had properly discharged his or her financial obligations and responsibilities toward each other" (Section 25). Husbands resent having to pay one-third of their gross income indefinitely to their first wives, especially if they do not feel responsible for the divorce. The second wife and family must accept a reduced standard of living. The second wife is often forced to get a job, while the first wife, even with no children at home, is free not to work. The court will even include the second wife's income as part of the husband's assets in making maintenance awards to the first wife. The first wives, despite the envy and resentment of their successors, aren't happy with the law either. All they can expect is one-third of joint resources of the first marriage, and it is not enough. The support orders are not enforced, pushing the first family toward poverty or welfare. Even if the husband pays, no cost of living adjustment is made to overcome the effects of inflation.

Law reform advocates criticize the law, because it contains inconsistencies and anachronisms. The divorce law has shifted away from guilt and misconduct, but these things can still affect maintenance awards. The goal of maintaining the ex-wife for life is rooted in the old-fashioned idea that marriage is a lifelong obligation. In fact, divorce and remarriage are becoming more and more prevalent. Furthermore, they argue, the changed economic role of women has made lifelong support unnecessary and unfair. Women have many opportunities to be self-supporting. The number of employed married women has grown, and new legislation for equal pay and against sex discrimination has strengthened their position in the labor force. It is unfair to ask a man to support his ex-wife when she is capable of supporting herself. As Ruth Deech pointed out, with divorce on the rise it is more and more difficult to enforce support orders. "We cannot afford easy divorce and perpetual maintenance."[13] What is worse, the maintenance laws reinforce archaic stereotypes of the husband as provider and the wife as full-time housekeeper and mother. Women should not be forced to be economically dependent:

> Marriage is no longer a secure lifelong career for a woman, and her retreat into the home and motherhood during marriage ought to be treated as her own choice and not forced on her by her husband. The vicious circle of dependence followed by work handicap can now only be broken by changes on maintenance law.

The commission offers a number of models for the law on financial consequences in divorce, ranging from retaining court discretion in making awards to repeal of the section about placing parties in the position they would have been if not divorced to American models of rehabilitative alimony. It concludes, however, that the division of opinion on the issue is too wide at this time for any particular reform to settle the conflict.

Clearly, tension is building due to the implementation of current laws based on conflicting values about marriage and divorce. The view that marriage is an equal partnership with shared roles seems to be gaining support. Spokesmen for interest groups such as the Campaign for Justice in Divorce and the National Council for the Divorced and Separated keep their demands before the public from within and outside Parliament. However, the real problems of economic dependency, reinforced by disadvantages women suffer in the work place, produce competing claims for better treatment of women in divorce.

Complete removal of fault. Contradictions in family law values persist most blatantly in the divorce law itself. The ease of procedure, changes in families, and relaxation of church opposition have made divorce a choice available to all. Most couples end their marriages by consent (or at least most do not contest divorce petitions). Courts are no longer required to make decisions about the morality of conduct. As the previous discussion shows, courts are most heavily involved in decisions about sharing family assets. Still, the divorce law itself retains a healthy chunk of old-fashioned morality. Despite the adoption of marital breakdown as the "sole ground for divorce," adultery, cruelty, and desertion remain as three of the five proofs of breakdown. They are the basis for 60 percent of the divorces. All of the problems that these grounds produced before 1969, such as perjury, collusion, and bitterness, remain. With them persist remnants of the nineteenth-century views of proper roles of women and men in marriage.

A committee of the Law Society has recommended that all traces of fault be done away with completely and that one clear, objective test of marital breakdown be used: separation for one year "after which real prospects for reconciliation can no longer be said to exist."[14] It also recommended that the three-year bar to divorce, still in the law since the Herbert Act of 1937, be reduced to two years, to be waived under specific circumstances. The Law Commission has begun its own discussion of the three-year rule, publishing an invitation for views in late 1980. However, although it recognized the interest among solicitors in removing fault grounds, it announced in its fifteenth annual report the same year that the commission has no plans to proceed with further review of the proposals.

FEMINISTS AND MARRIED WOMEN

Despite official indecision about further changes in public policy toward women in the family, feminists in the 1970s continued the work of their predecessors. For a moment they succeeded where the Fawcetts, Pankhursts, and M'Larens had failed: they won inclusion of women's rights planks in the platforms of the two major political parties. All too soon, however, their issue receded from official notice, and feminists—be they socialists, moderates, radicals, or emancipationists—fell back to lay seige to policymakers once again from the outside. The Women's Liberation Movement, with its focus on theory and academic feminism, harbored both conventional and daring proposals for change. For the first time, feminists have led the political left in offering visions of a society based not on classlessness but on new relations between the sexes and the family.

THE PARTIES

The Women's National Advisory Committee (WNAC) of the Conservative party works with women MPs of the party to develop policy proposals. In the mid-sixties it was interested in women in families and published several pamphlets. *Fair Shares for the Fair Sex* appeared in March 1969. It included a number of recommendations with respect to women's legal rights. Those on rights of the wife to family assets were consistent with Law Commission proposals that, at the time, were being prepared pursuant to the agreement between the Bishop coalition and the government.

16. On any distribution of property on termination of marriage a wife's non-financial contribution in running the home should be as fully recognized as any cash contribution she may make out of earnings.
17. "Family property" should be divided equally on breakdown of marriage normally but with a discretion to the court to vary this in appropriate circumstances.[15]

The recommendations of the WNAC became important when the Conservatives won the election in 1970; by then, however, most of their recommendations were already part of the law.

Unhappy Families was evidence prepared by the Conservative Political Centre (CPC) for the Finer Committee on Single Parent Families. It criticized the enforcement of the MPPA, claiming that it did not eliminate the notion of separate property. Recommendation 14:

On termination of marriage, the wife should have a statutory right to half the proceeds of the sale of the matrimonial home subject to certain provisions. The matrimonial home should only be sold with the consent of both spouses.[16]

In 1967 the National Labour Women's Advisory Committee recommended that the National Executive Committee set up a study group on the entire question of discrimination against women. The two reports *Toward Equality: Women and Social Security* (1969) and *Discrimination Against Women* (1972) covered a broad range of policy toward women in employment, education, the family, and politics. The Labour Party Study Group criticized the law for sustaining the notion of married women's dependency in marriage and suggested reforms:

We recognize marriage as a partnership and believe that the contribution of both spouses, whether in the form of financial support or of work in the home and caring for the family, needs to be taken into account.[17]

Since under present law wives do not have the same opportunity to acquire property as men, the group recommended that married couples should have joint ownership of the matrimonial home, goods, and property acquired during marriage; that property owned by spouses before marriage would be excluded from joint ownership; and that earnings of both spouses should be regarded as a "common pool." The Labour party committee's recommendations go further than the CPC in advocating a "community of gains" matrimonial property law, similar to the proposals by Olive Stone. The Conservative party in *A Fairer Deal for Women* (1973) officially endorsed the Law Commission's proposals for coownership of property, limited to the home. A plank endorsing the larger principle of coownership of property was included in the *Labour Programme,* 1973.

Both parties supported legislation for equal pay and against sex discrimination. After these policies went into effect in 1976, the parties lost interest in women's rights. In 1979 the Labour party manifesto included a perfunctory statement about equality for women, generally referring to reforms proposed by the Finer Committee and reiterating approval of the family court. The Conservatives dropped even a ritualistic reference to equal rights for women and gave social policy and families scant attention. Parties have always found it difficult to come to terms with women's rights issues (not that they have tried very hard). This barrier was briefly overcome when issues were seen in terms of economic policy. Feminists will have to rely on contacts with the Law Commission, MPs, and public relations to get their demands on the public agenda again.

THE OLD ACTIVISTS

The established women's organizations continue to be interested in women's rights, and a few of the old-style feminist groups linger on. The National Council of Women (NCW), although suffering from financial difficulties, prepares position papers on public policy issues. It overwhelmingly supports guaranteed rights to ownership of the matrimonial home. A slight majority of branches favor complete community of gains or property with the right to contract out of the system.

The NCW also seeks a legal means to provide the nonearning spouse with income. It agrees that one of the principle causes of marital breakdown is financial inequality, and thus it suggested "the establishment of a legal presumption that in a marriage partnership, earnings should be devoted primarily to payment for household and family expense, and that any surplus should be divided between the spouses on an equitable basis, with recourse to the courts in case of difficulty."[18]

The Married Women's Association is circulating a bill for equal partnership in marriage, incorporating the principle of joint income. Spouses together would decide expenditure of the common income for household and family expenses, and the remainder, if any, would be equally divided between the spouses and treated as separate property. The bill also provides for joint ownership of the matrimonial home. "An enactment of this kind would be educative, it would be a guide and directive to the selfish and unthinking and the dissident would feel the enforcement of the law. Women would then have the force of legal persuasion in support of justice." The Law Commission disagreed: "It would be unrealistic to underrate the fierce hostility such proposals would arouse, not only from those who would resent any legislation regulating the manner in which husbands spend their income, but also from a far larger class of people who think that the intrusion of the law into this sphere would be more disruptive of existing marriages than educative."[19]

The Six Point Group also suppoorts "Equal Partnership in Marriage":

> Traditionally and in general, the wife and mother occupy relatively an inferior position in the family. Her status should be raised to one of equal partnership with the husband and father. There should be joint ownership of the matrimonial home and pooling of financial resources and management effort for the benefit of the family unit.

However, the Six Point Group has no specific proposals to make. It has not been very large or well organized, and interest in it has waned with the passage of the Sex Discrimination Act.

THE FEMINISTS

At first, most of the feminist groups inspired by the Women's Liberation Movement were not directly concerned with the legal and economic status of married women. They concentrated on policies having to do with abortion, rape, battered wives, equal pay, and the status of working women. The demands from the first national women's conference in 1971 demonstrate these priorities: equal pay; equal education and opportunity; twenty-four-hour nurseries; and free abortion and contraception on demand.

With respect to the status of women in the family, two schools of thought developed, both of which militated against campaigning for changes in family law. One view is represented by the Women's Section of the National Council for Civil Liberties (NCCL). Anna Coote reported in an interview that the NCCL was reluctant to take up the issue of legal rights for married women, because the law could do little to change their status.[20] In English law, it points to the courts' reluctance to interfere in people's lives during marriage to enforce legal rights. The NCCL prefers to work on policy areas dealing with social services or criminal law such as rape, abortion, and battered wives and to educate the public by publishing position papers on these issues.

The other school of thought places the family structures as basic to the status of women: the only way to change that status is through a complete overhaul of the family itself.[21] Most of the proposals for change involve the elimination of the distinction between public and private spheres in society: the politicization of family roles. This would be part of a drastic reorganization of society along socialist production lines. Housework would be considered socially as useful and as necessary as any other productive work. Feminist socialist ideology is not concerned with family property issues, since the principle of private property itself is alien to the expected social transformation.

However, in the mid-seventies, new feminist organizations appeared, calling for the removal of all assumption of women's dependency from law and social policy. The Women's Liberation Campaign for Legal and Financial Independence successfully included a demand for independence as part of the Women's Liberation Movement (WLM) in the Edinburgh Conference of 1974. The Independence Campaign seeks to eliminate public policies that reinforce women's dependence on men, most of which involve matrimonial and family relationship.[22] In 1978 Rights of Women (ROW) formed as an advocacy and information group specializing in women's legal rights. Subgroups in family law and cohabitation respond to Law Commission working papers. ROW holds conferences to monitor the working of acts such as the Domestic Proceedings and Magistrates Courts Act as they apply to women.

ROW has been joined by the Claimants Union in demanding change in the social security legislation and practices. The regulations concerning family benefits are based on the assumption that women will mind children and take care of homes and that men will support them while they are doing it. These views are reflected in the hated "cohabitation rule," which permits benefits to be cut off to a single woman if she lives with a man, while not affecting the benefits of a man who cohabits. A woman cannot file separately or on behalf of the couple; only the man can apply for supplementary benefits. The social security administration accepts involuntary role reversal in marriage or cohabitation, such as where the woman is forced to support the family due to the man's absence or inability to work, but no voluntary role duplication. Thus unless her mate is disabled or disappears, a woman has no right to claim benefits in her own right. The feminists view this rule as the clearest indication that the government intends to maintain a male-dominant nuclear family among the poor with a sexual division of labor.

The Wages for Housework Campaign Committee has brought a radical perspective to an old demand. Direct payment to housewives either by husbands or by the state in return for their work in the home has been a recurring dream. However, feminists have never agreed on the idea. Some argue that it would make women more dependent; others fear wages would perpetuate women's role as housewife and the servant of men. Single women thought it ludicrous to pay married women for work that they were expected to do for themselves. However, demands by the Wages for Housework Campaign and its allies Wages Due Lesbians and Power of Women Collective are part of an international drive to undermine the sexual division of labor, not perpetuate it.[23] The demand is to persuade men that women consider housework and love for their men as work, not something given freely. When the slaves of men rebel, men will follow, opening the way for a true liberation from all exploitation. The Wages for Housework Campaign is based on socialist feminist theories being developed within academic feminist circles. Great need exists now to find those common themes that will unite the movement in seeking changes in policy.

Feminists at all political levels are beginning to realize the connection between the status of women in the family and the status of women on the job. As Christine Delphy stated in a British feminist newsletter, "The appropriation and exploitation of their labour in marriage constitutes the oppression common to all women." As long as women are considered to be dependents of their husbands (and as long as they consider themselves that way), they are, as a group, in a poor bargaining position for equal pay and equal employment opportunity. In turn, discrimination on the job makes marriage the only viable economic solution for many women. All through the public debates on divorce and matrimonial property reform, the dependence of wives and mothers has been assumed. Only recently has the point been made that equality in marriage will mean shared roles—that the wife may need to be as financially responsible as the husband and even that husbands may assume child care roles by choice.

There are barriers to achieving the kind of equality on the job and in the home envisioned by a complete sharing of roles. Politicians are not willing to face up to the need to invest in adequate child care facilities. Employers have benefited from controlling men through the enforcement of their economic responsibilities at home and relying on women as a cheap reserve labor force. Women, especially those who have been financially successful on their own, are afraid of sharing with men, believing that men are still in a favored position. These women balk at paying adults to do housework and feel little sympathy for problems of unemployed wives and mothers. Some men and women still believe that the socially enforced separate sex roles in marriage are basic to the continuity and stability of British society. They suspect that unless women are required to be dependent, they will not carry out their childbearing and childrearing responsibilities, and unless men are required to support their families, they will neglect them. The conflict over the sex-role pattern in the family and society will continue. It is difficult to say when the issue will again reach the public agenda. Nevertheless, the political leaders, through legislation passed so far, have shown themselves willing to consider a society with shared family roles and equal legal and financial status between men and women.

NOTES

1. The practice could not become widespread based on judge-made law alone. The House of Lords declined to accept the concept of family prop-

erty in the absence of an enabling statute. Pettit v. Pettit, 1970, A.C. 777 (H.L.).

2. Bernard Passingham, *Law and Practice in Matrimonial Causes* (London: Butterworths, 1974).

3. W. Barrington Baker et al. *The Matrimonial Jurisdiction of Registrars: The Exercise of the Matrimonial Jurisdiction by Registrars in England and Wales* (Oxford: Wolfson College, Social Science Research Council, Family Law Studies 2, 1977).

4. Interview with Colin Gibson (13 February 1976), Bedford College, London. Gibson has also published with Oliver R. McGregor and Louis Blum-Cooper their book *Separated Spouses* (London: Duckworth & Co. Ltd. 1970), a study of magistrates courts.

5. Parliamentary Debates, Official Report, V *Hansard* (House of Commons) 947, c. 1595-1636. Rights of Women, *Newsletter* (1978), Gray's Inn Rd., London.

6. The Law Society, "A Better Way Out: Discussion Paper Prepared by the Family Law Subcommittee of the Law Society" (January 1979).

7. Law Com. Working Paper No. 42/1971, *Family Law: Family Property Law,* 14.

8. J. E. Todd and L. J. Jones, *Matrimonial Property,* Survey of the Office of Population Censuses and Surveys, Social Survey Division, 1972.

9. Law Com. No. 52/1973 *Family Law: First Report on Family Property: A New Approach* (H.C. 274), 19.

10. Law Com. No. 86/1978 *Third Report on Family Property: The Matrimonial Home (Co-ownership and Occupation Rights) and Household Goods.* The second report led to the Inheritance (Provision for Family Dependents) Act of 1975, which empowers courts to award lump sum or property from a deceased person's estate to individuals (wife, ex-wife, or mistress, presumbly) who were dependent on him.

11. V *Hansard* (House of Lords) 401, c. 1432-48; 405, c. 112-54.

12. Law Com. No. 103/1980 *Family Law—The Financial Consequences of Divorce: The Basic Policy, A Discussion Paper* (Cmnd. 8041).

13. Ruth Deech, "Why Maintenance in a Bad Bargain for All Concerned," *Times,* 14 February 1980, 8.

14. Law Society, "A Better Way Out."

15. Conservative Party, *Fair Shares for the Fair Sex* (1969), 49, Conservative party, London.

16. Conservative Party, *Unhappy Families* (1971), 40, Conservative party, London.

17. Labour Party Study Group, *Discrimination Against Women* (1972), 31, Labour party, London.

18. National Council of Women, *Memorandum on the Law Commission Working Paper, No. 42, Family Property Law* (July 1972), Appendix, 6, NCW Archives, London.

19. Married Women's Association, *Newsletter* (May-June 1974), Fawcett Library, London.

20. Coote has drafted several reports for the NCCL and has coauthored with Tess Gill the book *Women's Rights: A Practical Guide* (Middlesex, Eng.: Penguin, 1974).

21. Eli Zaretsky, *Capitalism, The Family and Social Life* (London: Pluto Press, 1976); Lee Comer, *Wedlocked Women* (Leeds, Eng.: Feminist Books, 1974); Roberta Hamilton, *The Liberation of Women: A Study of Patriarchy and Capitalism* (London: Allen & Unwin, 1978); Annette Kuhn and Ann Marie Wolpe, ed., *Feminism and Materialism: Women and the Modes of Production* (London: Routledge & Kegan Paul, 1978); Ann Oakley, *The Sociology of Housework* (London: Martin Robinson, 1974).

22. The Women's Liberation Campaign for Legal and Financial Independence, *The Demand for Independence* (November 1975), Women's Resource and Research Centre, London.

23. Silvia Federici, *Wages Against Housework* (London: Power of Women Collective, 1975).

Bibliography

GOVERNMENT PUBLICATIONS AND RECORDS OF GREAT BRITAIN

Parliamentary Debates, Official Report. *Hansard,* Series II, III, IV, V.

Parliamentary Papers. Bills and Proceedings of Committees.

Statutes at Large:

Divorce and Matrimonial Causes Act of 1857, 20 & 21 *Vict.,* 85.

Married Women's Property Act of 1870, 33 & 34 *Vict.,* 93.

Married Women's Property Act of 1882, 45 & 46 *Vict.,* 75.

Matrimonial Causes Act of 1923, 13 & 14 *Geo. 5,* XIX.

Law Reform (Married Women and Tortfeasors) Act of 1935, 25 & 26 *Geo. 5,* 30.

Matrimonial Causes Act of 1937, 1 *Edw. 8* & 1 *Geo. 6,* LVII.

Law Commission Act of 1965. *Public General Acts,* 1965, 22.

Divorce Reform Act of 1969, 17 *Eliz. 2,* LV.

Matrimonial Proceedings and Property Act. *Public General Acts,* 1970, 45.

Law Commission Reports and Working Papers:

Law Com. No. 1/1965. *First Programme of the Law Commission.*

Law Com. No. 6/1966. *Reform of the Grounds of Divorce: The Field of Choice* (Cmnd. 3123).

Law Com. Working Paper No. 9/1967. *Family Law: Matrimonial and Related Proceedings: Financial Relief.*

Law Com. No. 15/1968. *Third Annual Report, 1967-1968* (H.C. 312).

Law Com. No. 25/1969. *Family Law: Report on Financial Provision in Matrimonial Proceedings* (H.C. 448).

Law Com. Working Paper No. 42/1971. *Family Law: Family Property Law.*

Law Com. No. 52/1973. *Family Law: First Report on Family Property: A New Approach* (H.C. 274).

Law Com. No. 71/1975. *Tenth Annual Report, 1974-1975.*

Law Com. No. 86/1978. *Third Report on Family Property: The Matrimonial Home (Co-ownership and Occupation Rights) and Household Goods.*

Law Com. No. 103/1980. *Family Law—The Financial Consequences of Divorce: The Basic Policy, a Discussion Paper* (Cmnd. 8041).

Law Com. Working Paper No. 76/1980. *Law Reform? An Invitation for Views: Divorce in the Early Years of Marriage, a Summary.*

Law Com. 107/1981. *Fifteenth Annual Report, 1979-1980.*

Law Revision Committee Report No. 4/1935. *Married Women's Property.*

Lord Chancellor's Office. Records:

Married Women's (Torts) Bill, 1925/LCO 2 777.

Matrimonial Causes Bill, 1933/LCO 2 1194.

Law Revision Committee, 1934-1935/LCO 2 1969, 1977, 1978.

Marriage Bill, 1936-1937/LCO 2 1195.

Royal Commission Reports:

First Report of Commissioners Appointed by Her Majesty to Inquire in the Law of Evidence, More Particularly into the Mode of Obtaining Divorces a Vinculo Matrimonii (1604), XL 249, 1852-1853.

Royal Commission on Marriage and Divorce, 1912-1913 (Cmnd. 6478).

Royal Commission on Marriage and Divorce, 1956 (Cmnd. 9678).

Civil Judicial Statistics for England and Wales, 1950-1974.

The Registrar General's Statistical Review of England and Wales, 1963-1978.

Report of the Committee on One Parent Families, Vols. I and II, 1974 (Cmnd. 5629).

Todd, J. E., and Jones, L. J. *Matrimonial Property.* Survey of the Office of Population Censuses and Surveys, Social Survey Division, 1972.

Cases:

Brett v. Brett, 1969, 1 WLR 487

Curtis v. Curtis, 1966, WLR 422

Edwards v. Porter, 1925, A.C. 1 (H.L.).

Fribance v. Fribance, 1957, AER 357 (C.A.)

Gissing v. Gissing, 1969, 2 WLR 525

Pettit v. Pettit, 1969, WLR 966, 1970, A.C. 777 (H.L.).

Rimmer v. Rimmer, 1953, QB 63 (C.A.)

Scott v. Morley, 1887, 20 QBD 120.

Wachtel v. Wachtel, 1973, 2 WLR 366 (C.A.)

PAMPHLETS, RECORDS, AND JOURNALS

Bodichon, Barbara Leigh Smith. *A Brief Summary in Plain Language of the Most Important Laws of England Concerning Women, Together with a Few Observations Thereon,* 1854, 1869.

Claimants Union. *Women and Social Security,* 1978, Women's Resource & Research Centre, London.

Conservative Party Pamphlets, Conservative party, London.
Work for Married Women, 1966.
Fair Shares for the Fair Sex, 1969.
Opportunity for Women, 1969.
A Fairer Deal for Women, 1970-1973.
Unhappy Families, 1971.
Widening Horizons: Women and the Conservative Party, 1975.

Council of Married Women. Minutes, Committee Files. 1952-1970, Fawcett Library, London.

The Englishwoman's Journal
"On the Condition of Women as Affected by the Law" (October 1862), 124.
"Property of Married Women" (March 1858), 58.
"The Working of the New Divorce Bill" (July 1858), 339.

The Englishwoman's Review
"History of the Married Women's Property Bill" (July 1873), 177.
"The Married Women's Property Act, 1882" (September 1882), 25.
"The Property, Earnings and Maintenance of Married Women" (October 1867), 263.
"The Proposed Measures for Improving the Laws Relating to the Property of Married Women" (April 1868), 418.

Hastings, G. W. *The History and Objects of the National Association for the Promotion of Social Science,* 1861.

Labour Party Conference Reports, 1918-1923, Labour party, London.

Labour Party Pamphlets, Labour party, London.
Towards Equality: Women and Social Security, 1969.
Discrimination Against Women, 1972.

Law Amendment Society, Annual Report. *The Law Review.*
"Divorce" 1 (1845), 375.

"Divorce" 8 (1848), 347-53.
"Sixth Annual Report" 10 (1849), 442-49.
"The Laws Relating to Women" 20 (1854), 1-34.
"The History of the Law Amendment Society" 21 (1855), 326-37.
"Review of C. Norton's A Letter to the Queen" 23 (1855), 181-85.
"Woman's Law: Mrs. Norton's Letter to the Queen" 23 (1855), 334-35.

Law Society. "A Better Way Out: Discussion Paper Prepared by the Family Law Subcommittee of the Law Society," January 1979.

Married Women's Property Committee Pamphlets, Fawcett Library, London.
Anonymous. *The Lords and the Married Women's Property Bill,* 1870.
Hobhouse, Arthur. *On the Forfeiture of Property by Married Women,* 1870.
Minutes of the Third Annual Meeting of the Married Women's Property Committee, 1870.
Third Annual Report of the Executive Committee for Promoting the Married Women's Property Committee, 1870.
Fifth Annual Report of the Executive Committee for Amending the Law with Respect to the Property of Married Women, 1872.
Sixth Annual Report of the Executive Committee, 1873.
Binney, Frederich A. *Marriage Law Injustice,* 1876.
Seventh Annual Report of the Executive Committee, 1876.
Speech of Rt. Hon. Lord Coleridge on the Married Women's Property Act Amendment Bill, 1877.
Arnold, Arthur. *The Honorable Mrs. Norton and Married Women,* 1878.
Report of the Executive Committee, 1878.
Eighth and Ninth Annual Reports of the Married Women's Property Committee, 1879.
Mr. Hibbert and the Married Women's Property Acts, 1879.
Tenth Annual Report of the Married Women's Property Committee, 1880.

National Association for the Promotion of Social Science, British Library, London.
Sessional Proceedings, 1881.
Transactions, 1857-1884.

National Conference of Labour Women. *Report.* 1932-1972, Labour party, London.

National Council of Women, NCW Archives, London.
Working Party: Abortion Act; Social Security Act, Compensations for Personal Injury; Rape Law; Oral Contraceptives; Law Commission

No. 53; Law Commission No. 42; Battered Wives; Anti-Discrimination Bill.
Women in Council, 1934-1970.
Annual Report, 1974-1975.

National Union of Societies for Equal Citizenship. Records. 1920-1935, Fawcett Library, London.

National Women's Citizen's Association. Minutes, Reports. 1952-1970, Fawcett Library, London.

Norton, Caroline E. S. *A Letter to the Queen on Lord Chancellor Crawford's Marriage and Divorce Bill,* 1885, Fawcett Library, London.

Rendel, Margherita et al. *Equality for Women.* Fabian Research Series 268, 1968, Fabian Society, London.

Rights of Women. Occasional Papers. 1978-1981, ROW, Grays Inn Rd., London.

Six Point Group. *Newsletter,* 1960-1970, British Library, London.

Women's Leader and Common Cause, 1921-1923, Fawcett Library, London.

INTERVIEWS

Daniel Awdry, MP, London, 4 February 1976.
Edward Bishop, MP, London, 16 February 1976.
Ronald Briggs, Justice, by telephone, London, 29 January 1976.
Anna Coote, National Council for Civil Liberties, London, 16 February 1976.
Juanita Frances, Married Women's Association, London, 19 January 1976.
Lord Gardiner, London, 3 February 1976.
Colin Gibson, Bedford College, London, 13 February 1976.
L.C.B. Gower, University of Southampton, London, 27 January 1976.
Elsie Hargreaves, National Council of Women, London, 19 February 1976.
Joseph Harper, Justice, London, 17 February 1976.
Anne Hopkinson, Mother's Union, London, 17 February 1976.
Hazel Hunkins-Halliman, Six Point Group, London, 28 January 1976.
Joseph Jackson, QC, London, 9 February 1976.
Lady Johnston, Law Commission, London, 16 January 1976.

Ruth Lister, Financial and Legal Independence Group, London, 18 February 1976.
Norman Marsh, Law Commission, London, 16 January 1976.
Margherita Rendel, University of London, London, 12 February 1976.
Shelagh Roberts, Conservative Party, London, 6 February 1976.
Sheila Rothwell, Equal Opportunity Commission, London, 29 January 1976.
Sir Leslie Scarman, Royal Court of Justice, London, 2 February 1976.
Lady Seear, London School of Economics, London, 30 January 1976.
Cartwright Sharp, Law Commission, London, 3 February 1976.
William Wilson, MP, London, 16 February 1976.

BOOKS AND ARTICLES

Abse, Leo. *Private Member.* London: Macdonald, 1973.
Acland, Alice. *Caroline Norton.* London: Constable, 1948.
Adam, Ruth. *A Woman's Place, 1910-1975.* London: Chatto & Windus, 1975.
Allan, Sandra; Sanders, Lee; and Willis, Jan, eds. *Conditions of Illusion: Papers from the Women's Movement.* Leeds, Eng.: Feminist Books, 1974.
Allyn, Emily. *Lords vs. Commons.* New York: Century, 1931.
Altholz, Josef Lewis. *Victorian England, 1837-1901.* Cambridge: Cambridge University Press, 1970.
Archbishop's Group. *Putting Asunder: A Divorce Law for Contemporary Society.* London, 1966.
Arnold, Sir Robert. *Social Politics.* London, 1878.
Atlay, James. *The Victorian Chancellors.* London: Smith, Elder & Co., 1906-1908.
Ausubel, H. *In Hard Times: Reformers Among the Late Victorians.* New York: Columbia University Press, 1960.
Baker, W. Barrington et al. *The Matrimonial Jurisdiction of Registrars: The Exercise of the Matrimonial Jurisdiction by Registrars in England and Wales.* Family Law Studies, No. 2, Oxford: Wolfson College, Social Science Research Council, 1977.
Banks, Joseph and Olive. *Feminism and Family Planning in Victorian England.* New York: Schocken Books, 1964.
———. "Feminism and Social Change: A Case Study of a Social Movement." In *Explorations in Social Change,* edited by G. K. Zollschan and W. Hirsch, 547-69, Boston: Houghton Mifflin, 1964.
Barkun, Michael, ed. *Law and the Social System.* Chicago: Aldine-Atherton, 1971.
Basch, Francoise. *Relative Creatures: Victorian Women in Society and the*

Novel, 1837-67. London: Allen Lane, 1974.

Bauer, Carol, and Ritt, Lawrence. *Free and Ennobled: Source Readings in the Development of Victorian Feminism.* Oxford: Pergamon, 1979.

Best, Geoffrey. *Mid Victorian Britain, 1851-1875.* London: Weidenfeld & Nicolson, 1971.

Birkenhead, Lord. *The Life of F. E. Smith, First Earl of Birkenhead.* London: Butterworth, 1933.

Black, Eugene C., ed. *British Politics in the Nineteenth Century.* London: Macmillan, 1970.

Blake, R. *The Unknown Prime Minister: The Life and Times of Bonar Law, 1858-1923.* London: Eyre & Spottiswoode, 1955.

Branca, Patricia. *Silent Sisterhood.* Pittsburgh: Carnegie-Mellon Press, 1975.

Bromfield, S. W. *The Married Women's Property Acts of 1870, 1874, 1882.* London, 1883.

Brookes, Pamela. *Women at Westminster, 1918-66.* London: Peter Davies, 1967.

Brougham, Henry Peter. *The Life and Times of Henry Lord Brougham: Written by Himself.* Edinburgh: Blackwood, 1871.

Bryce, James. *Studies in Contemporary Biography.* London: Macmillan, 1903.

Burton, Hester. *Barbara Bodichon, 1827-1891.* London: J. Murray, 1949.

Butler, David, and Sloman, Ann. *British Political Facts, 1900-1971.* London: Macmillan, 1975.

Butt, J., and Clarke, I. F., ed. *The Victorians and Social Protest.* Hamden, Connecticut: Archon, 1973.

Campion, Lord et al. *British Government Since 1918.* London: Allen & Unwin, 1950.

Chapman, A. Beatrice, and Chapman, Mary Wallis. *The Status of Women Under English Law.* London: Geo. Routledge, 1909.

Clokie, Hugh M., and Robinson, J. William. *Royal Commissions of Inquiry.* 1937. Reprint. New York: Octagon Books, 1969.

Cobbe, Frances Power. *The Duties of Women.* London: Williams & Norgate, 1881.

———. "Social Science Congress and Woman's Part in Them." London: Macmillan, 1861. Reprinted in her *Essays on the Pursuits of Women,* 7-38. London: Emily Faithfull, 1863.

Cootes, David. *The Labour Party and the Struggle for Socialism.* Cambridge: Cambridge University Press, 1975.

Conacher, James B. *The Aberdeen Coalition, 1852-55.* Cambridge: Cambridge University Press, 1968.

Cook, Chris. *The Age of Alignment.* Toronto: University of Toronto Press, 1975.

Crofts, Maud E. *Women Under English Law.* London: National Council of Women, 1925.
Crosland, Anthony. *The Future of Socialism.* New York: Schocken, 1964.
Crow, Duncan. *The Victorian Woman.* London: Allen & Unwin, 1971.
Currell, Melville. *Political Woman.* London: Croom Helm, 1974.
Dangerfield, George. *The Strange Death of Liberal England.* London: Constable, 1936.
Davidoff, Leonore. *The Best Circles: Women and Society in Victorian England.* Totowa, N. J.: Rowman & Littlefield, 1973.
Delamont, Sara, and Duffin, Laura. *The Nineteenth Century Woman: Her Cultural and Physical World.* London: Croom Helm, 1978.
Deech, Ruth. "A Tide in the Affairs of Women." *New Law Journal* 122 (1972), 742.
Dicey, A. V. *Law and Opinion in England during the Nineteenth Century.* London: Macmillan, 1905.
Doughan, David. "Lobbying for Liberation: British Feminism 1918-1968." Mimeographed. London: City of London Polytechnic, 1980.
Dowrich, F. E. "Lawyers' Values in Law Reform." *Law Quarterly Review* 79 (1963), 556.
Evans, Richard J. *The Feminists.* London: Croom Helm, 1977.
Farrar, John H. *Law Reform and the Law Commission.* London: Sweet & Maxwell, 1974.
Fletcher, Ronald. *Britain in the Sixties: The Family and Marriage.* Bath: Penguin, 1962.
Friedman, Gil. *How to Conduct Your Own Divorce in England and Wales.* London: Wildwood House, 1978.
Friedman, Lawrence. *The Legal System.* New York: Russell Sage, 1975.
Friedmann, W. *Law in a Changing Society.* Middlesex: Harmondsmith, 1964.
———. *Legal Theory.* New York: Columbia University Press, 1967.
Fulford, Roger. *Votes for Women.* London: Faber & Faber, 1956.
Gardiner, Gerald Lord. "The Role of the Lord Chancellor in the Field of Law Reform." *Law Quarterly Review* 87 (1971), 326.
Gardiner, Gerald, and Martin, Andrew, eds. *Law Reform Now.* London: Gollancz, 1963.
Ginsberg, Morris, ed. *Law and Opinion in England in the 20th Century.* Berkeley: University of California Press, 1959.
Gollancz, Victor, ed. *The Making of Women: Oxford Essays in Feminism.* London: Allen & Unwin, 1917.
Graveson, R. H., and Crane, F. R., eds. *A Century of Family Law, 1857-1957.* London: Sweet & Maxwell, 1957.
Guttsman, W. L. *The British Political Elite.* New York: Basic Books, 1963.

Halevy, E. *A History of the English People in the Nineteenth Century, Vol. VI.* London: Ernest Benn, 1952.

Hamer, D. A. *Liberal Politics in the Age of Gladstone and Rosebury.* Oxford: Clarendon Press, 1972.

Hammond, J. L., and Foot, M. *Gladstone and Liberalism.* London: English Universities Press Ltd., 1967.

Hanham, H.J. *The Nineteenth Century, 1815-1914: Constitution, Documents and Commentary.* Cambridge: Cambridge University Press, 1969.

Hanser, Charles J. *Guide to Decision: The Royal Commission.* Totowa, N.J.: Bedminster Press, 1965.

Hayek, F. A., ed. *John Stuart Mill and Harriet Taylor: Their Correspondence and Subsequent Marriage.* Chicago: University of Chicago Press, 1951.

Herbert, A. P. *The Ayes Have It: The Story of the Marriage Bill.* London: Doubleday, 1937.

———. *Holy Deadlock.* London: Doubleday, 1934.

Hewitt, Margaret. *Wives and Mothers in Victorian Industry.* London: Rockliff, 1958.

Holdsworth, Sir William. *A History of English Law, Vol. XVI.* London: Sweet & Maxwell, 1966.

Hollis, Patricia, ed. *Women in Public, 1850-1900: Documents of the Victorian Women's Movement.* London: Allen & Unwin, 1979.

Hopkinson, Diana. *Family Inheritance: A Life of Eva Hubback.* London: Staples Press, 1954.

Iremonger, Lucille. *And His Charming Lady.* London: Seeker & Warburg, 1961.

Jackson, Joseph. *The Formation and Annulment of Marriage.* London: Butterworths, 1969.

———. *Matrimonial Finance and Taxation.* London: Butterworths, 1972.

James, M. H., ed. "Bentham and Legal Theory." *Northern Ireland Legal Quarterly* 24 (1973), entire issue.

Kaye, J. W. "Outrages on Women." *North British Review* 25 (May 1856), 233-56.

Killham, John. *Tennyson and the Princess: Reflections of an Age.* London: University of London Press, 1958.

Koss, Stephen E. *Lord Haldane: Scapegoat for Liberalism.* New York: Columbia University Press, 1969.

Lee, B. H. *Divorce Law Reform in England.* London: Peter Owen, 1974.

Lewis, Jane. "The Decline of the Organized English Feminist Movement During the 1920's." Mimeographed. Memorial University of Newfoundland, January 1975.

Liddington, Jill, and Norris, Jill. *One Hand Tied Behind Us.* London: Virago, 1978.

Lindsey, T. F., and Harrington, Michael. *The Conservative Party, 1918-1970.* London: Macmillan, 1974.

Ling-Mallison, E. *Law Relating to Women.* London: Solicitors Law Stationary Society, 1930.

Maccoby, S. *English Radicalism, 1853-1886.* London: Allen & Unwin, 1935.

Martin, Sir Theodore. *A Life of Lord Lyndhurst.* London: J. Murray, 1883.

McCrone, Kathleen. "The Assertion of Women's Rights in Mid Victorian England." In *Historical Papers,* 39-53. Canadian Historical Association, 1972.

McGregor, Oliver R. *Divorce in England: A Centenary Study.* London: Heineman, 1957.

———. "The Social Position of Women in England, 1886-1914: A Bibliography," *British Journal of Sociology* 6 (1955), 48.

———. "Social Research and Social Policy in the Nineteenth Century." *British Journal of Sociology* 8 (1957), 146.

McGregor, Oliver R.; Blum-Cooper, Louis; and Gibson, Colin. *Separated Spouses.* London: Duckworth & Co., Ltd., 1970.

McKie, David, and Cook, Chris. *The Decade of Disillusion: British Politics in the Sixties.* London: Macmillan, 1972.

Mill, John Stuart. *Autobiography.* New York: Columbia University Press, 1924.

———. *The Subjection of Women.* London, 1869.

Mitchell, Juliet, and Oakley, Ann. *Rights and Wrongs of Women.* London: Penguin, 1976.

Moore, Katharine. *Victorian Wives.* London: Allison & Busby, 1974.

Morgan, Janet P. *The House of Lords and the Labour Government, 1964-70.* Oxford, Clarendon Press, 1975.

Morris, David. *The End of Marriage.* London: Cassell, 1971.

Mowat, Charles L. *Britain Between the Wars, 1918-40.* Chicago: University of Chicago Press, 1955.

Mullins, Claud. *Wife v. Husband in the Courts.* London: Allen & Unwin, 1935.

Nagel, Stuart. "Law and Social Change." *American Behavioral Scientist* 13 (1970), 483.

Nesbitt, George L. *Benthamite Reviewing: The First Twelve Years of the Westminister Review.* New York: Columbia University Press, 1934.

Pankhurst, Emmeline. *My Own Story.* London: E. Nash, 1914.

Parry, Edward Abbott. *Law and the Woman.* London: Arthur Pearson, 1916.

Perkins, Jane Gray. *The Life of Mrs. Norton.* London: Murray, Albemarle, 1910.

Pinchbeck, Ivy. *Women Workers and the Industrial Revolution.* London: Frank Cass, 1930.

Proudfoot, Mary. *British Politics and Government, 1951-70.* London: Faber & Faber, 1970.

Puxon, Margaret. *Family Law.* Harmondsworth, Middlesex: Penguin, 1971.

Rathbone, Eleanor F. et al. *Our Freedom and its Result, by Five Women.* London: Hogarth Press, 1936.

Raymond, John, ed. *The Baldwin Age.* London: Eyre & Spottiswoode, 1960.

Reiss, Erna. *Rights and Duties of Englishwomen: A Study in Law and Public Opinion.* Manchester: Sherott & Hughes, 1934.

Roach, John. *Social Reform in England, 1780-1880.* London: Batsford, 1978.

Rowbotham, Sheila. *Hidden From History.* London: Pluto Press, 1973.

Rowntree, R., and Carrier, N. "The Resort to Divorce in England and Wales, 1858-1957." *Population Studies* 11 (1958), 188-233.

Rover, Constance, *Women's Suffrage and Party Politics in Britain: 1866-1914.* London: Routledge & Kegan Paul, 1967.

Sachs, Albie , and Wilson, Joan Hoff. *Sexism and the Law.* Oxford: Martin Robertson, 1978.

Scarman, Sir Leslie. *Law Reform, the New Pattern.* London: Routledge & Kegan Paul, 1968.

Schwartz, R. O., and Skolnick, J. H., eds. *Society and the Legal Order.* New York: Basic Books, 1970.

Simon, Viscount John. *Retrospect: The Memoirs of the Rt. Hon. Viscount Simon.* London: Hutchinson, 1952.

Six Point Group. *In Her Own Right.* London: Harrap & Co. Ltd., 1968.

Smellie, K. B. *A Hundred Years of English Government.* London: Duckworth & Co. Ltd., 1950.

Stansky, Peter, ed. *The Victorian Revolution: Government and Society in Victorian Britain.* New York: Franklin Watts, 1973.

Stenton, Doris May. *The English Woman in History.* London: Allen & Unwin, 1957.

Strachey, Ray. *The Cause.* 1928. Reprint. Bath: Cedric Chives, 1974.

Tennyson, Alfred Lord. "The Princess." In *Poems of Tennyson.* London: Oxford University Press, 1918.

Thickness, Ralph. *The Rights and Wrongs of Women.* London: Women Citizen Publishing Society, 1907.

Thompson, William. *Appeal of One Half of the Human Race, Women, Against the Pretensions of the Other Half, Men.* 1828. Reprint. New York: Source Book, 1970.

Tingston, Herbert. *Victoria and the Victorians.* London: Allen & Unwin, 1972.

Travers, R. L. *Husband and Wife in English Law.* London: Duckworth & Co. Ltd., 1956.

Underhill, Sir Arthur. *The Law Reform (Married Women and Tortfeasors) Act, 1935.* London, Butterworth, 1936.

Vallance, Elizabeth. *Women in the House: A Study of Women Members of Parliament.* London: Athlone Press, 1979.

Vicinus, Martha, ed. *Suffer and Be Still: Women in the Victorian Age.* Bloomington, Ind.: Indiana University Press, 1972.

———, ed. *A Widening Sphere.* Bloomington, Ind.: Indiana University Press, 1977.

Vincent, John. *The Formation of the British Liberal Party.* New York: Charles Scribner's, 1966.

Ward, J. T., ed. *Popular Movements, 1830-1850.* London: Macmillan, 1970.

Watson, George. *The English Ideology.* London: Allen Lane, 1973.

Wilding, Norman, and Laundy, Philip. *An Encyclopedia of Parliament.* London: Cassel, 1972.

Wilson, Elizabeth. *Only Halfway to Paradise: Women in Postwar Britain: 1945-1968.* London: Tavistock, 1980.

Wilson, Trevor. *The Downfall of the Liberal Party: 1914-35.* Ithaca, N.Y.: Cornell University Press, 1966.

Williams, Glanville, ed. *The Reform of the Law.* London: Gollancz, 1951.

Winnett, A. R. *The Church and Divorce.* London: A. R. Mowbray & Co., 1968.

Young, G. M. *Victorian England, Portrait of an Age.* London: Oxford University Press, 1953.

Index

About the Author

DOROTHY M. STETSON is Associate Professor of Political Science at Florida Atlantic University in Boca Raton. Her articles on marriage and family law reform have appeared in the *Journal of Marriage and the Family, Policy Studies Journal,* and the *Journal of Comparative Family Studies.*